Better Bouldering

The long, sloping
hand traverse
of Grain de
Poussiere *(7b)*,
Fontainebleau.
JO MONTCHAUSSÉ

HOW TO CLIMB™ SERIES

Better Bouldering

Second Edition

John Sherman

FALCONGUIDES

GUILFORD, CONNECTICUT
HELENA, MONTANA
AN IMPRINT OF GLOBE PEQUOT PRESS

FALCONGUIDES®

FalconGuides is an imprint of Globe Pequot Press.

Falcon, FalconGuides, and Outfit Your Mind are registered trademarks of Morris Book Publishing, LLC.

All interior photos by John Sherman unless otherwise noted.

Text design: Casey Shain
Project editor: David Legere

Library of Congress Cataloging-in-Publication data is on file.

ISBN 978-0-7627-7031-1

Printed in the United States of America

10 9 8 7 6 5 4 3 2 1

Jeff Johnson on Tarface, Swimming Hole, Southern California. This problem is only for the best boulderers—a fall from the delicate crux here will deposit the climber into the creek below with a high risk of being sucked under the boulders and drowned.

Contents

Preface ix
Introduction xi

1   **Gear**   1

2   **Safety**   19

3   **Bouldering Basics and Static Movement**   51

4   **The Art of Dynamic Movement**   103

5   **Jamming**   121

6   **More Bouldering Tricks**   137

7   **The Mental Game**   155

8   **Strategy**   171

9   **Gym Bouldering and Competitions** *by Paul Robinson*   179

10   **Highballs**   185

11   **First Ascents**   193

12   **A Woman's Perspective** *by Angie Payne*   205

13   **More Bouldering Games**   211

14   **Physical Training** *by Dave MacLeod*   219

15   **Injuries and Injury Prevention** *by Nico Brown, PT*   241

16   **Taking It to the Next Level**   259

17   **Paths to Success**   269

Appendix A: Bouldering Ratings 276
Appendix B: Suggested Reading 278
Index 279
About the Author 285

Preface

When I wrote the first edition of *Better Bouldering* back in 1996, the idea of writing a how-to book on bouldering seemed ridiculous. Most climbers then considered bouldering a fringe activity, and the market seemed minimal. It was rare to see more than one bouldering pad under a problem. Dedicated bouldering gyms were still years off. Bouldering competitions were few and far between. Women were noticeably underrepresented. Bouldering videos didn't exist. And of course there was no money in the sport (some will whine that that's still the case). Nevertheless, for the few devotees back then there was an abundance of passion for the sport. Take that passion, add pads and V grades, a pinch of money, and an eventually enlightened media, and the sport has taken off to levels none of us imagined fifteen years ago.

Going bouldering is one thing, bouldering well and enjoying it quite another. The time-honored path to bouldering success depends on learning from one's mistakes. The more mistakes you make, the more you learn. A better way is to learn from my mistakes—this book is bursting with thirty-six years' worth.

When I first started bouldering, there were no books on the subject. There was, however, a terrific community of boulderers at Indian Rock who befriended and taught me despite my bumbling.

Though I learned much of what's in this book after those formative years, it was the Indian Rock crew that taught me the most important lesson: above all, bouldering should be fun.

The following people still have my thanks for their comments on the first edition's manuscript: Jeff Achey, Jim Belcer, Scott Blunk, Chris Dunn, Chris Jones, and Neal Kaptain. My thanks go out to the following people who made suggestions for the second edition: Chad Foti, Adam Markert, Paul Robinson, Dave Winthrop, Hillary Haakenson, and Tania Jackson. I also thank all the people who appear in the photos. Thanks too to John Gill, Jim Holloway, Dawn Kish, Derek Thatcher, Andy Mann, Lisa Hathaway, John Dickey, Jo and Francoise Montchaussé, Pat Goodman, Ben Ditto, Wills Young, Chris Summit, Adge Last, Nico Brown, Steve Woods, Paul Robinson, Eric Odenthal, Isaac Pallatt, Shadow Ayala, Sandra Stuckey, and Arjan DeKock for use of their photos. To check out more of the pros' pics, visit the following sites: andymann.com, eric denthal.com, dawnkishphotography.com, dickey photo.com, and bendittophoto.com. Yet more thanks, this time to those who wrote chapters: Angie Payne, Nico Brown, Paul Robinson, and Dave MacLeod; and those who shared words and thoughts: Lisa Rands, Diane French, Mary Gabrieli, and Fred Nicole; and to Crusher Bartlett for the illustrations.

The author on **Edge Direct,** *Indian Rock, Berkeley, California, late-1970s.*

Introduction

In 1975 I was a pudgy high school junior who couldn't do a single pull-up. Outside of knocking down a few beers with my buddies, I had few interests I can remember, and no passions. Then one day a couple of drinking buddies took me bouldering at Indian Rock, in Berkeley. I was pathetic; it took me multiple days just to scale *Beginner's Crack,* a route most newbies do on their first outing. Nevertheless, I persevered. A few visits later I pulled off a tricky move around an arête that was thwarting much better climbers. For the first time ever, I felt I possessed some athletic aptitude. I was hooked. I bought a pair of rock shoes and bouldered nearly every day after school until I graduated. By that time I was cranking sixteen chin-ups off the door jamb in the English classroom, and my wannabe beer belly had turned to a six-pack. Bouldering became the defining passion in my life. Where I chose to live, the friends I made, the jobs I took, the mercurial sex life—all were influenced by my obsession. Bouldering changed my life forever: It gave me focus, healthy exercise, an outlet for stress, a positive self-attitude, and some cool scars. It can give you all of these as well.

Rule One

Before we even get into the introduction proper, we need to hit on Rule One of Bouldering—prior to climbing a boulder, walk around it and find the descent. Nothing quite as humbling as busting out that big line, then finding yourself stuck on top and meekly asking a passerby for directions down. We call that a Rule One Violation, and much to our embarrassment it happens all the time.

Rule One Violation? Russell Wilson jumps from Chez Peron Spire, Hueco Tanks, Texas.

The author back in 1980 on his testpiece **Germ Free Adolescence**, *Eldorado Canyon, Colorado. Crash pads and sticky rubber were still years off, and so too it seems was my footwork.*

Bouldering is a difficult and sometimes frustrating pastime. I know. I nearly quit after making it up only one problem on my first day (this one even easier than *Beginner's Crack*). Yet the success on that one problem, as well as the fear and exhilaration, kept me going, as did each subsequent success. I realize now that the problems I failed to climb drove me as well. Somewhere a marvelous transition took place: I was no longer "at war" with the rock; I was "at one" with it. The boulders became my friends, not my

adversaries. Hopefully, the techniques and strategies in this book will improve your bouldering and help you to become "at one" with the rock.

I'm sure we'd all like to be the LeBron James of bouldering. Realistically, few, if any of us, possess that kind of athletic ability. I'm of only average athletic ability. Fortunately, so too was Larry Bird, and it never stopped him. At one point I did get strong. When I was twenty, I could snap off fifty pull-ups, but I was lousy at utilizing that strength. Ten years later, I could do less than half as many pull-ups, but I was doing problems I wouldn't have dreamed possible when I was twenty, because I was using my brain as well as my arms. In 2007 I swept first place in my age division in all three legs of the Triple Crown bouldering series despite having both hips replaced a year before and climbing on a partially paralyzed left arm. The point is that being smart will get you up more boulders than being strong. This book aims to make you smarter, stronger, and more skilled. We'll focus on climbing movement and techniques specific to bouldering, such as spotting and pad placement. We'll also discuss some of the most common movement mistakes and how to cure them. Ditto for mental bugaboos. In addition, we will delve into the nature of the sport, the gear used, and bouldering ratings. For this second edition of *Better Bouldering,* the injury prevention chapter has been completely revamped by sports medicine expert Nico Brown. Trad superstar, sports physiologist, and climbing coach Dave MacLeod (who climbs V13s for the training benefit) has written the chapter on physical training. I've added a chapter on highball bouldering, ace boulderer Paul Robinson has contributed a chapter on gym bouldering and competitions, and leading boulderer Angie Payne has contributed a section on female bouldering. To wrap it up, we'll explore a number of ways top boulderers have approached the sport, and how you can use these approaches to improve your own bouldering.

This book gives you all the how-to tips and

tricks to bust into new levels of bouldering. If you're looking to climb up the grade ladder, show off to your friends, or win the next competition you enter, this book will serve you well. But it's my great hope that this book will instill in you a love and respect for the sport and the places where you practice it. In most boulderers' careers a minimal percentage of time is spent actually sending big projects or winning the local gym comp. The vast majority of our bouldering careers is spent warming up, training, practicing, spotting, recovering from injuries, approaching boulders, brushing off chalk, scouting new lines to try, spraying smack, and the like. Only when we appreciate the beauty in those moments do we make the leap from bouldering as mere sport to bouldering as a lifestyle. In line with exploring the philosophical aspects of the bouldering lifestyle, some of the sidebars contain various "hero stories" taken from my personal experiences. Their purpose is to further illustrate points made in the text, as well as demonstrate the growth of a boulderer. If you would rather not bathe in the glow/stench (circle one or both) of my foibles, accomplishments, and ego, you can safely skip these asides and rest assured that you are not missing out on vital technical information. Please note that other sidebars often contain information vital to your understanding of the rest of the text and should not be skipped over.

You'll notice the photos in this book feature boulder problems spanning the gamut from V0 to V-gazillion. That's because the techniques and concepts used by the Big Name Boulderers to crush V13s, 14s, and 15s are the same techniques they acquired when they were gumbies learning on V1s. The only thing that changes is that the walls get steeper and/or the holds get smaller or more sloping or maybe farther apart. So if you see a rating tossed in a photo caption, don't attach any significance to it as it relates to the technique illustrated; it's just there in case you fancy the look of the problem and care to add it to your tick list.

The Bouldering Game

Bouldering has the reputation of being the simplest of all climbing games: You don't need an expensive rack or rope, you don't need a lot of time, you don't even need a partner. All you need are boulders and desire.

In its broadest sense, bouldering is defined as unroped rock climbing close enough to the ground that a fall would not be fatal. Most people would add that bouldering is usually highly gymnastic and relatively low risk.

At its simplest, bouldering can be nothing more than playing on rocks. Despite what you may have gathered from the climbing rags, you don't need to be a twenty-year-old white male college dropout to excel at bouldering. Bouldering is great for people of all ages—if you can climb out of your crib or into your coffin, you're invited. Carried to extreme levels, bouldering can be an intense engagement between climber and nature. Because you can try dozens of different climbs each time you go out bouldering, you can steer each session to match your mood. You can pack in more hard moves in a day than with any other kind of climbing. On the other hand, you needn't always throw yourself at the hardest problem around. The following very incomplete list hints at the variety the bouldering experience can provide: climbing a problem with the most holds; climbing a problem with the least holds; off-routing selected holds to add difficulty; trying the lowest possible start; playing follow-the-leader; trying to do a problem faster or the fastest ever; doing laps on a problem; searching out first ascents; repeating a problem in fewer tries than has been done before; wiring a problem until it is effortless; doing the longest problem, the shortest problem, the prettiest problem, or the most strenuous problem; seeing how many times you can do a given problem in a single session; trying to do the most problems you can in a session; climbing one-handed or hands-free; seeing who can do the longest jump between boulder tops; climbing blindfolded . . . and

*Two ends of the spectrum: Paul Robinson (left) uses a sit-down start to explore very difficult territory on **Monkey Wedding (V14), Rocklands, South Africa**, while the author (right) takes it high off the deck on the Sierra East Side, California.*

so forth. You might approach bouldering as training for roped climbs, or you might sell your harness and devote your life to the small stones.

Usually bouldering is practiced above a good landing—no higher than the boulderer is willing to jump from. The advent of bouldering pads has opened up territory once only ventured into by the boldest of the bold. Some of the trendiest new areas sport awful landings now made safe by multiple pad use. Risk is minimized; hence the boulderer can

concentrate on the moves and not the danger. That said, bouldering is not risk-free, and a good portion of this book is devoted to risk management and injury prevention and treatment.

High bouldering (aka highballing), in which a fall is long enough to cause injury, has provided me with some of the most intense experiences in my climbing career. But as the rewards are so great, so is the risk. Jumping off is not an option. When asked where I draw the line between high bouldering and soloing, I say, "If you fall high bouldering, you *will* get hurt. If you fall soloing, you *will* die." Obviously this is a perilous game and only recommended for boulderers exercising outstanding judgment. For some climbers it is a small or negligible part of their bouldering experience. Nevertheless, because the techniques and tricks of the high boulderer are worth learning for every boulderer, a portion of this book is devoted to them.

Style Versus Difficulty

In this era of high-speed Internet and instant gratification, it's easy to get wrapped up in just trying to chase the biggest number you can bag. The sad fact is that the vast majority of climbers who only chase numbers without regard to style or personal growth end up quitting the sport as soon as some young punk joins the same gym and starts climbing circles around them. Today's V-Holy Grail is tomorrow's V-warm-up—always has been, always will be. I want the readers of this book to develop a lifelong love of bouldering, and this comes not just from pushing one's physical limits but also from developing one's mental powers, acquiring a kinesthetic appreciation for bouldering movement, and gaining a rapport with the stone. The boulderers who have left the biggest mark on the sport, climbers like John Gill and Jim Holloway, did so only because they freed their minds of the expectations of others and the standards of the day to chase a personal dream of mastery. Gill and Holloway established problems that went unrepeated for twenty to thirty years, and they did it in primitive footwear, without pads or spotters. Their vision went beyond numbers.

The first edition of *Better Bouldering* delved into matters of style. This second edition does too, and I'm not about to apologize for it. I think people who chip holds in boulders are losers and those who lie about their climbs are no better. Most climbers agree with me. Beyond that I personally choose not to use cheater stones or power spots.

Some climbers agree with me on this, others don't. I use chalk. Some climbers frown on this. The point is that everyone should follow the style of climbing that makes them happy, not some style dictated to them by me or others. My comments on style are just a starting point to get the reader thinking about what style makes them happy. How you choose to climb is a reflection of your character. If you choose a style out of character with your principles, your bouldering career, or any career, will be miserable and/or short-lived.

Shortly after the publication of the first edition of this book, my bouldering career hit a wall. I'd grown happily accustomed to being one of the country's top boulderers in the 1980s and early 1990s, but was experiencing nerve damage in my left arm. I had surgery to fix the problem, but the surgeon botched it. I awoke from surgery with no feeling in half of my hand and very little function. My hand was so messed up I couldn't pick up a book, work nail clippers, or even turn a doorknob. My days were awash in suicidal thoughts and self-pity.

I'm a stubborn guy, however, and soon shifted into rehab mode and got back on the rock. At first I was climbing pretty much one-handed, and it seemed like getting back to 5.8 would be a major accomplishment. As I climbed those easy boulder problems and roped climbs, I realized that I was enjoying climbing at a reduced level. Really enjoying it. I was rediscovering what had initially appealed to me about the sport when I first started: being outside in beautiful surroundings, feeling the flow of the moves, enjoying the camaraderie of my partners, surprising myself when I did a move that seemed beyond me. Instead of experiencing the creeping indignity that comes with the inevitable gradual erosion of an athlete's skills, I got the magic bullet, an injury both career-ending and life-restoring.

Since the partial paralysis of my hand, I have learned to adjust my technique to accommodate my

handicap. Different muscles have been recruited and trained to do old tasks. Discovering and developing new bouldering areas has filled in the gap left by losing the edge in the numbers game. Even if I never do another first ascent, I can be happy just with the feeling of moving on the rock smoothly. I know this because it was only four years ago that I had both hips replaced. I was worried that another botched surgery would end my bouldering career forever. At that time I had not yet bouldered at Fontainebleau, the most historic and revered boulder garden in Europe. When I visited Fontainebleau prior to my surgery, I was in such bad shape that I had to climb the stairs to the second floor of the B&B on all fours, but I had one of the best bouldering trips ever, doing easy problems over perfect sand landings in a fairy tale forest. Had difficulty meant more to me than style, I would have retired many injuries ago and missed out on these experiences. I'd probably be some fat office slob trolling EwePorn.com, not a grizzled boulderer typing advice on his rest days.

From Gym to Outdoors

These days, many readers will likely have started their bouldering careers inside a gym. Some of you may have yet to boulder outside. If this is the case, I encourage you to go bouldering outside as early and as frequently in your career as you can. The predictably steep angles of the walls make gyms good places to gain strength. However, the relatively huge size of bolt-on footholds fosters lazy footwork, and the forced nature of artificial route setting retards the acquisition of body awareness. Outdoor bouldering, due to its infinite variety of hold types and wall angles, is the fix for this.

Indoor and outdoor bouldering may appear on the surface to be the same pursuit, but for both to flourish they need to be approached differently. Bouldering outdoors has a tradition that dates back to the 1800s. An essential part of the tradition is respect for the natural habitat and the other user groups that share an area. While as modern boulderers we may view the boulders as gymnastic apparatus, we mustn't treat them as merely an outdoor version of the bouldering gym. The routes outside are not set one day only to be pulled down a few weeks later. The features have been there for eons and will be there long after we depart, so it's imperative that boulderers never alter or manufacture holds outside. What would we be left with if all of today's V15s had been chipped down to be cutting-edge V4s back in the 1940s? Deciphering moves and sequences is at the heart of outdoor bouldering (as opposed to indoors, where every hold is marked out to force certain sequences). Don't ruin the fun and learning aspect by drawing lines at every hold you see. If sharing the area with other users, keep the screaming and cussing down. Remember there is nobody outside waiting to pick up your trash at the end of the night—clean up after yourself and others. Chipping, tick mark abuse, rude behavior, and littering are all a threat to access. Anyone who has been in this sport for even a short time has probably seen access to a favorite area either threatened or lost. Between the time I write this book and it hits the shelf at your local climbing shop, some of the problems pictured may possibly be closed to climbers. Send problems, don't create them.

Others are watching us while we boulder outside, including "The Man." Behave accordingly.

Gear

The only gear really needed to go bouldering is boulders (or a climbing wall). But since we live in a high-tech age of smart phones that can land a space shuttle, it's only natural that specialized gear exists to help us scale boulders.

Essential Gear

At the minimum, a modern boulderer should carry rock shoes, a bag of gymnastics chalk (though some purists eschew this aid), a toothbrush to clean chalk and dirt from holds, and a bouldering pad. A carpet patch on which to wipe your shoes is handy when your bouldering pad isn't positioned at the start of the problem.

Shoes

This is a very personal matter. On bouldering trips I've carried up to six different pairs of shoes to be prepared for any problem: stiff edging boots; loose, comfy warm-up boots; heel-hooking shoes; slippers for thin cracks and pockets; high-tops for bad landings; and an all-around shoe.

If you can only afford one pair of shoes, buy the brand that fits your foot best and is most durable. None of us are born with good footwork, so our first pair of shoes usually wears out the fastest. A resoler who's been in business for years and has resoled hundreds of pairs of shoes is a good person to ask about the most durable brands. Don't get stuck on the brand your hero wears—his or her foot may not be shaped like yours. Moreover, the climbers in the ads get their shoes for free, so they don't care how durable they are. Don't buy the "Our rubber is stickier" claims either. These days different rubbers are so similar as to be indistinguishable in blind tests. Ignore the ads and believe your feet. You can always resole them with different rubber if you desire.

The current trend in climbing shoes is toward low-top slipper styles. These soft shoes smear very well and excel at precise footwork on overhanging rock. Slippers have thin soles that allow you to better feel the rock beneath your toes. The disadvantage to slippers is they do not edge as well as stiffer boots and provide negligible support for landing after falls.

There are a few stiff-model boots available, but they're not near as stiff as in years past. Stiff boots excel at edging and really let you drive hard off tiny footholds. Because they don't bend as easily as slippers, they can actually gain you an inch or more of reach when going for that next hold. However, they lack sensitivity and require more trust (thus helping develop more trust) in one's footwork. Most stiff boots are cut higher than soft boots, lending some protection from ankle scrapes and strains.

Boots are classified as symmetric or asymmetric. Symmetric boots have toe boxes that are generally rounded, extending farthest around the second or

Essential gear for safe bouldering—a good pad.
DAWN KISH

1

The left shoe has a pointed asymmetric toe box, the right shoe a more rounded symmetric toe box. While asymmetric shoes are often marketed as higher performance models, the actual performance characteristics of each style will vary depending on your individual foot shape and toe lengths.

The left shoe has an aggressively downturned toe, good for pulling in on toeholds on overhangs. The right shoe has a flat sole, good for all-around use and comfort.

middle toe. These are generally most comfortable for all-day use. Asymmetric boots have toe boxes that extend farthest at the big toe, forcing more weight there for increased performance on tiny footholds. These are generally less comfortable than symmetric shoes. The different styles require different techniques to get the most out of them. Symmetric

Bouldering involves more heel hooks, toe hooks, and rand smears than other styles of climbing, thereby favoring shoes with ample rand coverage. Audrey Hsu on Shipwreck, Joshua Tree National Park, California.

boots edge better with the outside of the big toe placed on a hold—this forces the inside of the ankle closer to the rock, an advantageous posture on vertical and less than vertical faces. Asymmetric shoes edge better with the tip of the toe driven onto the foothold—this works best on overhanging rock.

Some asymmetric shoes have "downturned toes." These are specialty boots designed to help you pull on toeholds on overhangs. In general these are less comfortable to walk around in between problems—Velcro closures are nice as you'll be slipping them off frequently. Even if you aspire to only crushing roof projects, there will be time spent warming up on lower-angled stuff where a second pair with a more forgiving shape will be desired.

A shoe with ample rands (the rubber along the sides) is a plus for heel hooking, toe hooking, and instep smears.

The tighter the boot fits, the better it will perform up to a point—that point being when it hurts so bad you can't even walk up to the boulder. Most boots have leather uppers that stretch a bit, or a lot, after a few sessions. Some are made of faux leather that doesn't stretch at all, so be sure to ask the

No, his right foot isn't smaller than his left. He's just a masochist cramming his foot into the smallest boot he can pull on in hopes of gaining a performance edge.

salesperson how much stretch to expect. Shop for boots in the afternoon, as your feet can swell up to a full size in the course of a day. You will be jumping from boulders frequently. Shoes that pinch your toes may edge a bit better but will hurt like hell whenever you hit the ground.

Do you want a pair of shoes for all-day use, or megaproject sendmasters you'll have to remove after every attempt? If you only own one pair, I suggest sizing for comfort—there's nothing quite like a painfully tight pair of shoes to take the fun out of bouldering. Once you get hooked, you'll doubtless invest in a tighter or more specialized pair for your projects. As mentioned earlier, your first pair of shoes will probably wear out faster than subsequent pairs. As your footwork improves, so will the life of your shoes.

Resoling

The time to send your boots in for a resole is when the sole gets really thin, but before you grind a hole in the rand. It's much easier (not to mention cheaper) to retain the shape of the shoe if a rand repair isn't required. If you find your rands wear out before the sole, then this is a sign of sloppy footwork.

Chalk and Chalk Bag

Climbers use gymnastics chalk to keep hands and fingers dry and to reduce the greasy feel on handholds. It is composed of magnesium carbonate and comes in blocks, powder, a combination lumpy powder, or liquid form. Which form you choose is a matter of personal preference; they all work well. Powder, however, is more prone to blowing out of chalk bags on windy days and to spillage if a chalk bag tips over. Some companies distribute "chalk socks," which are porous fabric sacks filled with powdered chalk and kept in one's chalk bag. (These are commonly called "chalkballs," though one company has trademarked that name.) Chalk socks help prevent spillage and keep chalk dust to a minimum,

Shout Out to the Climbing Shoe Industry

As of 2011, not a single shoe manufacturer was making a safety-oriented bouldering shoe. Ankle sprains have reached epidemic proportions of late. The use of low-top shoes with thick bouldering pads is a formula for disaster. At present the industry takes sport climbing shoes and markets them as suitable for bouldering. These shoes excel at climbing rocks but suck at landings. The only "high-top" shoes currently on the market barely cover the ankle bone, so only provide protection from scrapes when crack climbing (thus are often marketed as trad climbing shoes), but they do not extend high enough above the ankle to trigger the proprioceptive muscle-tightening response to help control ankle roll when the joint is about to exceed its normal range of motion. Basketball players are constantly jumping and landing on others' feet, and you don't see them wearing low-tops. Ditto goes for football linemen who tape well above the ankle bone to protect their livelihoods. A proper bouldering shoe would extend about 2 inches above the tip of the ankle bone and allow normal range of motion. How do I know this? Because I got so tired of taping my ankles or trying to squeeze ankle braces inside my boots that I've taken to modifying my boots to provide ankle support, and now they work fine with no loss in range of motion. It would be easy to manufacture high-top versions of the current top sport climbing shoes with their aggressive high-performance shapes and characteristics (I've confirmed this with designers from several different companies). However, the honks at the shoe companies tell me they could never market such a shoe because of the stigma attached to high-tops as Gumby boots. A load of malarkey, I say—I remember when wearing a harness with leg loops marked you as a complete dweeb. Now you can't buy a harness without leg loops. So shoe companies, here's your opportunity to quit hating on us boulderers and our ankles—and become the first to bring out a bouldering shoe for the twenty-first century.

This is a 1960s-version of the PA, named after its designer and noted French alpinist and boulderer Pierre Allain. The original version came out in the late 1930s and was the first smooth rubber-soled shoe for climbing. It was designed especially for the needs of bouldering on the sandstone blocks of Fontainebleau. Because Allain designed the shoe for bouldering, he got it right when it came to ankle protection. None of the plethora of modern shoes in the background can claim as much.

the latter being an important consideration in climbing gyms or for climbers with breathing problems such as bronchitis or asthma.

Lately some manufacturers have added "secret drying ingredients" to their chalk. Some climbers find this improves performance, others can't tell the difference. If you already have dry skin, these "super chalks" may cause excessive drying and subsequent skin splitting. Hand lotion can relieve this.

Because the majority of chalk bags are basically the same, most people choose their chalk bags on the basis of how cool they look. Some people, especially those with big hands, like big bags they can sink their entire mitt into. Others prefer the light weight of a bag that accepts only fingertips. The only really essential feature to look for on a bouldering chalk bag is a slot, pocket, or loop to hold the toothbrush you'll use to clean holds. On most hard boulder problems, you will not be able to let go and chalk up. Therefore, I suggest finding a bag that will sit on the ground and not tip over and spill. Years ago most bags featured collapsible midsections that helped prevent spills—a good idea that fell victim to fashion trends. A few manufacturers make chalk pots—big, pear-shaped chalk bags designed to sit on the ground.

You wear two shoes, so why not wear two chalk bags? On longer problems where I have to chalk up during the climb, I like to wear a chalk bag on each hip. I look about as suave as Barney the purple dinosaur, but this system works great. I always know where to dip, and the energy I save not fishing around for my chalk bag while hanging from one hand more than makes up for the extra weight.

Liquid chalk has become my chalk of choice for most bouldering. It's simply magnesium carbonate dissolved in alcohol. Squirt a bottle cap's worth on your hands, rub it all over your palms and fingers (and backs of your hands if jamming), and watch as the alcohol evaporates and leaves a coating of chalk adhered to your hands. Liquid

chalk remains on your hands longer and leaves less residue on the rock—a win-win situation. I can give a problem three or four burns before I have to use more liquid chalk, whereas with dry chalk I usually need to chalk each attempt. Liquid chalk also minimizes the health concerns with breathing in chalk dust. For the ultimate in stealth bouldering, I add water-soluble cake coloring to tint my liquid chalk. Looks like goose poop when it comes out of the bottle, but it works great. I can fire off problems and only the savvy boulderer can tell I've been there—great for maintaining access. One safety note: Mixing liquid chalk yourself is not a good idea unless you have access to medical grade magnesium carbonate, as the block and powder chalk sold in climbing stores sometimes contains trace amounts of lead and arsenic—not something you want to dissolve and rub into your skin and scrapes.

Toothbrush

Your old retired brush with the black algae growing up the bristles will do, but given that this is the least expensive piece of bouldering gear, why not splurge and buy a specialized bouldering brush? The best are made of boar's hair—they lift chalk out of

An extendobrush in use.

textured holds well, leaving them super grippy for your next attempt.

To clean holds beyond your reach, make an "extendobrush" (or bubbabrush in the old-school boulderer's vernacular). This can be as simple as taping a toothbrush to a stick, or you can go all out with a telescoping handle and attached blow tube. My personal bubbabrush consists of an old golf club shaft (buy the longest club you can find in the barrel at the thrift shop) with a denture brush held on the end with small pipe clamps. Insert a plastic blow tube into the butt/handle end of the shaft. Because the shaft gradually narrows toward the brush end, the force of the air rushing through the tube is concentrated and does a great job of blowing loose chalk, dirt, and debris off holds.

Carpet Patch

A carpet patch is used to wipe the soles of your boots on immediately before getting on a problem. Carpet patches help improve the performance of

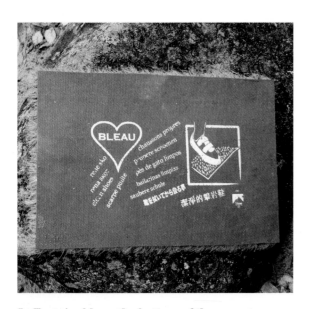

In Fontainebleau the bottom of the carpet patches urge you (in eleven languages) to love the rock by cleaning your soles before climbing.

your boots and protect the rock. Sticky boot rubber picks up a lot of dirt and grit—you don't want those little ball bearings between you and the footholds. Furthermore, grit stuck to your soles acts as an abrasive and hastens the polishing of footholds. You can either cut a square from an old carpet, or go to a carpet store and ask if they have any sample patches of discontinued lines they'd give you (or sell to you for a buck or two). The carpet store samples have finished edges so they won't unravel. Never leave your rug fixed at the boulders—they become dirty so quickly (and muddy if it rains) that they become useless. Furthermore, they are trash, plain and simple, and give a homeless hideout look to any boulderfield. By always keeping your personal rug with you, you can beat the dirt out every now and then, keeping it clean. In turn, it cleans your boots better, increasing your chance of succeeding on a given problem.

Bouldering Pads

Bouldering pads (aka crash pads) are foam-cushioned mats used to take the sting out of bouldering falls. Used intelligently, bouldering pads allow one to push harder on the boulders.

Some climbers view bouldering pads as devices merely to protect against bruised feet, but they do much more than that. Imagine jumping off your kitchen table and onto the tile floor fifteen times a day, three days a week, for ten years straight. Now imagine how bad your back, your hips, your knees, and your feet would feel after those ten years. The cumulative effect of bouldering falls can be crippling. Moreover, bouldering falls commonly create acute injuries such as bruised heels and broken feet. There's no sense in becoming an Advil poster child—investing in a good bouldering pad is an investment in your long-term health.

The most important component of any bouldering pad is the foam. Too soft and you'll feel like you just received a Singapore foot caning. Too stiff and your skeleton will take the shock before the

"Gnarly" Charlie Long on King Tut (V3), Buttermilks, California.

foam does its job. Your weight and bouldering style should determine which pad you buy. Having fallen on more bouldering pads more times than probably anyone else, I've come up with the following suggestions for checking foam quality and consistency: Stand on the bouldering pad with both feet. If your weight fully compresses the pad without jumping up and down, the pad is too soft. If you stand with all your weight on one foot, it should compress nearly all the way down—a 1-inch hop should compress it fully. Obviously, David Spade would pick a softer pad than Rush Limbaugh. If you only take very short falls, you can get away with a softer pad than if you frequently take very long falls.

Most pads have two densities of foam: a thick chunk of open cell and a thin slice of closed cell. There are two theories on using these: One says to lay the closed cell on the bottom as the final protection against stone bruises if you fully compress the open cell above. The other says to put the closed cell on top to distribute the force of a fall out over more of the open-cell foam below. Pads are made both ways, but in practice you can just flip them for the desired effect—closed cell down for a softer landing on short falls, closed cell up for a stiffer landing on long bombs or if your open-cell foam has gone mushy.

Quality bouldering pads are not cheap. Good, durable foam costs about as much per pound as filet mignon; it will last for years before wearing out. Cheap foam costs about as much per pound as hamburger. A pad made of cheap foam may work well for the first month or two, but will quickly deteriorate and soften. To assess foam quality, check the feel of the foam inside the pad before you buy—good foam will feel almost moist due to high latex content, cheap foam will have a slightly crunchy feel due to excessive use of clay filler.

The best size of bouldering pad is the biggest one you're willing to carry. By biggest I mean greatest surface area, not thickest. Overly thick pads, especially those thicker than 4 inches, have safety issues we'll touch on shortly. The longer the approach to your favorite area, the smaller a pad you might want to own. However, the higher off the ground you boulder, the greater you risk missing a small pad when you fall. While climbing the notorious Gill route on the Thimble, I remember my 3-foot-wide bouldering pad looking like a cocktail napkin.

The current trend in pads is to make them thicker and thicker, often to make up for inferior foam quality, but also as a marketing gimmick to make climbers think thicker pads must be safer. In fact, the thicker the pad, the greater the risk of ankle injury if you hit the edge of the pad—double that risk if you climb in low-top shoes. Some pads are so thick that people are rolling their ankles when hitting them dead center but with a sideways component of trajectory. I personally shy away from pads more than 4 inches thick.

The original homemade bouldering pads had carpet exteriors that were heavy but durable. The foam wore out before the carpet. Store-bought models save weight by using pack cloth exteriors. I have seen some of these wear out prematurely. Check for heavyweight pack cloth and for double-stitched seams. Some models also have some sort of carpet covering on one side to wipe your feet on. This is no substitute for carrying your own carpet patch, as your bouldering pad is often not positioned at the base of the problem. Therefore you need a carpet patch at the base anyway. Nevertheless, a carpeted side is desirable to provide extra friction for upside-down placements on steep slabs. (More on placing bouldering pads in Chapter 2.) Some pads feature rounded corners to reduce wear common on square corners. Few boulderers actually replace their pad's foam (Chinese pads flooding the market are frequently cheaper than domestically sourced replacement foam), so the durability of the corners is not that big an issue. More important is the fact that you can't butt rounded corner pads together (for multi-pad landings) without producing a gap where the corners meet. This gap is a huge safety hazard. Better to go with square corners and reinforce them with Shoe Goo or the like.

There are two basic styles of pads: those that fold with a hinge and those that fold like a taco shell. Hinge models will feel soft if you land on the hinge line unless the hinge line has straps or a flap to snug the gutter(s) shut (the little Velcro patches inside the gutter are nearly useless). You can find both bi-fold and tri-fold hinge models. Hinge models fold flatter than taco models—a plus when it comes to fitting in a trunk or storing in limited space at home. Taco-fold models are made of one thickness of foam, and you just fold the entire thickness over to shut the pad. These don't have the inherent soft spot along a hinge line, but with repeated folding the foam usually gets worked along the fold, creating a soft spot in the pad anyway. Storing the pad unfolded can help delay the onset of this soft spot. There are a few hybrid hinge/taco pads out there with a thin, uninterrupted sheet of closed-cell foam that fold taco-style atop a pair of open-cell chunks that are hinged. This reduces the softness of the hinge line, but not as well as a gutter flap. Of course the gutter flap/straps only work if you take the time to use them and seal the gutter tight—some folks are too lazy to do this every time they lay the pad out because the flap/straps need to be undone each time you fold the pad for carrying.

Check how convenient the closure straps are to use—some are a pain in the hindquarters. The terrain you travel through to the boulders influences the pack harness decision. For instance, if you boulder mostly in Boone, a pad that rides low is a plus because of all the branches you'll duck under getting to the boulders. If, however, you log most of your time in The Buttermilks, a high-riding pad will be better. Can you stash shoes and chalk bag inside without them falling out? Does the pad have handles for easy pickup to move between problems without strapping the whole shebang back together? On bi-fold pads, a handle inside the

Pictured left to right are a sub-pad, a hinge pad, and a taco pad.

gutter works well. Are the buckles metal or plastic? How comfortable are the pack straps and belt? You'll probably have a pack full of shoes and water stuffed inside the pad, so it will weigh more than just the pad alone in the store. If you're humping it out to Mount Evans, you'll be glad you checked. Some pads feature Velcro flaps to mate them side by side with other pads of the same make—alas it's a Tower of Babel when it comes to mating pads of different makes. Recently some manufacturers have started offering thin, firm sub-pads that can be used to cover seams between butted-together pads, among other uses.

As with much in life, you get what you pay for in a pad. Invest wisely.

There have been a few attempts to manufacture air pads, but so far none of these systems have gained popularity.

Pad Slitting: Calling Out the Manufacturers, Part Deux

Ah, here's another sidebar I hope to replace by the next printing of this book—how to make your pad safer. Circa 2000 I took a 6-foot fall off a problem in the Adirondacks, hit the edge of my pad, felt a horrid pop in my left ankle, and crumpled to the ground. Lying flat on my back, I looked at my out-stretched legs and found myself staring at the sole of my left shoe—my foot was on the side of my leg, not the end where it belonged. Luckily my bouldering partner was a Wilderness First Responder and did a crack job splinting the injured foot. My luck continued as I was taken to the Lake Placid emergency room, just down the road from the Olympic Training Center—no shortage of top sports medicine doctors there. They were duly impressed by the extent of the injuries—I'd popped all the ligaments off the outside of the ankle, tearing away some bone in the process, then rolled the ankle so tight as to crush ligaments on the inside as well. A "third-degree ring-around-the-rosey" sprain, as they called it. At first the doctor took me to be just a recreational climber, slapped an air cast on the foot, and told me to lay off it for eight weeks. "Wait a minute," I said, "is this what you'd do for one of your Olympians?" "No," responded the doctor, "but you won't rehab six to eight hours a day like they would." "Bullshit I won't." And with those words I was introduced to the joys of hardcore cryotherapy. The concept is simple: You immerse your foot in a bucket of ice water until it goes so numb you lose all feeling—only then can you stand to do the exercises. Then you knock out a bunch of exercises, upping the difficulty and intensity each session until the injury is healed. The catch is you get to do this every three hours from breakfast till bedtime, only taking enough time off between sets to avoid frostbite. Yep, six times a day the pain of the foot freezing. Six times a day the much greater burning agony of it thawing out. Multiply by a couple months. Hence the start of my search for a safer bouldering pad.

It's sad to say that since then, in the last decade plus, pads have only become more hazardous, not safer, as manufacturers engage in megamaxipad marketing, producing ads that sound like Enzyte com-mercials. "Enjoy the throbbing surge of confidence that comes with packing the biggest, thickest rig in the klettergarden. This product has not been evaluated by the FDA and is not intended to treat any threats to your safety." To increase my safety, I modify my pads to soften the perimeter and reduce ankle roll on edge falls. The process takes under an hour, perfect for your next rest day. Here's how I do it:

First, grab a long knife—this is the only tool you'll need. (A bread knife with wide smooth serrations cuts foam smoothly, whereas knives with tiny sharp serrations snag and tear at the foam.) Pull the foam out of your pad. This is easier if you fold the pad in a U shape. Note that some pads will have open- (soft) and closed- (hard) cell foam bonded together; others will have separate sheets of foam. If the former, the instructions below apply to the entire bonded mass. If the latter, the slicing instructions below apply to the open-cell foam, not the closed cell.

Make a cut parallel to the edge of the pad. This cut will be three-quarters of the depth of the pad and $1\frac{1}{4}$ inches from the edge, and will run the length of the foam. Do this around the entire perimeter of the

*The pad slits
get shallower
as one moves
toward the cen-
ter of the pad.*

pad, but do not cut any slices along the gutter edges in hinge-model pads. Repeat the process, slicing parallel to the edge but $1\frac{1}{4}$ inches farther in toward the center of the pad. This slice should be one-half the depth of the pad. Make one more set of slices $1\frac{1}{4}$ inches in, but only one-quarter the depth of the pad.

Next, start making angled slices perpendicular to the edge and spaced $1\frac{1}{4}$ inches apart. The angle at the bottom of these cuts should just intersect the bottom of each of the cuts made in the preceding step.

You should be left with a pattern of individual cubes along the edges that act like individually wrapped mattress coils. Fold the foam in half, making sure the unsliced edge goes toward the gutter, then reinsert in the nylon sleeve. This modification is not a cure-all, but helps reduce the severity of an ankle roll on an edge hit.

Other Useful Gear

Skin Kit

A honking flapper the size of a nickel need not end your session if you have a skin kit along. A skin kit contains a roll of breathable athletic tape, nail clippers, an emery board or patch, a tube of Krazy Glue, and a can of Tuf-Skin or bottle of tincture of benzoin. Band-Aids and antibacterial ointment (such as Neosporin) are needed for post-session treatments. An extra roll of tape can be a huge help if there's an injury that needs splinting.

Knee Pads

Knee bars are often the key to success on many problems, but can be painful without knee pads. Big soccer-style knee pads are clumsy and have a tendency to rotate when smeared against the rock. More stable are the thin neoprene knee braces (without stays) that look like a small section of a wet suit. Better still are the neoprene knee braces with a patch of 1 millimeter-thick rand rubber glued to the front. In Europe these are available in climbing shops (by the time this reaches print maybe in the United States as well, otherwise you can get a resoler to make you a pair). You can easily

Flappers and Skin Care

A flapper occurs when the rock gouges up a chunk of skin that remains partially attached to your finger or elsewhere. First we'll discuss how to treat an existing flapper, then we'll talk about preventative skin maintenance.

If you've gouged up a choice divot and you want to continue bouldering, clean out the wound, then trim off any dangling leftover skin (the flapper itself) with your nail clippers. Okay, you've just clipped off the lid of the crater, now look around the walls. Is there any loose skin you can see under? Often there is. Many flappers are just the torn-up lid of a thick blood blister. Slip the clippers under the edge of any loose skin (taking care not to irritate the sensitive raw patch at the base of the crater) and bevel the side of the crater. You don't want any loose overlapping skin left to initiate another possible snag. Tape over the crater and continue bouldering. Tuf-Skin or tincture of benzoin can be used to help the tape stick—and the latter gives you a burning sting to let you know you're still alive.

When a cut is on your fingertip and you don't want to wrap the whole tip in tape, you can place a thin strip of tape just over the cut itself with Krazy Glue. Put the glue on the skin, then press the tape on, taking care not to glue your fingers together.

If the gouge is really deep and you still want to continue bouldering, you can clean the wound and leave the flapper intact. Press it back into place or glue it down with Krazy Glue (not Super Glue, which is toxic), then tape over it. The chunk of flapper will provide some extra padding for the wound. (Some people might find that Krazy Glue irritates their skin. Use this technique sparingly.)

When you finish bouldering, pull the tape off, then trim off the dead skin and bevel the crater with your nail clippers (if you haven't already done so). You can further bevel and smooth the edges of the cra-

make these yourself. If you don't have access to rand rubber, you can use Stealth Paint, which is just ground-up climbing sole rubber mixed with contact cement. Get a bigger can of contact cement, as the tube that comes with the kit is woefully inadequate. Instead of mixing a goopy mess of rubber and cement, spread a coat of contact cement on the front of the knee pad, then cover it with rubber dust. Brush away the excess dust that didn't bond and save it for the next coat. Do three coats this way. Reapply as needed as it will gradually wear away after heavy knee-barring action. I've done this trick with a pair of Stonemaster stretch climbing jeans—because they are anchored to your waist, the rubberized patches can't slide down on really cranking knee bars as sometimes happens with separate knee pads. Knee bar specialists carry duct tape to tape the pads in place on their legs to avoid pad spin and slip. Great fun when the tape comes off.

Helmet

Despite allegations that my skull is thicker than the former Berlin Wall, I have suffered multiple concussions from occasionally landing on my head instead of my feet. These days I frequently wear a helmet when bouldering without a spot, when I'm unsure

ter with an emery pad or board. Put an antibiotic ointment, such as Neosporin, on the wound, then bandage it. Keep it covered. If you boulder within the next three days, tape over the wound while bouldering, then apply ointment and bandages afterward. If treated right, on the fourth day the finger should be ready for climbing without tape.

To prevent flappers from occurring in the first place, remove all "pull tabs" (tiny flaps of peeling skin) from your fingers with the emery pad or nail clippers. Keep the surface of your fingers smooth, with no pull tabs or ridges to snag. Also keep the skin moist and pliable. Those prized calluses you worked so hard to develop will last longer if they

Can you say "Welcome to Hueco"? Classic flappers, yummy.

don't dry out. Furthermore, dry skin flappers easily. Pliable skin doesn't. To keep skin pliable, wash off chalk as soon as possible after each session. Use hand lotion after washing your hands. Before going to bed, rub a little petroleum jelly on your fingers to help prevent splitting. Keeping your skin soft may seem counterproductive to climbing. Some folks fear it may shorten the duration of their sessions. Session length, however, is a function of pain endurance, not skin toughness. Your nerves will adapt to long sessions and they, not your skin, will tell you when your fingers have had enough.

SHADOW AYALA

as to the spotter's skills, or when there are just plain too many objects (nearby rocks, tree limbs) to hit. Wearing a helmet has improved my bouldering by allowing me to concentrate on the moves and sending the problem instead of worrying about fall consequences. The best part? Wearing a helmet at the boulders announces that you have cool to spare. So much, in fact, that you can dumb it down a bit to make the less confident at the rocks feel less intimidated by your presence.

I feel that a skateboard helmet is a better choice for bouldering than a climbing helmet. Bouldering falls are very much like falls off a skateboard, and skateboard helmets are designed to withstand blows both to the sides, back, and top of your head. Climbing helmets, on the other hand, are designed to stop falling rocks from caving in the top of your skull. Most climbing helmets provide little side or back impact protection, though some of the newer models are trending in this direction. There are some exciting advances in material technology that will make for more protective, less obtrusive helmets soon.

I have no spotter here. If my fingers cut loose, I'll be going headfirst to the deck. Good time to rock the lid.

Pie in the Sky

Chris Summit tells the story like this: "so the pic of my bloody scalp—funny shit. I was pulling off the ground on a brand new just brushed little warm up V3ish sit lowball piece of crap really but with a perfect square cut starting hold campus move. we were at my new found granite area "spicer". i knocked on the hold with one hand and held it with the other hand to feel for vibrations to test for solidity before pulling off the ground and it felt solid so i pulled off and Pop! it snapped off in a sharp little pie shape, i still have the piece, it hit me in the noggin and it felt like someone threw a drink on my head the blood spilled out so fast! rad. my bro ryan took his shirt off and put it on my head so most of the blood came off on it then we took it off and took the pic, it was even bloodier at first, it was in my mouth and eyes even! we taped my head up and i looked like a [dork] climbing all day. blood kept leaking threw so we figured it needed to be maybe stitched or at least butterfly bandaged and also it would be good to clean it better than we had so i went to the free med clinic at the ski lodge and they put butterflys on it and cleaned it with no pain killer—ouch, but good fun! hell yeah you can use the pic in your book, im honored! i think?"

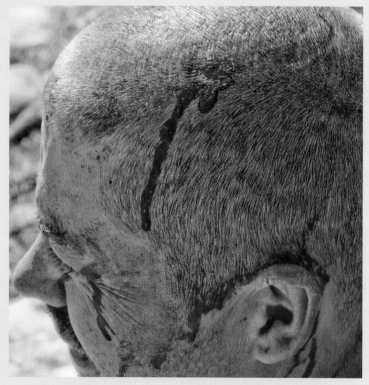

CHRIS SUMMIT COLLECTION

Ego-Swelling Combat Tale #1

One of the most satisfying first ascents I've ever done is called *Best of the Best*. The forty-minute approach, the longest in Hueco Tanks, put off most potential spotters, so several times I went up there alone. This 25-foot roof ran above a stepped slab landing with potential for serious injury if one landed on the edge of a step. To protect myself I positioned a bouldering pad over the most hazardous step. Then I stuffed a folded Ensolite pad down the back of a pair of baggy shorts and inside my T-shirt to protect my spine. In addition I wore a bicycle helmet. A couple of knee pads and I could have been taking snaps in the NFL. These precautions allowed me to try moves I wouldn't otherwise have tried without a spotter. Despite looking like a rodeo clown, I eventually succeeded. As I sat atop the boulder, all that protective gear strapped to me could not stop the good feelings from soaking in.

Cell Phone

If there's cell phone reception at the boulders, bring your phone in case somebody gets hurt. A head injury or fractured femur can prove fatal if help doesn't arrive pronto. Turn the phone off or at least the ringer as a courtesy to your fellow boulderers. Or play the cell phone game (I do this when I give slide shows)—first person's phone to ring and disturb everyone gets to buy the beer (I can hear you readers tapping your partner's number into speed dial right now—sneaky, sneaky—bottoms up!).

First-Aid Kit

No brainer.

Safety

In case you go bouldering before you finish reading this book, let's get to the most important information right now. Safety should be the prime concern of all boulderers. Much of what is written in this chapter is here to prepare you for the worst-case scenario of a long fall onto a bad landing. Some of this might make bouldering sound overly scary and serious, yet the chances of a bouldering session ending in a closed casket funeral are virtually nil. Nevertheless, twisted ankles and broken bones are common bouldering injuries. This chapter discusses the risks of bouldering and how to minimize them.

Falling and Jumping

In bouldering, virtually every fall is a ground fall. If it isn't, you've probably either ledged-out or fallen into a tree. Naturally, either scenario can be about as fun as a kick to the goolies. Fortunately, there are techniques to minimize injury.

Good Landings

I consider a good landing to be flat or only slightly inclined, free of obstructions, and relatively soft (e.g., dirt or sand—not a rock slab or concrete sidewalk).

With a good landing, ideally you will fall feetfirst and onto a bouldering pad. If possible, keep your eyes on the landing as you fall. When you land, suck up the impact with your legs like a skier hitting a mogul. In extreme cases you might bottom out, your legs fully bent, butt to heels and knee to chin.

If your body hits a good landing at an angle, you will not be able to suck up the impact with the knees. Instead, roll with the fall like a judo master. Be sure the landing is free of obstructions before you get on the problem. You don't need to be rolling over a half-full beer, your ghetto blaster, and/or into some dog poop.

On less than vertical faces, you might hit the wall as you fall. Push off the wall as you fall so you land clear of the base of the rock. On low-angle slabs (50 degrees or less) you can turn around (face away from the rock) and run down the slab as you fall. Be sure you have room to run after you hit the ground. Scope the scenario first and have your landing planned before you attempt the problem.

WARNING: **A nice flat landing doesn't guarantee a safe fall. The North Face of the Mushroom Boulder in Hueco Tanks (before Texas Parks closed it to climbers) had one of the smoothest, flattest dirt landings around,**

Incoming! Cody Roth takes a man-size whip off the top moves of **The Hatchling (V11), Rocklands, South Africa. Fabrice Clair** *provides the fearless spot.*

Alan Carne doing a textbook job of sucking up impact with his legs.

yet many climbers broke wrists when they failed to land on their feet. Two climbers even broke both wrists. (You find out who your friends are when you can't wipe for yourself.)

Don't take good landings for granted, and maintain a measure of respect for the dangers involved in bouldering. When available, always use a spotter and a bouldering pad.

A split second after his feet start sliding, Adam Massey turns outward to run down Initial Friction *in Yosemite Valley. Had he faced toward the rock and slid down, he would have lost rubber off his shoes and maybe some skin off his hands as well as risked smashing his shins on the lip at the base of the slab.*

Bad Landings

Some sickos, like me, believe a nasty landing adds spice to a problem, heightening the adrenaline buzz and increasing the feeling of accomplishment when one succeeds. Some of the best boulder problems in the world have bad landings. There are two basic ways to approach problems with bad landings: run away or deal with it.

Running away is also known as discretion and is not a bad quality to have. Be honest with yourself when it comes to your abilities. Hurtling headfirst toward a stack of broken blocks is a bad time to find out you aren't ready for a given problem. Boulder problems rarely disappear at night, so you can always come back later. For every twisted highball problem I've done, I've seen a dozen I wouldn't try because I felt the risk was too great.

Dealing with it involves carefully analyzing the landing and the directions you might fall—in other words, risk management. The first thing to check is if your head or spine will hit anything. If so, pad that surface, alert your spotter, and/or wear

The author on the first ascent of ICBJ, Independence Pass, Colorado, circa 1990. These days this abysmal landing could be made safe with multiple pads.

a helmet. Next, check for branches that might skewer you, tree roots you might twist an ankle on, and so forth. Know where these hazards are before you go up on a problem. I have some nice scars on my back from tearing a hold off a traverse and not knowing there was a splintered tree stump right behind me.

Some bad landings consist of multilevel landing spots, neighboring walls, or boulders you might bounce off of. Some even result from carelessly stacked bouldering pads—more on this later.

Clearing Bad Landings

One way to cope with bad landings is to clear them of obstructions and turn them into good landings. This job is commonly left up to the first ascensionist. If he or she chose to clear away more or less than you would have, then that was his or her decision and you should respect it. If you don't like the landing on an established boulder problem, go to a different problem that suits your tastes. Alternatively, ask first ascensionists if they mind if you clear the landing more. They might say go for it. Other than

Paul Robinson grew up always using a pad. Here he takes the opportunity to try a Richi Signer problem in Chironico, Switzerland, in the pad-free style of the early 1980s first ascent. His falling technique has been inhibited by his climbing gym upbringing—see how he corkscrews into the rocks, legs barely bent to suck up the impact. Even if you never go outdoors to boulder, it's worth practicing good falling technique in the gym.

Risk Management

Every time we start up a boulder we consciously take a risk. Risk management skills are key to maximizing safety. There are three steps:

1. **Assess the situation/identify the risks**. Is the landing bad? How many pads do we have? Which direction will the boulderer fall? How far away is help if something goes wrong?

2. **Develop a plan/strategy to deal with the risks**. Make priorities based on minimizing the worst outcomes, such as "above all, don't let Jimmy fall in that gap between rocks and snap his femur." Lesser outcomes, like Jimmy landing on his iPod, go to the bottom of the list. Have a plan in case all your preparation is in vain and there's an accident. Who will run for help, who will stay? Where are the car keys stashed? Communicate the plan with each other.

3. **Apply the plan/strategy.**

The above procedure might sound daunting to apply on every problem, but all it really requires is a vigilant attitude and soon it will become second nature. If you boulder at the same spot repeatedly or with the same partners, you probably have most or all of the strategy in place from past sessions.

removing cheater stones (whoever left them there should have done this) or recent debris (say a fallen tree limb), it's best to leave landings as you found them. This way everyone can have the same experience as the first ascensionist.

But the Landing Sucks and I Just Gotta Do That Problem . . .

A given problem may captivate you so much that you feel you must climb it. Unfortunately, the macho jerk who put it up opted not to clear away the rusty ship anchors and barnacle-encrusted stones at the base. Somehow he felt this added to the thrill of the problem. You, however, would prefer not to risk a trip to the hospital. What do you do? You can toss a toprope on the problem, you can wait until you are good enough to do it unroped over the bad landing, or you can try and clear the landing. The first two options show respect for the first ascensionist and the climbing community. They are your best choices. If the problem really means a lot to you, then it's probably worth waiting for until you can do it cordless. Some folks will justify the third choice, claiming they are doing a public service by making the problem safe. But unless the first ascensionist has granted you permission to rearrange the landing, you're better off leaving it as is. If you disagree with the style of a first ascent, then make a statement with your own first ascent of a virgin line in the style you choose. How you climb is a reflection of your character. If you don't respect others' first ascents, don't expect anyone to respect yours.

Predetermining Fall Angles

This is one of the keys to safe bouldering. Visualizing sequences to a problem is a common technique that helps one psych up and climb efficiently. It is also important to visualize falling off a problem. Imagine as many scenarios as you can: If that left-hand layaway snaps, I'll end up in the bushes to the right; if I can't push the mantel, I might topple over backward; if my left foot pops off that nubbin, I'll shoot down and to the left; and so on. Experience and/or a degree in physics will help you figure out the angles. Discuss these possibilities with your spotters. Tell them which moves you feel you might fall off of. Then they can already be in position.

Visualizing falls is only a safety precaution. Don't let it psych you out. Do it for every problem and it will become standard operating procedure.

Fall angle analysis #1: *Lisa Rands on the Checkerboard Boulder, Buttermilks, California. If her right toe hook pops, she'll pirouette outwards and left and fall into the arms of the spotter on the left. If her left hand comes off, she'll pivot out and right, falling into the arms of the spotter on the right.*
WILLS YOUNG

Fall angle analysis #2: *Adam Markert on a difficult roof lunge at Rocklands, South Africa. Adam is pushing hard with his feet to propel him to the target hold on the lip to the left. If he fails to reach the target hold, he'll pivot back and right around his right handhold. If his feet popped an instant before this photo was taken, his right arm would launch him to the right. However, at the point captured in this photo, his feet are staying put and he's already generated substantial momentum from right to left—the greater worry is if his right hand slips or the hold snaps, then his momentum will carry him violently headfirst to the left. If he latches the target hold and his feet leave the holds, his legs will swing to the left and threaten to pull his right hand off.*

NOTE: These sample analyses don't take every contingency into consideration. For example, if the space shuttle was to crash into the back of the Checkerboard Boulder, Lisa would probably land somewhere in Oregon. As well, these samples only analyze a single move. Out in the field you'd analyze fall angles for the entire problem, paying extra attention to the hardest and most hazardous moves. The idea behind these samples is to introduce you to the thinking process involved in fall angle analysis. As you look at the other pictures in this book, try to analyze them as well.

Fall angle analysis #3: *This climber is just getting into the meaty crux of* **Creaky Heights** *(V4) in Rocklands, South Africa. He's smearing some warty bumps with his feet and pulling hard with his hands on thin sidepulls. Should his feet creep off the smears he'll rocket down and left, possibly missing the left pad. The more frightening scenario is if his fingers give out, then his legs will catapult him horizontally toward the rock behind the spotter's leg.*

Pre-Jumps

The more experience you have, the easier it will be to predetermine fall angles. Sometimes, however, you can't figure out where you'll land by looking at a problem. In this case I will sometimes climb up to the move in question, give it just enough effort to put my body into the position it will be in when trying the move, then jump off from that position. Because I am forcing the fall, I am prepared to land on my feet and suck up the impact, hopefully with the help of my spotter. This simulated fall, or pre-jump, should give you a very good idea of the trajectory a real, unexpected fall from that point will take. You can then position your spotter and bouldering pads accordingly. In certain situations where you might strike a wall or neighboring boulder before hitting the ground, you may pre-jump, not from the move itself, but from the point you will bounce off the wall or that neighboring boulder (given you can establish yourself at this point). This will make for a shorter, less dangerous pre-jump.

I have yet to be injured from a pre-jump, but that is because I use it sparingly. If a landing is so bad that the risk of injury during a pre-jump is nearly as great as that from an unrehearsed fall, I will not do a pre-jump.

The Stone Toss

This is a good trick to use with, or instead of, a pre-jump to determine where one might land. It is generally less accurate than a pre-jump but virtually free of risk. With the stone toss, I toss a stone, stick, or other object up the boulder to the point where I think I might fall off. I watch its trajectory after it bounces off the boulder and where it lands (hopefully in the middle of a bouldering pad). I repeat this several times. The best results come when the stone bounces a short way out from the wall before landing, instead of ricocheting straight down. This is because climbers usually pop away from the rock when they first fall, then drop. This technique works best for straight-down falls, and is of limited use for falls with a component of sideways trajectory.

Spotting—The Sacred Trust

Spotting is the technique used to break a boulderer's fall and steer him or her to a safe landing. Spotting is a technique that takes time to master. As a spotter, your partners count on you for their safety. *SPOTTING IS NOT A CHORE, IT IS A SACRED TRUST.*

Go back and read the last sentence again. Now let me pound the point in a bit harder. A good attitude is the most important characteristic of a good spotter. Many of the greatest ascents in the history of bouldering were done only because the boulderer had a trustworthy spotter who took pride in his or her assignment. The "I'll spot you on your project if you'll spot me on mine" attitude is sure to generate listless, ineffective spots. You are the spotter now, not the climber. Focus on your job.

The ideal spotter would have the reflexes of Bruce Lee, the lateral movement and quickness of Serena Williams, and the strength and size of Shaquille O'Neal. Of course no such person exists, but Scott Blunk comes close at 6 feet 7 inches, 220 pounds, and a master of martial arts. Still, those qualifications would be all for naught if it weren't for Scott's superior attitude and technique. These anyone can develop, even if you're built like Napoleon Dynamite. A superior attitude comes from taking pride in one's duty and striving to always better one's technique.

Spotting Priorities

When spotting, you are not required to catch the falling climber like a football or a ballerina. The spotter's number one priority is to protect the boulderer's head and spine.

The spotter's priorities, in order of importance:

- Protect the boulderer's head and spine. If the spotter fails to protect the boulderer's head and/or spine and an injury results, then the spotter has failed in the worst way. Better a broken ankle than a broken skull.
- Steer the boulderer toward a good landing. By steering the falling climber toward a good

Ego-Swelling Combat Tale #2

I was bouldering on Scott Blunk's ranch in Wyoming several years back, trying to bag the second ascent of a wild diagonal lunge problem he had put up. I would fly for the lip, come up short, then arc over to the left where Scott would break my fall. This happened many times as I continued to work on the problem. On my last try I was all coiled up, ready to blast for the lip. Suddenly the finger rail I was yarding on snapped. I launched backward and headfirst like a backstroker starting a race. My noggin was on a trajectory to land in a patch of stones and cactus several yards right of where I had been previously landing. There was no warning, unlike the previous falls, but because he focused his entire attention on spotting me, not just watching me, Scott made a save that would have made ESPN's highlight reel. I didn't even nick the ground.

landing, the spotter protects the boulderer's ankles, knees, etc.

- Break the boulderer's fall. By absorbing some of the force of a fall, the spotter lessens the force of the boulderer's final impact.
- Protect oneself—the worst-case scenario is if both climber and spotter get injured and nobody is left to call 911.
- Do not interfere with the ascent. The spotter should interfere with the fall, not the ascent. Avoid touching a boulderer while he or she is climbing. Some climbers get very upset if touched by the spotter—they just know someone will witness the dab and call them out on 8a.nu.

First Things First

To start the spot, be sure you're positioned where you need to be as discussed above in predetermining fall angles. Get your hands up in position ready to make the catch. Keep a slight flex in your knees; otherwise a falling climber might flatten you like a jackboot crushing a cockroach. This knee flex will also help you absorb some of the climber's fall.

Keeping your fingers together and your thumb close to the index finger can help prevent injuries

due to snagging on the falling climber's clothes or simply from a climber coming in too hot.

Watching the Climber

When spotting, focus on the boulderer's center of gravity. With most men this is a few inches above the belt line. With most females, it is at the belt line. Think tramp stamp and you'll focus on the right spot. If you see this point rapidly dropping, then the boulderer is surely falling and it's time to do your thing. Many spotters make the mistake of watching the hands, arms, feet, or legs. These have a tendency to fly about and give the appearance that the climber is falling, when really he or she is still hanging on and busting a nut (or an ovary) trying to send the problem. If you grab the person at this point, he or she will doubtless be upset and bust you in the reproductive units. Just because a hand doesn't hit the hold it was shooting for does not automatically mean the climber will fall. The temptation to watch hands and feet to discover sequences is great, but if you want to do that, do your partner a favor and let somebody else spot.

When watching the boulderer, try to establish a sense for which way he or she might fall from any given move. If he or she doesn't discuss probable

Fingers together and thumbs tucked in, Chad Foti about to make the catch on Masaya Ogata, Schwupp (aka Roadside Dyno) (7a), Rocklands, South Africa. Chad is in good position with a proper amount of bend in his knees. Thin anti-fatigue mats seal the gaps between pads.

falling angles before the climb, don't be afraid to ask the boulderer where he or she expects to fall from and where the anticipated landing is. Even with these clues, one must still be alert at all times. Unexpected falls are often the worst.

Making the Catch

In most situations the spotter will actually grab hold of the falling boulderer to break the fall and steer the body to a good landing. When falling from vertical or less than vertical terrain, the boulderer's body will usually be aligned vertically, heading toward the ground feetfirst. In this case, grab the boulderer by the hips and steer toward a good landing. Absorb some of the fall with your arms and legs. Let the boulderer absorb the rest of the fall with his or her legs when hitting the ground. Keep hold of the boulderer, if possible, so he or she doesn't roll away after landing. A climber's worst injuries may come not from the initial impact, but from impacts taken while rolling.

When one is climbing overhangs or falling over backward (say due to a snapped layaway hold), the body often falls at an angle to the ground, instead of feetfirst. Sometimes it can even go headfirst. In these hazardous cases, grab farther up the body (above the center of gravity), along the upper lats or in the armpits. This will cause the body to rotate feet downward. Steer the climber to a good landing and absorb the impact as above.

Chris Kelk grabs Fabrice Clair and steers him toward a safe landing.

Pat Goodman keeps his focus on Elaina Arenz-Smith's center of gravity while she tries **Picture Perfect Arête,** *Joshua Tree National Park, California.*

Spotter Rachel Strate knows climber Harry Crews greatly outweighs her. Furthermore, this crux lip sequence is situated at the end of a pumpy hand traverse and over an abrupt ledge. Hence Rachel stays very focused and keeps her hands just inches away from Harry's lats should his fingers fail. **Barracuda Rail (7b), Rocklands, South Africa.**

The Bump-and-Catch

This is a more advanced technique than those above, but has the advantage of absorbing a lot of fall force. It is a good technique for spotting longer falls, but should only be done when the climber is falling feetfirst. When the boulderer comes toward you, hit the boulderer's buttocks with the palms of your hands like you're setting a 200-pound volleyball. Keep your fingers together and thumbs tight in. This should absorb much of the speed and force of the fall. Done correctly, the boulderer will slow down and you can quickly grab his or her hips and steer toward a good landing. If both climber and spotter agree in advance that a bump-and-catch is called for, the falling climber can lift his or her knees during the fall to better expose the butt for the bump. Done incorrectly, the bump-and-catch can cause the climber to flip over backward on top of you, a dangerous situation for all parties concerned. Practice this with a backup spotter.

Shoving

In some situations, the best a spotter can offer is a redirection of the falling boulderer's trajectory away from a hazard. In this case the spot consists of a quick shove away from the hazard and toward a better landing. If there is not a second spotter, the falling boulderer is then responsible for breaking the rest of his or her fall. This may involve rolling. Often a bump-and-catch is more like a bump-and-shove.

Gang Spots

This is when more than one spotter is watching the boulderer. If coordinated well, a whole gang of spotters can be more effective than a single great spotter. It's a good tactic when there are multiple hazards to contend with. All spotters must be clear as to what their assignments are. Let's say Latrina is climbing. Joe, being light but quick, is in charge of shoving her away from the broken branches on the right; Manuel, because of his surefootedness, stands on the slab to the left and keeps her from falling in the Indian grinding holes; Bertha, a trigonometry major, tends the bouldering pad and moves it between potential landing zones as Latrina moves out the roof; and Bubba, being state power-lifting champ, is in charge of the final catch. Be sure to discuss who will do what *before* someone falls. Two or three spotters getting in each other's way can lead to more injuries than if there were no spot at all. It's like those baseball bloopers where two infielders and an outfielder all collide and the ball drops untouched to the ground between all three. Communication is key—tell fellow spotters if you have the spot or need help. Sometimes instead of multiple spotters all trying to follow the climber on every move, it works better for them to split responsibilities, again discussing it before the attempt. For instance, "I've got Lucrushus until he gets to the undercling and steps left—you take over at that point." If another spotter is getting in your way and you are in the superior position to spot the climber, call the other spotter off and tell them that you have the spot.

Paul Robinson on the second ascent of Evangalion (V13), Hueco Tanks, Texas. Should Paul fall, the spotter atop the boulder to the left is there to shove him toward the other spotters on the ground.
ISAAC PALLATT

Walker Kearny punches out another big overhang at Hueco Tanks, Texas. The uneven landing makes it hard for one spotter to follow all the moves; therefore the spotter in white is in charge of spotting the lower half of the problem. When Walker gets higher the spotter in orange takes over.
DAWN KISH

Room for Improvement

One of the most frustrating things about compiling this book was trying to get photos displaying good spotting technique. The sad fact is nine out of ten spotters do a lousy job, primarily because they are looking at holds, trying to absorb beta, or just have a lazy attitude. Look at the photos in the book and see how many spotters are not focused on the climber's center of gravity. It's an alarming number.

The spotter is focused on the climber's hips, which is good, but there are several things that could be done better here. First, the spotters shouldn't be afraid to step closer to spot the lower moves of this problem; they can then move back as the climber gets higher up the overhang. Second, the climber is perilously close to a dangerous "edge hit" on the pad; if she fell a few inches to her left, she could easily sprain her ankle, so the pad should be relocated about half-a-pad's worth to her left, or there should be a spotter close to her left to redirect her to the center of the pad. Third, the pads are askew, creating a dangerous gap between them. The pad in the background should be slid over and butted right up next to its mate.

This spotter is obviously transfixed by the hold Adam Markert is about to lunge for. The spotter has zero chance of making the one-handed grab.

Well, if it isn't Mr. One Arm Spot again, this time trolling for foot beta. He'd better hope Chad's toe hook doesn't blow or he might spill his Coke.

Ego-Swelling Combat Tale #3

You may be protecting your partner, but you have to look out for yourself too. Once I was involved in a two-man spot at a lakeside boulder in southern Illinois. We were spotting a guy named Alan, who was bigger than either of us. He was climbing out a roof with his heel hooked at the back and his body extended out to reach the lip. He cut his heel hook loose and his feet swung outwards toward us. He lost his grip and came flying over our heads like Superman in reverse. We were there to keep him from falling in the lake, but it was obvious to both of us that we couldn't reel that big a guy back in. Without words, we made the same decision. With hands over our heads we each pushed Alan as hard toward the lake as we could, hoping deep water would absorb his fall. The trick worked and I was howling to see Alan emerge like a swamp creature from the water, pouring what looked like a quart of milk from his chalk bag. My laughter soon ceased, however, when I realized my spotting partner was in terrible pain. When we twisted around to redirect Alan's fall, my spotting partner's foot got stuck between some roots and didn't twist. It broke in several places and required surgery to fix. The trajectory of Alan's fall had surprised us. Had we examined the footing though, the surprise would not have been so costly.

Spotting Beta

It is a good idea to plan a spotting sequence for each problem. On a simple straight-up problem, the spotter might never change stances. On traverses and overhangs, the spotter might move many times. These moves may require negotiating obstacles such as boulders, bushes, tree roots, or street curbs. Know what is underfoot so you don't trip and fall. Plan the moves between stances so you can move when the boulderer is least likely to fall and need your services. Practice these moves between stances so you can switch positions quickly. If you are gang spotting, you can leapfrog between stances and never leave the boulderer unprotected. Know at each point in the problem which way you will direct a fall. If you don't have enough pads to protect all the potential landing zones, you may want to move one in mid-problem. Prepare for this in advance so you can reposition it when the climber is least likely to fall (discuss this interruption in spotting with the climber before the attempt).

Spotting Low Problems

There are stacks of gruesomely hard sit starts and close-to-the-ground roof problems out there now. Slip off your handholds on one of these and its skull bongo time. For such problems the spotter should get on his or her knees to get more directly under the climber and keep the head and shoulders off the deck. Catching a climber from a stooped-over standing stance is nearly impossible.

Calling Off the Spot

Sooner or later some psycho will talk you into spotting him or her on a ridiculous problem. Before you know it the climber's feet are fifteen feet up, knees doing the Elvis, and the confident, challenging voice that coaxed you into this has turned into a high-pitched whimper. If there is a fall, you will end up 2 feet shorter. When you put yourself in as much danger as the climber you're spotting, you have every right to call off the spot. The high boulderer may not like this, but understands it's

*Jesse Althaus gets low to spot McKenzie Long on the steep start to **Morning Dove White** (V7), Happy Boulders, Bishop, California. When the climber gets higher, the spotter will rise to a standing position.*

part of the game. Ideally you will explain the situation before he or she starts up the problem: "I'll spot you until you reach that mantel, then you're on your own," or even just, "I might have to bail on you if you get too high for my spotting ability. I'll yell if I'm chickening out." What is inexcusable is to leave your post without warning the climber. This is a violation of the sacred trust. I've topped

out on more than one tall problem not to be elated at succeeding, but pissed because my spotter had vamoosed without telling me.

Spotting Recap

Putting this all together:

- Analyze the potential fall angles and communicate with the climber; figure out your spotting beta.
- You're spotting now, not climbing. Keep your attention on spotting, not on your partner's beta.
- Position yourself correctly.
- Keep a slight knee flex and fingers together.
- Focus on the climber's "tramp stamp."
- Make the spot.

Uh oh, this dude's a load and he's coming right at you. If your focus isn't 100 percent on spotting, he'll drive your ass into the ground like a tent peg.

Bouldering Pad Use

It's funny that modern bouldering—which is essentially gymnastics using boulders for apparatus—quickly borrowed dynamic moves and spotting from gymnastics, but was slow to incorporate padded landings. In the old days we'd pad a sharp stone or a tree root with a pack or a sweater. In an extreme case in Yosemite in the 1970s, climbers pilfered mattresses from employee dorms, then dragged them over to the Camp 4 boulders to cover the jagged blocks under *Bachar Cracker*.

Marcie Puskarik and Hillary Haakenson at The Elephant sector, Fontainebleau, France. Because it is straight up and doesn't overhang much, a single pad is adequate for this problem.

Nevertheless, portable, custom-made pads didn't arrive on the scene until around 1990, over thirty years after the advent of gymnastic bouldering.

If you're new to the sport and coming from a gym background, you'll be used to landing on fully padded floors and/or mats the size of wading pools. This is definitely not the case outdoors where you may have only one 3 x 4 foot pad. Pad placement is absolutely key to safety. Bouldering pads don't work if you don't hit them.

Single Pad Use

Proper placement of your bouldering pad is most important. In 1994 I took a mere 4-foot hop off some pissy variant to an otherwise easy problem on Mount Sanitas in Colorado. I landed on my bouldering pad with all of my right foot and the heel of my left foot. The ball of my left foot hit a walnut-size stone and I broke the peanut-size sesmoid bones that protect that joint. That foot gave me problems for years.

Some people make the mistake of leaving the pad at the base of the first moves so they can wipe

Even covered with a bouldering pad, this unassuming root could seriously twist an ankle if landed upon; hence I mark a "no-fall zone" on my crash pad.

Shena Sturman on **Red Monster** *(V6), Ibex, Utah. A fall from this tough move would miss the pad, but the consequences of a fall turning the lip are greater, so she's positioned her single pad under those moves. Note how Thimble, being a smart crag dog, keeps her distance.*

their feet before starting. On vertical to less than vertical straight-up problems, this will work. On overhanging, angling, or traversing problems, this probably won't be the case. Assuming you don't have a partner who can move the pad as you climb, anticipate the most likely place you will fall and place the pad there. (See the Predetermining Fall Angles section for advice.) Use a carpet patch to wipe your feet.

The most important consideration is to place a pad where it will most reduce the risk of injury. This is not necessarily under the crux moves. In some cases there might be a nice, cushy, natural landing where you are most apt to fall, but a nest of punji sticks under the easy moves. Automatically placing the bouldering pad under the most likely spot you'll fall can be a mistake. If the bouldering pad can be used to protect a more hazardous landing on an easier move, and you think you can survive falls elsewhere on the problem unaided, then use the pad to reduce the bigger risk as much as possible. Better yet, go with a buddy who has a pad too, and cover all the hazards (see Multiple Pad Use below).

Bring the greatest surface area pad you are willing to carry.

On steep, slabby landings the pad may try to slide out of position. If the pad has carpet or other textured facing, flip it upside down so the higher-friction side contacts the slab. If this doesn't stop the sliding, rig a leash to anchor the pad. Note that this will expose the pack straps and possibly create a tripping hazard—the straps will be offset to one side—so position the pad to minimize that hazard. If the pack straps are removable, by all means remove them for added safety.

In some cases an unevenness, such as an embedded stone or tree root, may lurk under only part of the pad, but you definitely want the pad covering the area surrounding it. In this case I will take a chunk of chalk and outline the "no-fall/don't-land-here zone" on the pad. When I jump or fall off, I try to make every effort not to land in that outlined area. In some cases a pack or sweater can fill the unevenness, then the bouldering pad is placed on top.

Multiple Pad Use

These days it's common to have more than one pad at the boulders. While more pads might always sound like a good thing, they present their own hazards if not laid out with care. Avoid haphazardly tossing pads into a random stack just to add thickness. Exposed pad edges are ankle enemy number one. Determine the area that needs padding, then carefully butt pads together end to end to cover the landing. Push them together tight—if they have Velcro mating flaps, use them. The goal is to have no gaps between pads (hence the desirability of pads with square corners). A few manufacturers now offer lightweight, thin (less than 1-inch thick) yet firm sub-pads to cover the meeting edges of pads—these sheets are not tall enough to create an edge-striking hazard. Alternatively, carefully position the softest pad of the lot on top, which will help cover any gaps and constitute the lowest edge-fall hazard. This is a good use of that pad you retired but just couldn't stand taking to the recycler. When butting

The spotter, Fred Nicole, has a good knowledge of how his partner might fall off **Slashface (V13)**, **Hueco Tanks, Texas**; after all, Fred did the first ascent of this line. Fred's hands are in good position to make the catch, but what's with the haphazard pad stack?
DAWN KISH

pads end to end, put pads of similar thickness and stiffness together. Two pads of the same thickness that look good butted together may still be of radically different stiffness. Carefully step on the meeting edges of the pads to see if one side is way squishier than the other—this could be an edge-fall hazard. Align the pads so the softer pads are under the moves with the shortest falls and the stiffer pads are under the tall moves. Remember, most pads are

Ah, this is much better. Note the pads are well placed next to each other to minimize any gaps (except the first pad, which was just used to sit on to get started). Stefan Hofer flies for the lip on Black Velvet (8a), Rocklands, South Africa.

The Fireman Catch

This technique requires several spotters all grabbing a corner or two of a large bouldering pad suspended above the ground. In theory the falling climber hits the pad, it sinks under him, decelerating his fall before he hits the ground below (preferably also padded). In practice it's hard to pinch the fat corner of a pad hard enough that it won't rip instantly from your grasp when the climber falls into the pad. Nevertheless, some force of the fall is absorbed and some deceleration is better than none.

The Pad Waiter

This also involves the climber falling toward a pad raised above the ground, but in this case there is no effort to hold onto the edges of the pad to absorb the fall. Instead the pad is held aloft by one spotter, much like a waiter holding a tray of food. The pad waiter then quickly positions the raised pad under the falling climber so the climber hits it dead center and rides it to a cluster of well-placed pads on the ground. The advantage of this is it eliminates the dreaded edge hit one might get by falling into any gaps between pads on the ground. *See photo sequence on next page.*

Talus Fields

The advent of bouldering pads grandly expanded the boulderable terrain of the world by opening up the talus fields of the high mountains. Mount Evans and Rocky Mountain National Park are two currently in vogue venues that host sweet bouldering in the talus. Just add padding. With greatly uneven landings you can fill in the gaps between rocks with pads, packs, and the like until a relatively flat surface presents itself upon which you can arrange the top pads. Be creative while leaving the beautiful mountain terrain as you found it. There have been cases of climbers engaging in what amounts to large-scale bricklaying, rearranging rocks into unnatural flat perches, much to the chagrin of the rangers. Without prior approval of the land manager, this is a proven recipe for losing access.

stiffer when positioned with the closed-cell side up and softer with the open-cell side up—use this knowledge to fine-tune the landing. Be mindful of exposed straps causing a tripping hazard.

James Morris getting a perfect pad waiter spot on **Jaws (V8), Flock Hill, New Zealand.**
DEREK THATCHER

Magic Wood has arguably the worst landings of any bouldering area on the planet. Here a stick platform has been rigged on which to set a pad. This may pass muster in Switzerland but would give most U.S. land managers an aneurysm.

Pad Tossers—Tosser Being the Operative Word Here

Unless you've cleared it with the climber first, don't come rushing up to a climber halfway up a problem and toss another pad on top of the stack thinking you're doing him a favor. He has probably carefully stacked his pads to minimize edge-fall hazards and now you've just messed that up. I absolutely loathe when climbers do that to me—there I am ready to commit to a tough move, now my mind is all twisted in the wrong direction wondering if I'll blow my ankle apart landing on a reconfigured stack. My focus is redirected from the sensational psyche for success into an animalistic survival move. I feel nothing but pure hatred for the jackass who ruined my landing zone, and when I get down that pad-tossing chump better hope he has a head start.

Way Bad Landings with Minimal Pads

With enough pads, any landing can be made soft and level. However, sometimes you might have

On this freaky problem near Fort Collins, Colorado, Mark Wilford opts not to pad the landing. This rock slopes enough so that a bouldering pad on top of it would skid out from under Mark's feet if he hit it, causing him to land on his face.

only one pad or none with which to work. On extremely uneven landings in such cases, I prefer not to use a bouldering pad so I can see exactly where I'll hit. This way I can aim for the top of the one flat, solid stone available, or straddle the tree root if necessary. When landings are this bad, it pays not to fall, but often one may be forced to jump. Before you go up, know the danger zones and the safety zones. Be prepared to jump for the safety zones.

When a landing is nothing but jumbled rocks, and no dirt safety zones or single boulders large enough to land on exist, the boulder run comes into play. It consists of falling or jumping from a problem, then running tiptoe across the tops of the rocks at high speed until one reaches safety or can stop oneself. Imagine Fred Astaire tossed into a mosh pit and dancing across the tops of everyone's heads to get away—that's the boulder run. Generally this technique is risky—one false step and you could break a leg. Hence this is a desperation tactic done only when one lands in such a place. It helps to have some kind of sideways momentum when you hit the landing, either from kicking off the rock face just before the landing, or by pushing off immediately from the first rock you hit. A spotter will only get in the way if you have to do a boulder run. If you think this is your best chance to survive a fall, then I recommend forgoing the bouldering pad and spotter and being prepared to dance.

When Not to Use a Bouldering Pad

A bouldering pad may give a false sense of security on problems with a jumble of boulders or a bevy of deeply exposed tree roots at the base. The pad will look nice and cushy, but when you land it will collapse or twist around that rack of bowling balls beneath it, causing your ankle to twist or collapse as well. If you don't have enough additional padding/stuffing to fill in the gaps under the pad, then it might be preferable to forgo the pad and the false sense of security it gives. When I forgo the pad, I go into "no-fall mode" but prepare myself for a boulder run should things go wrong.

When You Want One But You Ain't Got One

Do like in the old days: Pad the landing with a pack or a sweater. Put your sandwich over the coat peg of rock lurking behind you. Be creative. Heck, I've even stacked cow pies over a nasty stone spicing up an otherwise grassy meadow landing.

The author back in 1984 on **Mother of the Future *(V9), Hueco Tanks, Texas. Check out the cush landing—packs and sweaters jammed in the gaps between rocks to level out the surface.***

Puppy Love

I am desperately in love with my dog, Thimble. She's the most beautiful creature in the world, and I get warm and fuzzy just writing about her. This is why I absolutely refuse to let her lie down on any bouldering pad or carpet—even mine—whether it's being used or not. Call it "tough love," but my dog's well-being and safety must come before her comfort. Dogs who lie on bouldering pads will eventually be hit by a falling climber (the same goes for toddlers). I've heard of at least one canine fatality

Louis the dog chills out while Carrie Cooper (seven months pregnant) works out on the Triangle Boulder, Priest Draw, Arizona.
DAWN KISH

Sharka, on the other hand, has snuck into somebody's pack and guzzled a cold one, allegedly. Next thing you know, Sharka is aimlessly wandering underneath Kelsey Fair on this cool pocket traverse. If Kelsey comes off, Sharka will have to change her name to Spot. Fortunately Sharka escaped injury, but still needed a ride back to the car.

caused by a falling climber. Don't let this happen to your best friend: Teach him or her that bouldering pads are off-route. If need be, tie your dog up when you are bouldering, or bring your dog a separate blanket or pad on which to lounge. By the way, Thimble does get to sleep on my bed.

Downclimbing

Downclimbing is one of the best ways to get out of trouble. It saves wear on the joints caused by jumping, and it is a great way to get viciously strong. The legendary Jim Holloway attributed much of his bouldering strength to the fact that he downclimbed nearly every problem he could climb up. Downclimbing is often the only safe course of retreat from a problem. Consequently it is one of the foremost tools in the highballer's repertoire. Nevertheless, downclimbing requires strength, thereby using up energy that could be put into

another attempt—sometimes a disadvantage. Occasionally a muscle strain can occur downclimbing if one drops onto a hold too quickly.

Dealing with Loose Rock

Loose holds are out there, and at some point you'll have to know how to deal with them. Climbing on loose rock is not the crap shoot it might seem at first—it's a technique to be mastered like any other and an indispensable skill for other types of climbing, especially soloing. Learn to evaluate holds by the sound and feel they make when hit with the palm of your hand, rapped on with your knuckles, or kicked with your toe. Hollow sounds (generally a low-pitch, heavy, deadened sound or ringing) indicate loose holds; so too can vibrations. Be suspicious of holds when you can see cracks (hairline or otherwise) surrounding the hold—even if the hold doesn't sound hollow or vibrate. Learn to pull on

It will be more than Shadow Ayala's fingers feeling pain should he wrench off this dubious, hollow-sounding hold. Pulling outward might snap it (left), but it can be safely used by pulling straight down (right). Notice how the palm and forearm pushes the hold against the wall.

loose holds in the direction toward which they are supported. Don't pull out on them. Pull down (or sideways if supported from the sides and not from beneath) and push the hold against the rock. Sometimes it's better to go with a smaller solid hold and do a harder move than to risk snapping a hold.

Distribute your weight among several holds. In this way you can use holds that by themselves won't support full body weight. It also prepares you to catch yourself on another hold should the unstable hold break. I tense my muscles more when climbing on loose holds so they will be prepared to

A close look at this hold reveals a hairline fracture. If one has no choice but to pull on it, the pull should be parallel to the fracture.

instantly absorb the shock of catching full weight on a hold should another hold snap.

When you let go to reach for a hold, only one hand will be on the rock. To avoid overweighting that handhold, you can dyno to the next hold, even if you could reach it statically. In this way you can generate the force for the move with your weight distributed between arms and legs. When you let go to reach up, you "float" through the split second when one hand is off the rock, and consequently don't overload the loose hold on which your other hand is placed.

Situational Awareness

This is simply paying attention to what is going on around you—looking out for your safety as well as others.

It's a good thing Adam Markert is hanging on strong here on the finishing moves of Vlad The Impaler, *because the dude wandering below could get crushed if Adam comes off. Wait a minute, isn't the dude below bouldering superstar Paul Robinson? In this case Paul's V16 ability is no substitute for basic situational awareness.*
ARJAN DE KOCK

Accidents

Despite all your risk management efforts, accidents can and will happen. An accident might not happen to your party, but to another boulderer you meet at the rocks. Carry a cell phone and know the exact location of the boulders (GPS coordinates will help rescuers immensely). Take a first-aid class, or better yet become a Wilderness First Responder (WFR). On the hike in to the boulders, ask yourself what you will do if there's an accident. Formulate a plan in case of an emergency situation. Where's the nearest cell signal? Is

A Mother's Ankle Injury Story (aka The Mother of All Ankle Injury Stories)

When I wrote the first edition of this book, I was proud to include a picture of Diane French bouldering. She was one of the few serious female boulderers at the time. She kept pulling down all these years, but recently sustained a horrific ankle injury. Here is her story in her words.

Dear John,

I apologize in advance for the gore to follow (this was a bit more than a sprain), but here's the story, in all of its remarkable unremarkable-ness. I say that because it was a garden-variety fall (more of a controlled missing of the lip) that turned swiftly into what could have been an absolute game-changer. I was just starting the session on a tricky but not superhard problem. I'd tried it twice before and jumped off it. The third time, I got a few moves higher to go for the lip, which I did. Missed the hold, had time and composure to say, "Nope," oriented my body for the fall, and came down the 8 to 10 feet to the deck. Something must have been slightly different in my trajectory because it went all wrong. No one knows if I hit the edge of the crash pad or missed it altogether, but I heard/felt a giant pop, and ended up with my back on the pad, feet in the air. The next thing that registered was that I was looking at the bottom of my right foot alongside the inside of my right leg. That, and the unmistakable shock and half-concealed horror on my husband's face, as he stood there breathing, "Okay, okay, okay . . ."

The long story short is that Sacha (my husband) and Matt (our buddy) had to take turns carrying me out (never has a single mile of steep, rocky trail felt so long), while whoever wasn't carrying me was carrying my three-year-old son (yep . . . he witnessed the whole thing). I think his presence was the thing that kept me from passing out. Half of me was yelling involuntarily every time I got jostled too hard, the other half was mothering the scared little boy just ahead of me. ("It's a really big owie, honey, but mommy's going to be fine . . .").

My foot was attached with nothing but a (flap of) skin and some very stretched tendons. We were

there a snowpatch or cold stream nearby to ice a twisted ankle? Do you have an extra roll of tape to splint an injury? Are splinting materials around—say branches, pack stays, or a bubbabrush handle? I took a fall in the Adirondacks in which I ruptured multiple ligaments in my left ankle. My friend Pat had recently become a WFR. He used tape and the closed-cell foam taken from a crash pad to splint the ankle. The ER docs were impressed with his ingenuity and splinting skill. In my WFR class we made an inflatable splint from a Camelback bladder. (Drink the water or put it in other bottles—don't pour it out—you might need it.)

able to get service enough to call 911 at the trailhead, and sooner or later the ambulance reached us. Thirty miles later we were at the ER in Canon City. Have you ever seen an emergency doc blanch? I have.

It was three and a half hours from time of accident until they finally, blessedly, put me under for the first of two emergency surgeries. The surgery report reads that I had an open dislocation of my right ankle. Miraculously, I broke no bones, but the risk of infection was extreme, since the whole open mess went right into the dirt on the trail. Both surgeries were primarily to clean out the injury. The surgeon looked not at all happy when he came to see me after the first operation. He said he had me on the "Farm Mix" of antibiotics in hopes of keeping anything from setting in, but told us that if we couldn't stave off infection, there was a good chance of my losing my foot.

One does a lot of thinking after news like that. For as long as I've been bouldering, for as long as I've loved bouldering, it all suddenly seemed so ridiculous. Eight feet of air, a chance combination of angle and force, and I was contemplating life with a prosthetic. Right about then, you weep in the company of your own worst fears for a few minutes—and then you call the nurse for more morphine.

So, the great news is that the surgeon gets full marks for the job he did cleaning me up and beefing up my defenses. To date I've had no infection to speak of. After two months of casts, crutches, painkillers, and incredible family and friends to support me, I'm in PT and *walking* (okay, limping) around on my own foot. The only real vestige of my ordeal is the frighteningly precise scar that runs from 12 o'clock to 6 o'clock around my right ankle. Not an incision scar, but an injury scar. Every doctor I've seen has told me that I should have shattered this, blown apart that, have pins here, screws there. But instead, I got lucky. Ridiculously lucky. It's the same sort of luck that seems to protect all of us, through no real effort of our own, through so many years of bouldering.

So that's my story, John, and no, I will not share with you the picture that was taken of the injury at the hospital, lest I become known as some twisted purveyor of gore. Though I've actually never looked at it myself, I've watched it literally sicken too many people when they see it. I think the story should be enough . . .

Bouldering Basics
and Static Movement

Most techniques for moving on rock come naturally and are just extensions of the climbing instincts we have as children climbing trees, ladders, and jungle gyms. In this chapter we'll hit on some real basic stuff for readers new to the sport of bouldering as well as delve into more advanced techniques of static movement. Our hands and feet are our primary attachment to the rock, but as we'll see the whole body also comes into play.

Footwork

In the early 1990s an elite crew of European boulderers created a splash at Hueco Tanks in Texas. Many of my fellow Americans were agog at how strong they were. Personally I felt I knew many boulderers whose fingers and arms were just as strong. What blew me away was how precisely these Europeans used their feet. Shame dealt me a low blow when I compared my own footwork to

Static versus
Dynamic Movement

In climbing, when we use the term "static move" we are referring to any move done in a slow, controlled manner that one can easily reverse. You can pause partway through a static move.

A dynamic move, aka dyno, is one that makes use of the body's momentum to propel you toward a hold. It is quick, gymnastic, and hard to impossible to reverse. If you throw a dynamic move and miss your target, you will likely fall. Prior to the 1960s, dynamic moves were considered heresy in the climbing world—how things have changed.

Kayla Dempsey bouldering at the Cul de Chien sector,
Fontainebleau, France.

to be done outside, not on a gym wall. I'll go up to the rock and point at an area about the size of a 42-inch TV screen and say, "Quick, show me five good footholds in this area." The student points to the five biggest holds. It takes a few seconds. "Good. Now five different ones. Quick, quick, the clock is ticking." This time it takes a bit longer as the obvious choices are gone. Then again and again, until we're pointing out edges no wider than a dime. Identifying footholds quickly on-the-fly is an essential skill to develop for outdoor bouldering. The holds aren't marked like in the gym, nor do they all protrude from the face. If you get halfway up a problem and the foothold you thought you were going to use doesn't work for you, then you need to be able to read the rock instantly to find the next one to try. Do this drill with a seasoned boulderer and see which holds he or she picks out. You'll be amazed what you can stand on given a little practice. As your skills, strength, and comfort level increase, you'll find that you instinctively know where your feet should be placed to stay in balance and move upward (or sideways if that's the case). You then take that instinct for where you want your foot, and combine it with your ability to read the rock to pick the best foothold for the move. The best foothold might not be the biggest one.

Edging

On basic edges one will usually place the side of the big toe on the hold to stand up. Some shoe designs make it feel more natural to "toe-in" by standing on the point of the toe—this makes for poorer leverage but often greater precision when it comes to standing on small holds and dimples, particularly on steep terrain. Adopt the style that feels most comfortable and natural to you. Learn to stand on the outside edge of your shoes as well—the best leverage will occur if you align the outside ball of the foot alongside the hold. You may feel a bit more control if you use the outside edge between the tip of the pinky toe and the outside ball of the foot.

theirs. It was obvious that these guys had spent a lot of time perfecting their footwork. One of the best ways to look outrageously powerful is to use your feet well.

The most basic tenet of climbing movement is to let the big muscles of the legs propel the body upward while using the smaller, weaker arm muscles for balance and positioning. The more overhanging the problem, however, the more the arms will be forced to support weight. Nevertheless, even on the steepest problems you should support as much weight as possible with your legs. Always think feet first.

Footholds range from glassy smears to ledges big enough to park a bike on. When I take somebody out bouldering for the first time, one of the things we do is a foothold recognition drill. This needs

Opposition and Compression

Opposition is any technique in which limbs pull (or push) in opposite directions to hold each other on the rock. Stems, laybacks, and underclings are classic examples.

Compression is a form of opposition technique formerly called bear-hugging. It involves pulling hands toward each other to provide the proper vector forces to hang onto very sloping holds. It also involves using the same squeezing together with the feet, usually through heel hooks, toe hooks, or rand smears. It is generally a very strenuous technique. Moving limbs while in a compressed position can often be a slappy affair that involves moving quickly to grab the next hold before sagging off the rock.

*James Morris on **Dirty Rascal** (V5), Flock Hill, New Zealand, feet stemmed in opposition, hands bear-hugging in compression.*
DEREK THATCHER

*The Happy Boulder's **Atari** (V6) is one of America's most exemplary bear-hug problems. Henry Schlotzhauer sending.*

The granite at The Buttermilks in California is known for its demanding footwork. The climber's left foot is "toe-in" on a dinky edge, while his right foot is edging on the side of the toe.

In general when edging, position the edge of the boot sole right up against the wall, then keep the foot in a fixed position while moving the body up. Keeping the foot still and heel neutral to low helps prevent the boot from rolling off the edge. The main cause of rolling off an edge is the bulging part of the rand bumping the wall above the edge and levering the sole off when the heel moves upward or the ankle rolls inward. Some moves require you to lift the heel while pushing on the hold (say to gain that last extra bit of reach) or to roll the ankle inward. If rand bump is repeatedly popping your foot off the hold, try placing your foot toward the outside of the hold. You'll have less of your sole in contact with the foothold and therefore less leverage, but you will free up space

An outside edge move on a roof at the Fortress sector, Rocklands, South Africa.

to accommodate the inward roll of the rand so the dreaded "rand bump" doesn't knock your foot off.

Standing on the toes for any length of time tires the calf muscles, especially on less than vertical slabs. If the edge is big enough, try placing the inside heel of the boot on the hold to reduce strain on the calves. On slabs, with practice you should be able to stand on your heel on an edge no thicker than a matchbook.

Smearing

When there is no edge on which to stand, just a rough patch on the rock or a glassy bump, it's time to smear. The key to smearing is placing and keeping as much rubber on the rock as possible, then really pushing hard into the smear to make the soft boot rubber conform around all the bumps and rough spots on the smear. Keep your heels low to force more of the sole in contact with the smear. Try to press the foot perpendicularly into the rock, not parallel to it. If you can work with opposition from your arms, say a layback or undercling hold, directing the perpendicular force on the feet is easy. On less than vertical friction slabs with dinky or nonexistent handholds, there is no possibility of applying opposition force, so the best you can do is to stand upright keeping your "nose over your toes."

Smearing can also be done over small edges, just treating the edges as a bit of bonus roughness to force into the boot rubber. This works well with soft slippers.

Fabian Haak keeping his heels low to smear a friction slab at Cresciano, Switzerland.

Bouldering Physics 101

A rudimentary understanding of physics with respect to coefficients of friction and vectors can help us understand how we stick (or don't stick) to the rock. To climb upward we need to counteract the force of gravity. Gravity pulls us in one direction, straight down toward the center of the earth. Friction between our skin and the handholds and between our boots and the footholds keeps us from peeling off. The following examples deal with the branch of physics called statics, the study of forces on objects not in motion.

Coefficient of friction μ is a unitless measure of how much two materials have trouble sliding across each other. For latex and personal lubricant most of us prefer a lower coefficient of friction than we do when it comes to skin or boot soles against rock. Teflon contacting Teflon has a coefficient of friction of around 0.04; a good tire on dry pavement checks in at around 1.4. For skin or boot rubber against rock it varies depending on how rough the rock is, how humid a day it is, etc. Tests of climbing rubber against cut, but not polished, granite countertop material yielded μ's between 0.54 and 0.68, and between climbing rubber and a gym hold 0.96 and 1.17. In real-life outdoor situations various bumps, crystals, or grains would increase μ. For instance, μ for polished limestone footholds at Castle Hill in New Zealand would doubtless be much lower than for the same-angled hold on Stanage gritstone or Joshua Tree granite.

Physicists and engineers use vectors to represent the direction and magnitude of forces. Vectors are represented as arrows. In diagrams the length of the arrow is the magnitude of the force, the direction of the arrow is the direction of force. We can break down a force (for instance, gravity acting on a climber) into multiple components to analyze how much force is being applied in any direction, such as the direction the climber is pulling on a handhold or pushing on a foothold. Vector diagrams are drawn to scale, so with just a protractor and a ruler one can measure vector quantities—no need for a calculator or big math skills.

Let's start with a simple example, Case 1a. Roscoe is a 141-pound climber, standing straight up, nose over toes, on a 45-degree slab. He exerts a 141-pound force (F) straight down toward the center of the earth equal to his mass (m) times the acceleration (a) of gravity (F=ma, one of the most basic physics equations). Breaking this 141-pound force of gravity into vectors parallel to the slab and perpendicular to the slab, we see that there is a 100-pound force urging Roscoe to slip down the slab and a 100-pound force (perpendicular to the slab—called the normal force) trying to make his boots stay put. (These illustrations are to scale, but if you want to check the math you can draw a 45-degree/45-degree/90-degree right triangle with the long leg 141 millimeters long, then measure the short legs—they'll both be 100 millimeters long. Or you can resort to the calculator and basic geometry and use a^2 (red slipping vector^2) + b^2 (green normal vector^2) = c^2 (gravity vector^2).

Another basic physics equation tells us that $F_f \leq \mu F_n$; in other words Roscoe is going to fall if the amount of force urging him to slip (F_f) exceeds the normal force (F_n) times the coefficient of friction (μ)

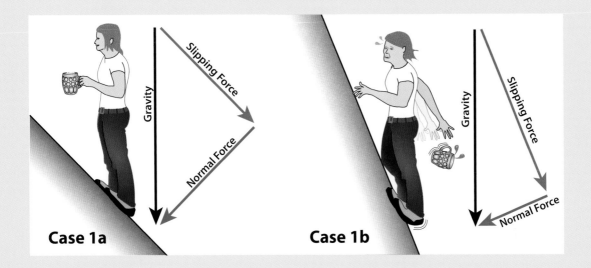

Case 1a   **Case 1b**

between his boots and the rock. Because I picked an easy example for the math (the 45-degree angle of the slab), the slipping force and the normal force are equal, and we can see that Roscoe will stay put if the coefficient of friction between his shoes and the rock is 1.0 or greater (realistic for a rock shoe against most rock types that aren't too polished).

What if the slab is 67.5 degrees steep, as in case 1b? Roscoe is in textbook upright posture, yet when we draw the vectors now, we see his normal force has been cut in half to only 50 pounds, while his slipping force has risen to 132 pounds. Uh oh, if the coefficient of friction between his shoes and the rock isn't 2.64 ($F^F/_{Fn}$ or $^{132}/_{50}$) or greater (an unrealistic number for climbing shoes against any rock type with less than cheese-grater texture), Roscoe is taking the plunge. Either way Roscoe is going to wish he cleaned his boots at the base, because the coefficient of friction of clean soles against rock is higher than that of dirty soles against rock. (Okay physics geeks, don't bother writing in to muddy up the discussion—I know this is oversimplified and discounts palms against the slab, the rotation of the earth, multi-asperity static friction models, and Roscoe's gravitational pull toward the mass of your ego. Nevertheless, it serves to illustrate the basic concept.)

When it comes to hanging sloping handholds on overhangs, the same concepts apply. Let's check out cases 2a and 2b. In 2a we see Roscoe when he was a plump newbie. He weighed 141 then, but most of it was flab. He lacked the core strength to pull any weight onto his foothold; therefore his center of gravity (red dot at waist) is positioned dead under his handhold. (The 0 to 1 scale represents the horizontal distance between the handhold and foothold.) The handhold slopes 45 degrees, just like the slab he was

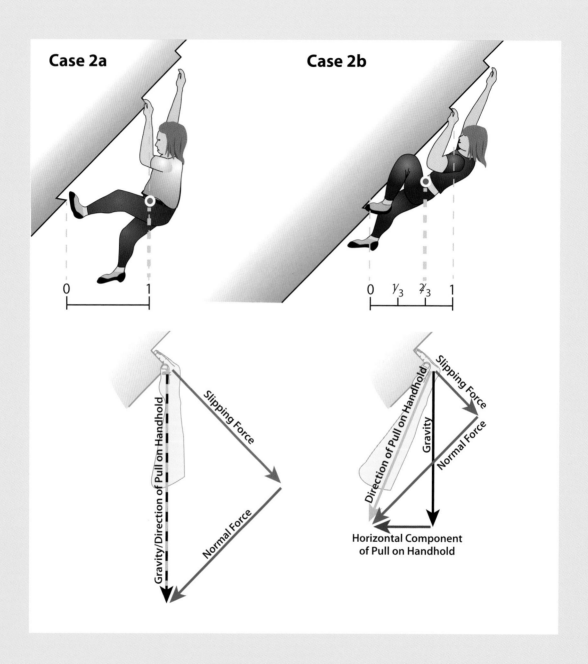

Case 2a

Case 2b

0   1

0   y_3 z_3 1

Slipping Force

Normal Force

Gravity/Direction of Pull on Handhold

Direction of Pull on Handhold

Slipping Force

Gravity

Normal Force

Horizontal Component
of Pull on Handhold

standing on earlier; hence the breakdown of slipping force and normal force is the same as before, each 100 pounds. Roscoe will whip unless the coefficient of friction between his skin and the hold isn't equal to 1.0 or greater (very unlikely unless the rock is very rough).

Fast forward a year and Roscoe has transformed his physique. He's replaced 15 pounds of blubber with 15 pounds of finely chiseled lean mass and has become a 141-pound cranking machine. He's on the same problem, but now he has the core power to use his foot to pull his hips in toward the wall. Before, his center of gravity hung below the handhold, now it's shifted one-third closer to the toehold. So how much weight is now supported by his hand and how much by his foot? We can think of the handhold and toehold as being points about which his body would like to pivot because the center of gravity is off-center with respect to either hold. Roscoe's weight produces a "moment of force" around each hold that equals the weight on the hold times the distance between his center of gravity and the hold. Basic statics tells us $\Sigma F = 0$, which means the sum of all forces on an object must cancel each other out (add up to 0), or the object will not stay in place. Hence the force on his handhold (F_h) times $1/3$ must equal the force on his toehold (F_t) times $2/3$. If $1/3 F_h = 2/3 F_t$, then $F_h = 2F_t$, or there is twice as much weight on his hand as on his foot. So 47 pounds are supported by his foot and 94 pounds are supported by his hand.

Because Roscoe has pulled his hips in toward the wall, he has changed his angle of pull on the handhold, in this case 22.5 degrees closer to the wall. This produces some amazingly positive results as the vector breakdowns show. The vectors are drawn to scale between the cases 2a and 2b. The slipping force trying to rip Roscoe off his handhold has dropped from 100 pounds to 33 pounds, due to both the reduced weight supported on the hold and the advantageous angle of pull. The "normal force" remains the same at 100 pounds, so now if the coefficient of friction between his finger skin and the hold is 0.33 or greater (very realistic on most rock types), Roscoe will stay put.

Even though Roscoe is only supporting 94 pounds on his hand, he has to pull harder than that not to fall. To visualize this, look at the gravity vector whose length represents 94 pounds. For the "pulling vector" (yellow arrow) to have a vertical component equal to the vertical gravity vector (black arrow), its point must extend down to the same level as the point on the gravity vector. Draw a vector in the line of pull on the hold until it reaches this length and measure it (or crank out the simple math) and find that its magnitude is 105 pounds. So Roscoe's fingers must be capable of pulling 105 pounds' worth on the handhold without unwrapping—good thing he's been hitting the fingerboard. If we now break down the yellow pulling vector into its vertical (gravity) and horizontal (blue arrow) components, we see that the horizontal blue vector has a magnitude of 47 pounds. What does this mean? Because $\Sigma F = 0$, it means Roscoe must pull outward (horizontally toward the handhold) with his foot with a force of 47 pounds, or the object (Roscoe's body) won't remain on the rock.

Getting on to the situation at Roscoe's foot: We know he has to support one-third of his body weight (47 pounds) on the toehold, which means he needs to exert a vertical component of 47 pounds, and as we know from above, he has to pull horizontally toward his hand with a force of 47 pounds. I'll leave it to you to draw the vectors and/or do the math, but the result is Roscoe will have to pull with a force of 67 pounds at a 45-degree angle to the ground and pointing toward his handhold. Depending on how steep the foothold is, this can be realistic (foothold is horizontal, $\mu = 1.0$), to you-got-to-be-kidding (foothold is sloped outwards 22.5 degrees, $\mu = 2.3$). In the latter case, to stay glued to the rock Roscoe will have to come up with some other trick, perhaps a bicycle move with a toe hook in opposition to his sloped toehold.

What should we take away from this basic physics diatribe? First, do everything you can to increase your coefficient of friction: clean your boots, clean the footholds and handholds, dry your fingertips, utilize the footholds with the roughest texture, and wait for crisp sending conditions. Second, use the tricks at your disposal to increase the normal force you apply on holds: adopt a better angle of pull on the holds (usually by sucking your hips in toward the wall), pull harder at that angle by utilizing heel hooks, toe hooks, etc. to create the opposition force to allow you to exert more force on the hold, and if available, add a pinch between thumb and fingers. Third, strengthen your core muscles.

What about the physics of dynamic moves? Well, that delves into the branch of physics aptly called "dynamics," which involves much more complicated math. Read all about it in *Mo' Betterer Bouldering*, 12th edition, due out in fall 2035. Until then, all you need to know is F=ma, which translates to Force equals Mass times Acceleration, which means the farther you fall, the harder you hit the ground.

Pockets

Duh, wear a low-profile shoe and stuff as much of the toe in as possible. If that doesn't work, consider going barefoot.

The volcanic rock of Bishop, California's Happy Boulders is riddled with pockets, presenting many potential footholds. Using body awareness, determine where your feet should ideally be to do the move in question, then pick the largest and/or closest pocket to that point and stuff the toes in deep.

Heel Hooks

When it gets steeper than 120 degrees, it's often easier to weight your feet by hooking your heel on a hold above your center of gravity. Frequently a heel is hooked even with or above one's hands. Between 90 and 120 degrees, hooking a heel below one's center of gravity can work well, say around the corner of an arête, provided the hook is positive enough to resist an outward pull. Heel hooks are also commonly used on rock-over topouts.

Alex Johnson at Stone Fort, Tennessee. Her left heel is pulling hard to keep her body to the left.
PAT GOODMAN

Inspect Her Gadget (V7) sports heel hook move after heel hook move just to get to the sloping slapfest at the end. Lee Payne cruising at Horse Pens 40, Alabama.
ANDY MANN

An outside rand smear with his left foot allows AJ Camelio to shuffle his right foot to the next heel hook on **Barracuda Rail (7b), Rocklands, South Africa.**

Rand Smears

This is when you smear the arch or outer edge of your foot on a protruding chunk of rock, commonly used on an arête.

Toe Hooks

A toe hook is when you use the top of the toe for placement on a hold. This is primarily done in compression situations on steep terrain to allow one to move a hand without swinging off. You can undercling with the toe in opposition to a hand pulling down to keep the toe in place. Alternatively, you can toe hook with one foot, then push the opposite direction with the other foot to keep the toe hook in place, a technique known as "bicycling."

Toe hooking can take a lot of abdominal strength.

Jenn Walsh pulling hard on a toe hook at Ibex, Utah.

A bicycle move: The climber pushes on his left foot and pulls on his right, thereby providing the opposition pressure to keep them both in place.

Heel-Toe Locks

This is a combination of a heel hook with a toe hook, requiring proper rock geometry to pull off. The heel presses down while the toe presses up in opposition, locking the foot in place. Heel-toe locks can be tremendously solid and take tons of weight off your hands. Often, what at first seems to be a

Marsha Tucker leans off a heel-toe lock on Karma (V6), Happy Boulders, Bishop, California.

marginal slopey heel hook or heel scum turns into a great heel-toe lock. Heel-toe locks should not be confused with heel-toe jams, which are used in wide crack technique.

Corner Torques

Corners or other depressions with walls perpendicular to each other offer a chance to jam your foot in the corner and support substantial weight. Paste the sole of the boot against one wall and the inside or outside rand (works either way) against the opposite wall. The edge of the boot sole should be as close to the back of the corner as possible and the heel angled away from the wall roughly 30 to 45 degrees. The heel is not in contact with the rock. Push hard on the sole of the boot and rotate your heel toward the opposite wall to apply

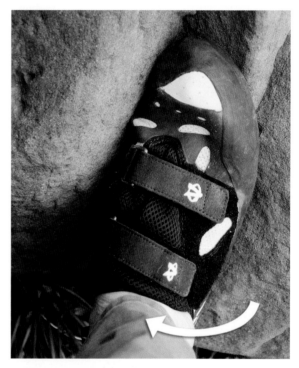

A corner torque—when the forefoot sole was placed on the rock, the heel was out at about 30 degrees from the left wall. The heel was then rotated to the position seen here, forcing the rand against the left wall to utilize the friction between the sole and right wall, and the rand and left wall. This can work with either foot in this placement.

Carrie Cooper stuffs and torques a right foot jam on **Floor Pie**, *Priest Draw, Arizona.*
DAWN KISH

rotation force around an axis between the ball of your foot. This will press the rand hard against the opposite wall—you should feel the frictional force on the rand pushing the opposite direction from the frictional force on the sole—the rand should be pushing upward and a bit outward, thereby forcing the sole to push down and dig into any roughness on the face. What initially felt like a marginal smear now feels like your foot is encased in concrete—better hope you didn't cross the Mob. You can practice this in the corner of a room to get the feel, but be careful about leaving boot marks on the walls.

Toe and Foot Jams

This involves torquing the toes or foot in a crack or between blobs of rock and is covered in detail in the jamming chapter.

Smedging

Smedging is a cross between smearing and edging, used for very tiny edges. The edge of the boot sole is positioned on the wall a couple millimeters above the micro-edge. The edge of the micro-edge digs into the sole of the boot, holding the sole in place, while the toe is rotated to force the edge of the sole to snap into place against the wall, basically forcing the rubber to compress a bit to squeeze it on top of the foothold. This is a neat trick when you need to drive a lot of weight off a tiny foothold on vertical to slightly overhanging terrain. It works best in stiff boots—the newer the better for a fresh abrupt edge on the sole.

Footwork Keys

Footwork is the key to finesse. Quite often you will do two or even three small foot moves to set yourself up for a single hand move. Precision, balance, trust, and practice are the keys to good footwork.

Pat Goodman on Space (V8), Stone Fort, Tennessee. A slab taller and balder than Kareem Abdul-Jabbar.
BEN DITTO

Precision

Keep your eyes on your feet until you paste them onto the holds. Usually a climber looks away from a foothold the second before touching a foot to it. Then he or she wiggles the foot around on the hold trying to get better purchase. By watching your foot as it settles on the hold, you will have more precise footwork, which means less time getting tired while your feet are dicking around.

Balance

Balance is the proper distribution of weight enabling the boulderer to remain steadily affixed to the rock, in this case the footholds. Balance is not

Kayla Dempsey in classic balanced position. Her center of gravity is around the belt loop her chalk bag is clipped to—notice how her center of gravity is between the support points provided by her hands and feet. Cul de Chien sector, Fontainebleau, France.

inherent, but a learned trait. As toddlers we learn how to stand and walk and our balance improves with repetition. The same holds true for bouldering moves, hence the value of trying a variety of moves and positions. (We have little organs inside our ears that act like plumb bobs and send information to our brain as to which way is down. Our brain processes this info and in general freaks out if our weight isn't equally distributed between our feet if we're standing, over our butt if we're sitting, or flat on a bed if we're sleeping. The experienced boulderer's brain has been trained to be comfortable when the body is in all kinds of crazy positions—it tells the boulderer just what direction gravity is trying to pull him or her off the holds, then the boulderer picks a move out of his or her vast repertoire to address the situation.)

When climbing statically we usually have three points of contact on the rock (our base of support), and maintaining balance is easy if we keep our center of gravity positioned between these three points. Of course our hands are used to help us maintain balance when moving our feet, but when that's not enough we can use momentum, speed, flagging, and a host of other tricks to stay in balance until we reach the next hand or foothold.

Trust

Weight your feet and trust them. From our physics lecture you know that more weight on your feet makes your shoes stick to the rock better. It also means less weight on your arms so more power is saved for harder moves. I remember a cobbler friend who had a client who couldn't wait for the newest sticky rubber to come in so he could get his boots resoled and finally send his project. He bugged the cobbler so much that the cobbler played a trick on him and resoled the client's boots with some horrid fifteen-year-old rubber that had never sold. He told the client it was the good new stuff. Sure enough, the guy sent his project and gave credit to the new rubber. What really

Your brain (and likely your body) will turn into an atrocious pile of goo if you don't trust your feet on problems like this. The author having fun slab bouldering in Cresciano, Switzerland.

happened is that his belief in the "new rubber" finally got him to trust his feet, and when he finally weighted them, they stuck and he sent.

It's easy to get in a rut of only trying spectacular power problems and ignoring slabs. Micro-edge slab climbing, however, does wonders for your footwork. Practice standing on all parts of your feet: inside toe, outside toe, heel—even arch smears on arêtes. Practice weighting your feet by consciously trying to do problems with as little support from your arms as possible. Find an easy problem and climb it with just your feet and your thumbs. Try doing problems one-handed or sans hands. Have a competition with your friends to see who can stand on the smallest foothold or steepest smear. Better yet, travel to the super-polished holds of Fontainebleau—it won't take long before you discover the key to standing on slick holds is to push hard *hard* HARD into them with your feet. The slicker the hold, the harder you need to push onto it (see the Bouldering Physics 101 sidebar). This practice will pay off later on all climbs, even the power problems.

Resoler extraordinaire Tony Puppo of Bishop's fabled Rubber Room has noted an epidemic of blown-out rands coinciding directly with the growing popularity of gym climbing. Go outside to get the most from your footwork practice. Footholds in gyms are relatively large, protruding, and already mapped out for you—they can do only so much for your footwork—gym feet are lazy feet.

Steve Moyles climbing **Falling Ant Slab** *sans hands, Jenny Lake Boulders, Wyoming.*

The Bleaussard

A Bleaussard is a Fontainebleau local of long-standing. Bleaussards are known for outstanding footwork and their eagerness to show young ladies the boulders when they aren't busy sandbagging foreigners. Jo Montchaussé, author of several bouldering guides to the forest, is a prime example. After watching several foreigners (myself included) get spit off by this sandbag on the Roche aux Sabots red circuit, the sixty-something Jo strolled up, cleaned his boots, subtly marked out the key foot smear, then walked the problem. Hmmph, that looked easy. But even having seen the beta, most of us still failed to send the problem. "I can't believe you stood up on that smear," I said. "Ah, but I am a Bleaussard," Jo replied with a mischievous smirk. "We use our feet on the rock like the way you touch a woman while making love." (Jo is very French.) All I could say was, "Damn, your wet-hold technique must be superb."

Looks like a desperate slap from a sick seam crimp to a sketchy pocket, but if that was the case Jo Montchaussé's chalk bag would be flying out from his ass. No, what's going on here is Jo moving slowly and deliberately. Body position and footwork are absolutely key. He's pulling his left leg inward with his hip flexors, exerting tons of normal force on his left foot on a glassy near-vertical slope—his right foot is just flagged around the corner.

Legwork

Besides propelling the body upward, legs can be used in many creative ways to take weight off the hands, control balance, etc.

Stemming and Bridging

Stemming is pushing with your feet in opposite directions to press them into place. This is a common technique used in dihedrals, but can be often used on flat walls when footholds face each other and are spaced far enough apart.

Bridging can be stemming, but also includes hands pressing in opposite directions from one another or hands pushing in opposition to feet.

Hands on one side of the scoop pressing in opposition to feet on the other side. Chaz Wilson hiking the Joshua Tree standard **Stem Gem** *(V4).*

Eric Decaria on the classic stemming problem **Streetcar Named Desire** *(V6), Joshua Tree National Park, California.*

Knee Bars and Knee Scums

Knee bars can make the difference between spitting blood on the crux or letting go on the same move to sign autographs. Look for them before you start up a problem. If a slot is about 2 to 6 inches too wide for your lower leg length, you can sometimes cross your free leg over the knee and bridge the gap, or stand with one foot atop the other to bridge a smaller gap (the latter can be pretty uncomfortable in tight rock shoes). Even if your knee does not lock into a bar, it can be "scummed" against the rock to take some weight off your hands.

Jesse Althaus rocks a nice knee bar on the Savannah Boulder, Happy Boulders, Bishop, California.

As an aside, if you should be so lucky to visit the famous boulders of Fontainebleau in France, understand that "knee bar" sounds just like the French term *nibard,* which refers to a woman's breasts. "Hey, nice knee bar!" might be the best or worst comment you could make. As with everything in bouldering, exercise good judgment.

Drop Knees

Drop-knee technique works well on overhanging walls with footholds one can stem between. It gets the feet high and the hips close to the rock. This posture puts your center of gravity close to your feet, putting more weight on your feet and less on your arms. The body is oriented sideways to the wall. The leg in front of you is straight to moderately bent, while the leg behind you pushes off a high hold with the knee bent moderately to sharply and pointing down. Often the dropped knee is lower than the foot. Reaches from this position are usually done with the arm on the same side as the knee that is dropped.

The author doing a right leg drop knee on the vintage V3 Solarium, Happy Boulders, Bishop.

Flagging

Flagging is crossing one leg across the other to shift one's center of gravity to maintain balance and avoid barndooring. The climber drops his butt toward the supporting foothold, moving his center of gravity closer to his foot, thus taking weight off his hands. The flagged foot is not placed on a hold but just waves out there like a flag and acts as a counterbalance. Flagging generally reduces how far you can reach vertically, but can help greatly when reaching horizontally.

*Textbook flagging on **Cholos (V9)**, Happy Boulders, Bishop, California—the left leg is straight out, providing balance but not actually touching the wall.*

Posting

Posting a leg is positioning a straight leg against the wall, often just smeared with no foothold. Because the leg is straight, there is no pushing motion, just a stabilizing supporting force that allows one to move the arms. Posting can be used to keep the body from sinking back down after gaining height.

On Your Knees

For decades there was a law written in all how-to climbing texts stating that under no circumstances should one place their knee on a hold and move weight onto it. Had I obeyed the law, there would be a slew of problems out there I never sent. Knees have a terrible tendency to slip off holds compared to feet, but sometimes you just won't be able to hoist your foot all the way onto a hold, but you can get your knee on it. My high step flexibility is shot, so I end up doing this all the time and I'm comfortable with it. Be careful with this—your knee-cap is not designed to push on, so there is a risk of injury.

This overhanging bulge is devoid of holds for over 6 feet. Cody Roth utilizes a left foot toe-heel lock combined with a right foot post to do a no-hands reach move near the DePakhuys campground, Rocklands, South Africa.

Okay, this is definitely one of the more embarrassing pics in the book, but just try and find someone who will let you shoot them pulling off this move. The author wallowing over the top of Pillow Talk (V6), Rocklands, South Africa.
SANDRA STUCKEY

Hip Scums

Hip scums involve simply pressing the hip against a wall in opposition with another support point. It's usually done in dihedrals but also works against any sizable protrusion.

Overhangs and Feet

Repeat after me: "I will put as much weight on my feet as possible at all times, especially on overhangs." Overhangs force weight onto your arms. The steeper the terrain, the quicker the clock is ticking toward ultimate forearm meltdown. To slow the clock, put as much weight on your feet as possible.

Use your feet like hands to pull your hips in toward the wall. This will shift your center of gravity closer to your feet, forcing more weight on the feet and also giving you a better pulling angle on sloping handholds. You need to both push down with your foot to make the boot stick to the hold, and pull outwards from the rock to shift your hips in. This takes great core strength, which is not just using the trunk muscles but also the glutes and hamstrings. Pulling on the toes works best if the foot is pointed in and toeing down on the hold—if your heel drops too low you'll lose purchase on the toehold. High footholds can work well because they

Lisa Rands pulling with her toes to keep her hips in close to the rock. **Mandala (V12), Buttermilks, California.** WILLS YOUNG

provide a support point closer to your center of gravity. Sometimes you can step up on a waist-high hold and sit on your heel. This takes a lot of weight off your arms, allowing you to utilize smaller fingerholds. Try not to get too stretched out between your hands and feet or it will be hell trying to pull on your toes.

If your feet aren't positive enough to pull out on, then it's time to use momentum to get your hips in by executing a controlled hip thrust toward the rock during a move. When the hips move in to the rock and force weight onto the feet, then it's time to push on those feet and nail the next handhold. (This is getting into the realm of dynamic moves discussed in the next chapter.)

The Gun Show

Chances are half of you readers skipped all that nancy footwork chatter and turned right to the glory pages. Yep, this is where we discuss how to use your hands and arms and impress the hell out of folks when your feet cut loose and you stay attached to the rock by the merest of handholds and the most massive of biceps.

For the neophytes, the types of handholds you'll hear discussed throughout this book are illustrated in the next few pages. Climbers used to snicker at laypeople who would call handholds "grips." However, the term "grip" has since morphed into some kind of retro-cool lingo in some circles. Use at your own peril—it will make you sound like either a complete dork or a sardonic elitist.

Daniel Woods on a variation to Skink, Rocklands, South Africa.
WILLS YOUNG

Edges

The term edge is usually reserved for flat to slightly incut or slightly sloping holds with a distinct outer edge. They range from dime-thick to hand-size and bigger, but in general the term edge is used for holds no bigger than a doorjamb. Thicker and wider than that and we call them "rails."

Flakes

Flakes are just what they sound like (no, not unreliable partners) and range from dinky fingertip rigs all the way up to elephant ears and bigger. Make sure they are solidly attached before yanking on them.

The author reaching for a finger edge on **When I Learn To Climb,** *Tamo, Arizona.*

Kelsey Sather reefing on a juicy flake at the Happy Boulders, Bishop, California.

Jugs

Jugs, aka buckets, aka Thank God Holds, are big enough for a full hand and incut so much they might as well be pull-up bars. Some can even be as big as bathtubs.

Knobs

Knobs are distinct rounded bumps protruding from the wall—if they're attached to the wall with a skinny neck, they're called chickenheads. Beware, if the neck is skinny enough or the rock otherwise fragile, knobs and chickenheads can be prone to breaking. Be careful how you leverage yourself on them. In some granites and pegmatites, distinct crystals form big enough holds to grab. Cobbles are rounded rocks in conglomerates that climb like slick knobs. Cobbles occasionally pop out of the matrix, forming scoop-shaped casts sometimes called anti-cobbles.

Now that's a bucket. Dylan Bogdan snags the welcome jug on the crux of **Ketron Classic** *(V4), Happy Boulders, Bishop, California.*

Chickenhead.

Slopers

Slopers are rounded holds with no positive edge into which the fingers can dig. They range from depressingly small to downright zaftig. To satisfy a sloper fetish, head to Alabama's Horse Pens 40.

Sidepulls

Sidepulls are vertically oriented holds. In general, the farther one's body is to the side of a sidepull, the easier the sidepull is to cling to.

France's Fontainebleau is known for its plethora of slopers. Pierre-Arnaud Chouvy on Surprise (7b+).
JO MONTCHAUSSÉ

Tom Herbert laying away hard on sidepulls at the Bachar Boulders, Sierra East Side, California.

Underclings

Underclings are holds with lips facing your feet (usually downward, but could be otherwise depending on body orientation). Ready for your graduate degree in undercling studies (and/or months of rotator cuff rehab)? Hit Horsetooth Reservoir's Eliminator Boulder and try the Holloway testpiece *Meathook*.

Pockets

Pockets come in all sizes. If you can only get one finger in, it's called a monodoigt (mo-no-dwah). If you get two fingers in, it's called a bidoigt (bidwah). If you get your whole fist in, it's called [radio edit]. Horizontally elongated pockets are known as "letter slots." Volcanic rock, such as that at Deadman's Summit on the Sierra East Side, is often riddled with pockets.

Audrey Hsu with fingers wrapped up into the undercling on **Turnbuckle (V2), Joshua Tree National Park, California.**

Pockets in volcanic rock near Bishop, California.

Huecos

Huecos refer to pockets, usually hand-size or bigger, that have a distinct lip and are larger inside than outside. They often form jugs. Hueco Tanks is the type location for these user-friendly holds. Hueco's Round Room Traverse (V0) is a must-do hueco-hauling for boulderers of any ability. This traverse is a 100-foot loop, perfect for pursuit races and time trials (join the elite by breaking the sub-minute barrier).

Pinches

Pinches are self-explanatory and range in size from nipples to big fatty love handles or even spans between two or more pebbles. Ease of pinching for any given pinch hold is hand-size and finger-length dependent. Britain's gritstone has some of the most

A hueco's-eye view of Julie Leino. Hueco Tanks, Texas (where else?).

Phil Schall putting a mighty squeeze on this pinch hold on Alma Blanca (V13), Hueco Tanks, Texas.

ANDY MANN

insanely small pebble pinches on the planet, often no bigger than a pencil eraser. On the other end of the spectrum is the brick-sized starting pinch on the John Gill classic, *Pinch Route,* at Horsetooth Reservoir, Colorado.

Tufas

Tufas are precipitate ribs and blobs found on steep limestone walls. They can form awesome pinches but are rarely found on boulders.

This pinch rib screams "tufa" but is actually a rare weathering phenomenon on the igneous syenite of Hueco Tanks. Jason Kehl on the first ascent of Bloodline (V8), Hueco Tanks, Texas.
ANDY MANN

Coming to Grips

Crimping

Crimping is the most common way to grab any edge one digit wide or smaller. When crimping, the first knuckles bend backward, placing a lot of stress on these joints but also applying a lot of force to the fingertips. If you are fortunate enough to have been born with long thumbs in relation to your other fingers, you can get even more solid crimps by crimping the hold, then wrapping the thumb over the index finger. This locks your index in place and allows you to pull on your thumb as well.

Crimping can also be done on slopers. You can direct more force to a certain part of the hold that way, but get less skin contact, which may lead to less ability to hang the hold.

The crimp position raises the position of the wrist, hence gains the climber a few inches of reach as compared to using an open-hand approach. Crimping is a major cause of tendon pulley injuries, especially in the ring finger.

Open-Hand Technique

Open-hand technique is when the fingers grasping the hold are curled inward. It is commonly used for slopers, pockets, edges wider than a single digit, and any big incut hold. Open-hand technique comes far less naturally to most climbers but is less stressful on the finger joints. It can also be used for edges smaller than a single digit, especially if the hold has some curvature to it that matches the lengths of one's fingers. It's a worthy drill to practice hanging and moving on the same holds both by crimping and open-hand technique until you are just as comfortable with either grip. Often you can stick a hold in an open-hand position and use that hand position while hanging straight-armed from the hold, then switch over to a crimp position when pulling up on the hold and locking off.

Biff Farrell crimps with his left hand and open-hands with his right on **Bertha (V9), Lost Cove, North Carolina.**
PAT GOODMAN

Laybacking

Laybacking, aka liebacking, involves pulling on your arms in a rowing motion to push your feet hard enough against the wall to make them stick, often in a relatively high position on a blank wall. Because it's an opposition technique, it requires a lot of power—plan your expenditure accordingly.

Gastons

Gastons (gas-stones) are moves where the hand is positioned thumb down on a sidepull. The name "gaston" derives from famed 1950s French mountain guide Gaston Rebuffat's rudimentary crack technique—unacquainted with the subtleties of jamming, Rebuffat would just grab either side of a crack and pull apart like he was trying to rip open a pair of elevator doors. Now gastoning refers to any such thumbs-down sidepull action.

Lev Pinter working a gaston with his right hand on **Loaded With Power** *(V11), Hueco Tanks, Texas.*
ERIC ODENTHAL

Pat Goodman on the classic Joshua Tree lieback problem **False Up 20** *(V0).*

Underclinging

Dust off the biceps and call the paparazzi. Feet pressing down, arms pulling up—I like to train for underclings by lifting trucks off babies. Underclinging is often a power-intensive opposition technique, but with the right holds can be relaxed.

Manteling and the Beached Whale

What the hell? There are no holds over the lip. Time for a press conference.

Manteling is pressing oneself up on a ledge like pushing down the lid on an overstuffed car trunk. Unless you do tons of push-ups and dips, chances

*Not only does the Happy Boulder's **Kling and Smirk** provide a good example of underclinging, at V2 it's also a quintessential sandbag. **Jesse Althaus** on the start moves.*

Clockwise from top left, Paul Robinson executing a textbook mantel at Magic Wood, Switzerland. Paul sets his feet well, then flips his left "elbow to the sky," presses with his arms and feet, then flips a hand around to help step up on the ledge.

are you'll be quickly learning to use your feet to help out. Run your feet up high before committing to the press. Once pressed out over a sloping lip, you'll find you can't see the footholds under the lip—best to have your feet on them before you get that far. If the lip is wide enough and not too sloping, huck a heel hook over the lip and roll onto it. If you've hooked your left foot, you will likely lock off with the right arm, then flip the left into mantel position and press over. Unless you possess unnatural shoulder flexibility, most mantels start with the palms situated so that the thumbs are pointing toward each other. After the initial press you may find it more stable to flip one or both hands around so that the thumbs are on the outside of the hands—this can help raise you an extra inch or two, enough to raise a stubborn foot onto the lip. Also look for any holds beyond the lip you can grab to help.

Manteling isn't reserved just for lip moves, but for any hold one needs to press off of until it is at waist level or below.

If you're just starting out bouldering and find mantels to be beyond your strength, you can practice by manteling out of a pool, using your buoyancy to help get started. Practice standing up on either foot to top out.

Some topouts are just too darn funky or strenuous to mantel, or maybe your feet popped off the holds under the lip after you pressed up and you

Jessa Goebbel throws a heel on the lip, then using mostly her right foot pulling and left hand pressing down, rocks over the top of **The Chube (V3)** *in Joshua Tree National Park.*

Back in the 1960s and '70s, gymnastic power was highly prized in the bouldering world thanks to sick-strong gymnast/boulderers like John Gill and Pat Ament. Mantel problems were favorites. Out in Colorado one-arm mantel problems were common tricks for showing off strength. In California boulderers adopted a different style. Yosemite's notorious climber hang, Camp 4, is bordered by a boulderfield with an abundance of mantel problems. Just pressing out one of these tough mantels wasn't cool enough. Style demanded the boulderer press it out with the fingers of both hands interlaced, then when fully pressed, raise those fingers to form a cup into which one inserted a toe and then stood up. Stand up with your foot outside your hands and suffer humiliation.

lack the flexibility to hoist them over the lip. Time for the least respected, but oft-employed, beached whale maneuver. This is whole upper body climbing at its ugliest and consists of rolling onto the lip as far as possible and smearing one's belly, thighs, arms, sometimes even face to stay put while desperately hunching up the rock with small hand presses and torso wiggles. It comes more naturally than you would like to think and is always a crowd pleaser.

Palming

Palming is any move where you press on the stone with your palms, most commonly when manteling, stemming, or wrapping a beach ball–size sloper. Sweaty palms cost you your chance at that executive position? Best be chalking up your whole hand, not just the fingertips.

Kayla Dempsey palming slopers on The Bilboquet boulder, Cul de Chien sector, Fontainebleau, France.

Wrist Hooks and False Grips

If the hold is big enough for your entire hand and has a distinct outer edge, or maybe you have a big chickenhead with which to work, you can employ a wrist hook or false grip to take weight off the fingers and put the arm in a position of more leverage. Wrist hooks are any move where the inside of the wrist is curled around a hold to support weight. The false grip is a type of wrist hook borrowed from gymnastics and is how gymnasts grip the still rings. Instead of grabbing the ring in the hand like a pull-up bar, the gymnast positions the ring to run between the encircled thumb and forefinger, along the palm parallel to the thumb muscle, then in between the two prominent wrist bones on the inside of the wrist, ending up wrapped around the pinky-side of the inside wrist. The gymnast's weight is then supported mostly on the wrist joint itself,

Melissa Lacasse using a false grip with her right hand on the first female ascent of Bierstadt (V10), Mount Evans, Colorado.
ANDY MANN

not farther out the palm toward the fingers—quite an advantage when busting out an iron cross. Wrist hooks work well for resting the fingers and shaking out on longer problems. False grips are great for gaining leverage on big front lever–type moves, but require the right size and shape hold to be a viable option. A standard false grip hooks the pinky-side wrist bone. A reverse false grip hooks the thumb-side wrist bone.

Skyhook

The skyhook grip is rarely used but can be employed for very tiny edges (less than one-quarter digit wide). Fingers are curled tight and weight applied to the very tip of the finger. You're not trying to crank on the nail itself. Instead force the flesh just under the nail to bear the weight. Just as comfy as it sounds. It works best if the hold is incut.

A skyhook grip on a ⅛-inch edge. The thumb is moving in to squeeze under the minuscule lip behind it to make this more secure.

The Match Game

"Matching" is when you use two limbs on the same hold, commonly both hands or both feet, but it could be a hand and a foot, or even both knees. If the hold is wide enough, it's a simple matter just to arrange the first hand or foot on the hold far enough to one side to leave room for the other. When the handhold gets narrower, it's time to overlap the fingers of the following hand over the first hand on the hold, then gradually wiggle the first hand's fingers to the side and let the following hand's fingers drop in place. When used on flat horizontal edges, this technique is called "piano-ing" and can be time consuming and energy burning. A quicker method when the hold is large and positive is to overlap the fingers, then make a small hop upward and slide the first hand out when your momentum takes weight off your hands. The following hand then falls in place. When matching feet on a narrow hold, one usually has to hop the first foot off, then quickly and accurately stab the following foot on the same hold. *See photos on next page.*

Figure Four

This is seldom used and falls more into the category of a circus trick than a core bouldering technique (though it is used frequently in ice climbing). Usually any situation that will allow a figure four is more easily solved with a simple dyno—the one exception being if the target hold is exceptionally poor and requires one to settle in on it statically. If you do a lot of comps, you might run into a figure four designed into the route to wow the crowd. Figure fours put a lot of stress on the wrist joint. To do one, get locked on your handhold well, then bring a leg up inside your arm and toss it over that arm, hooking it over the wrist, either just behind the knee or in some cases at the crotch. Post your other leg to stabilize and maintain height, then casually reach the next hold statically before your wrist snaps. Please don't tell anyone you learned this junk from my book.

Sopping wet topouts won't stop Brian Mancuso on this rainy day. Instead he works a traverse, off-routing the lip holds on this boulder at Rocher Fin, Fontainebleau, France. The pocket is great to sink four fingers in, but Brian only drops three in to make it easier to match fingers in the pocket. Note how the left fingers overlap the right ones, then drop in place when Brian moves his right hand to the next hold.

Foot-eye coordination. Above: Ben Connor has his left foot overlapping his right ready to match on the toe-hold as soon as the right vacates it. Below: Ben swings the right foot away and precisely nails the hold with the left toe.

Chad Foti does a heel/hand match on **Vlad The Impaler** *(V9)*, Rocklands, South Africa.

Posture

"Chest out, stomach in" is fine and good when going for that job interview or first meeting that blind date, but when it comes to bouldering, good posture means getting one's body aligned to force weight on the feet and maintain a balanced position. Generally this means keeping one's center of gravity aligned over and between one's feet. (**NOTE:** Don't confuse "good posture" with "climber's posture," a malady discussed in the training and injury chapters.)

Vertical and Less Than Vertical Faces

The key on these is to stay on your feet. On vertical terrain, try to keep your hips in close to the rock—good hip turnout helps here. If your hip turnout is poor, you can align your body sideways to the rock to keep one hip in. This usually requires

Above: The posture isn't bad, I'd grade it a "B"—heels are properly low, butt is over the feet (good), but the body is starting to inch into the wall. Below: Here the climber gets greedy and leans in attempting to reach a tiny edge. Seconds later her feet cut, causing a fall.

Maki Grossnick adopting a relaxed "nose-over-toes" posture as this problem turns less than vertical.

you to stand on the outside of one foot. On less than vertical walls, keep your "nose over your toes" and keep your heels low to force more rubber onto the rock. Don't lean into the rock or stand on tippy-toes—unless they are placed on positive edges, your feet will skate out from under you. On friction slabs, look for rough patches or subtly lower-angled spots to smear your feet.

Steve Bradshaw keeps his center of gravity over his right foot by turning sideways to the wall—a good trick for climbers with poor hip turnout. Planfontein sector, Rocklands, South Africa.

Overhanging Faces

On slightly to moderately overhanging walls, good posture means keeping the hips as close to the wall as you can and utilizing footholds close to your center of gravity. On very steeply overhanging walls

Jesse Althaus displaying textbook good posture on Solarium, Happy Boulders, Bishop, California. She has a very stable stance with her center of gravity between her feet. Her hips are close to the rock, forcing her weight onto her feet. Because she's properly weighting her feet, her fingers need not overgrip—instead they only have to pull hard enough to keep her from tipping over backward.

and roofs, the idea about forcing weight onto the feet is still valid, but trying to paste the hips close to the wall is usually a waste of strength. Instead, positioning one's center of gravity will vary a lot depending on if one is heel hooking, toe hooking, hanging slopes, working jugs, or whatever. The possibilities vary with every move.

Upper Body Technique on Overhanging Faces

When the rock overhangs, power becomes increasingly important. Attaining power is simply a matter of climbing lots of strenuous problems and/or putting in tons of gym time. The biggest mistake most boulderers make on overhanging stone is trying to use all power and no finesse. When you're climbing at your limit you need both. Dynamic moves are big energy savers and are discussed in the next chapter. Following are some additional tips for when the going gets steep.

Straight Arm It

Keep your arms as straight as possible. Allow your skeleton to support your weight, not your muscles. When moving up, use your legs to push your weight up. The arms are only there to hold your body in. Only bend them when necessary, after your feet are set. On vertical to slightly overhung faces, if you can't hang straight-armed to rest, try to get into a full lock-off position with hand next to shoulder and chest sucked into the wall. This is the next most restful position.

On horizontal roofs your arms don't need to pull up. Keep them straight and move between holds as if you were on a set of monkey bars. Use heel hooks, toe hooks, heel-toe locks, and knee bars to take weight off your fingers. If the holds are sloping, you'll need to employ compression either by bear-hugging with the hands or employing toe hooks and heel hooks.

Stephanie Bénard is saving energy by keeping her arms straight and weighting a heel hook on **John Denver (7a)** *(lots of climbers crash and burn at the end of this one), Rocklands, South Africa.*
PAUL ROBINSON

Daniel Woods on Black Shadow (V13), Rocklands, South Africa. Daniel has straight arms here. He's rocking a slew of techniques on this roof move: bicycle opposition between his feet, right foot toe-hooked to provide opposition with the hands, hands pulling in compression to each other, and a pinch with his right hand to increase the normal force his right fingers have on that sloping lip.
ANDY MANN

Many of today's sickest problems require intense compression moves like this one Daniel Woods displays on his problem The Game (V16), Boulder Canyon, Colorado. In this case Daniel's arms are bent to increase the leverage on the bear hug.
JOHN DICKEY

Torso Twists

On severely overhanging rock, one can progress between holds with torso twists while still keeping one's arms fairly straight. Your torso muscles are bigger and more powerful than your arms. Use those torso muscles to twist your upper body so the shoulder axis becomes perpendicular to the rock. Your supporting arm remains straight and crosses your chest and stomach. You'll be amazed at how far you can now reach up with your free hand.

*Using a torso twist, Whitney Boland barely bends her right arm to make this long reach on a problem on **Sherman Roof (V7), Rocktown, Georgia.***
PAT GOODMAN

Pure Power

The techniques discussed here all help take weight off the arms on steep rock. Nevertheless, you will have to pull up on your arms frequently. Use finesse to save your strength for these moves. Applying power is one thing, applying it at just the right time is another. To do power moves at your maximum ability, you need to time the use of that power exactly. After the power move(s), get your weight back on your feet as soon as possible. The best boulderers can go from technical and precise to powerful, then back to technical in an instant. As with all moves, focus on good execution.

Resting

Many boulder problems will have no rests, so it's up to you to sprint for the finish. However, there are some mighty long traverses and roofs out there where you won't stand a chance if you don't rest. Plan where you will rest in advance. Look for spots with big footholds, huge handholds, knee bars, over-the-head heel-toe locks, good jams, and so forth. A good knee bar is usually your best bet, but again, be creative. One time on a 50-foot roof, I copped a crucial rest in a 5-foot-diameter pod by stemming my feet out on one wall and pressing the top of my head against a scoop in the opposite wall. I was facing straight down with arms dangling free and my butt sticking up like a stink beetle. It was uncomfortable, but it worked.

Move fast between rests.

Working Slopers on Overhangs

Many modern testpieces have crux holds that slope so despairingly that it's impossible to just hang one's weight straight down off them. Time to cash in on those Pilates lessons. Use your core strength to suck your center of gravity in toward the wall thereby making the angle of pull more perpendicular to the sloper (see the Bouldering Physics 101 sidebar). Your hip flexors and hamstrings will be working overtime trying to pull outward on footholds to position your hips closer to the wall. Downturned shoes will help. Work any chance at compression (say a toe hook) to allow you to pull harder on the sloper. If the sloper has a certain grain or ripple pattern that feels rougher in one direction than the other, align your pull against the grain as much as possible.

Common Traps

Overgripping

Overgripping is hanging on holds harder than needed, thus wasting strength. Inexperience and fear are the major contributors to overgripping. The earlier in your career you address this issue, the better. Go to the boulders or gym and pick a slightly overhanging wall that forces weight on the hands. Staying safely close to the ground, grab a pair of holds and get on the wall in good posture. Now gradually relax your grip a tiny bit—you'll likely notice you're still on the wall. Relax it a bit more and a bit more—until your hands peel off. Get a feel for how little you need to grip the holds to stay on. Practice with different-shaped holds, at different angles, on problems you have wired, etc. When you start picking up crack technique, practice this with jamming as well.

Barndooring

Barndooring is not a technique, but a dreadful reality on some problems. It occurs when the angle of the rock in relation to the holds makes your body want to pivot around your hands and feet like a swinging door. Eventually the door swings wide enough to come off the hinges. This is commonly

Quentin Chastagnier working the heinous slopers of Moiste Maiste (V14), Rocklands, South Africa. At times like this it feels like an anvil is strapped to your waist trying to drag your hips away from the wall. To counteract this Quentin works toe hooks on the arête and uses heaps of core strength to lever his hips in close to the wall.

a problem with laybacks and arêtes, but can strike on just about any move. The key is using body position to align your center of gravity within your base of support. Flagging an arm or leg is the most common technique to deal with it, or moving quickly enough to grab a positive hold before you pitch. Alternatively, one can exert huge torque to counteract the swing. Body tension urges the hips toward the wall, and opposition between hands and feet pulling harder than normal applies the torque—anyone with a college physics class behind them can figure out how exhausting this is and why it only works if you're teetering right on the brink of losing balance, not a few degrees past.

Josh Vale joining the club as he barndoors off the notorious **Pope's Prow (V4), Buttermilks, California.**

The Art of Dynamic Movement

In 1958 John Gill started a revolution in rock climbing. He decided to approach rock climbing as an extension of gymnastics, rather than an extension of hiking or mountaineering. He took this new philosophy to the boulders and actively sought out problems that could only be climbed dynamically. Hence modern bouldering was born, and ever since, dynamic movement has remained the soul of the sport.

Standard Dynamics

When you don't have the strength to lock off and reach a hold statically, it's time to dyno. Alternatively, you may have the strength to crank to the next hold static; however, to do so will position your center of gravity outside your base of support, causing you to barndoor off. Even if you can crank a move statically, doing it dynamically can save a lot of energy and perhaps make the difference in doing the next move. Furthermore, dynamics, when performed correctly, are kinesthetically pleasing, downright fun, and crowd pleasers to boot. Dynamics are most commonly used on vertical to overhanging rock.

Five quick rules:

- Push with your legs, don't pull with your arms.
- Use your arms to pivot and direct.
- Crouch once, then fire—don't pump doubt.
- Commit.
- Don't overdyno.

Using Your Legs

The most important thing to remember when dynoing is to propel yourself with your legs. They are much stronger than your arms and will launch you farther and save your arm strength for other moves.

Determining which footholds to push off from requires experience. The more dyno problems you do, the better you will become at judging how high or low your feet should be for a given move. In general, use the biggest footholds available so you can push off harder. If, however, the bigger footholds are awkwardly placed, say too high, too low, or staggered, you may be better off using smaller footholds that feel better positioned. If the footholds permit, plant both feet equidistant from the hold you are shooting for. For example, if you're shooting straight up, a line drawn through both feet will be parallel to the ground (assuming the ground is level); if you're dynoing sideways, the foot opposite the direction you are dynoing in will be higher than the other. This will make it easier to push off smoothly and guide your trajectory.

If you are dynoing for a hard-to-grasp hold (small, sloping, or awkwardly angled), you'll have an

Justin Wood throwing a double dyno at Big Bend Boulders, Utah.
DAWN KISH

Commit! Maki Grossnick on the finishing dyno on **Ironman Traverse (V4), Buttermilks, California.**

Simon Collette sticks the finishing dyno on **Skink,** *Rocklands, South Africa. Note how his feet are at the same height, how his arms remain relatively straight as he pivots around the handholds, and how the upward thrust comes from his legs.*

easier time sticking it if your feet don't come off the rock. Keeping your feet on the rock will help kill any barndoor effect and will also take some of your body weight. Given multiple footholds of equal size to choose from, I will pick the lowest set that my feet will stay on when I hit the hold I'm shooting for. (See Sizing Up a Move in Chapter 6.)

There is a point of diminishing returns as you bring your feet higher and higher up the rock to do a dyno. This point varies from individual to individual, depending on leg strength and flexibility, but most folks will find it hard to push off their feet if they are placed any higher than their hips. Practice is the key to getting the feel for dynamics.

Adam Markert on Midnight Cowboy (7a), Rocklands, South Africa. Adam rises up a bit so he can drop fully down in a tight crouch, triggering the stretch reflex bounce to help propel him upward.

His arms remain straight as he pivots around the starting jug, then because this wall overhangs only slightly, he must bend his arms to keep his body in closer to the wall while his legs launch him to the sloping target hold.

Using Your Arms

Unless you have wings instead of arms, don't use your arms to propel yourself upward when dynoing. On a properly executed dyno, the arms are used to pivot and direct the body, not to propel it. Dynos done with the arms are usually sloppy, strength-wasting slap jobs. Done with the legs they are smooth, efficient works of art.

When dynoing, keep your arms relatively straight as you pivot around your starting handhold. The more overhanging the move, the straighter your arms can stay throughout the move. As walls get closer to vertical, your arms will bend more to keep your body in close to the rock. The more overhanging the wall, the less vertical component there will be to a dyno of any given length and the greater an arc you can let your body take. On vertical walls, flatten out the arc so as to give a maximum vertical component to your thrust. Use your leg power to push up, not out. Your arms will pull you in so your legs can push you up. Your arms are not pulling you up.

Crouch Once . . . Then Fire!

Sink down low enough to get the needed thrust from your legs, then fire for the hold. Exhale while you push off.

Commitment

Commit to the move. Imagine yourself latching that next hold with confidence. You own that move, now crouch and fire. Half-assed attempts give half-assed results.

Avoid Overdynoing

Only lunge as far as needed to hit the hold. Latch the hold at the "deadpoint" of the dyno, when the body has moved up as far as it will go and just before it starts to fall. This will make the transfer of weight to that hold easier and less likely to cause injury. If I find myself getting too "slappy" or over-lunging, I tell myself that I need to land on the hold softly, like a leaf dropping from the sky. It's kind of a mantra, and really calms me down and helps me focus on using good technique.

The Big Mistake

If we could harness all the energy wasted by boulderers unnecessarily pumping their bodies up and down before they lunged, we could keep the Vegas Strip lit up year-round for free. Many boulderers use a "One . . . two . . . three . . . go!" series of body thrusts before they actually take off for the hold. They justify this as "psyching up" and "building rhythm." More likely they are psyching out and wasting strength. I call this "pumping doubt." The proper place to psych for the dyno is not while bobbing up and down on the holds, but at the base of the problem before you step off the ground. Heck, why not psych up the night before while you're doing the dishes. When you get to the move,

crouch down once and fire. You'll be blown away at how much easier it is. Basically, if you pump three times before you shoot, you could have just tried the problem three times.

Four Cases Where an Extra Thrust Won't Hurt

Nine out of ten times, extra pumps are a big blunder. There are, however, four special cases where it isn't.

On your first time up a problem, an extra pump can be the right thing to do. It can give you a preview of how the move will feel. You might judge the distance to the next hold better or get some balance clues. You might decide you want to launch from different footholds. Once you've had your review though, it's time to get down to business—crouch once and fire. On subsequent attempts, forgo the pre-pump—again, crouch once and fire.

Case two exists on really long dynos where you need maximum thrust and your legs fold up completely, butt-to-heels, before you launch. In this case take advantage of the stretch reflex. This is the little bounce you get when you squat down quickly, maxing out that range of motion. Your body senses this and bounces you back up a few degrees to ease the stress. Use this bounce to initiate a more powerful deep leg thrust. Often you can get the bounce by just crouching down quickly, but sometimes a short pump upward followed by a quick drop gives a better bounce.

Case three occurs on roofs and very steep overhangs. On these it's hard to get into a crouched position before you fire. When you try to crouch down, your butt just drops toward the ground, not toward your feet. Push your legs straight once, then let your body pivot back downward. The momentum it has will carry your center of gravity past the low point of the arc and back up toward your feet into a crouched position. When your body reaches this position, push off on the footholds and blast toward the next hold. Usually one pump is enough to get into a deep enough crouch, but sometimes it

For this sideways dyno, the climber rocks left, away from the target, so he can create the maximum momentum on the swing back toward the target.

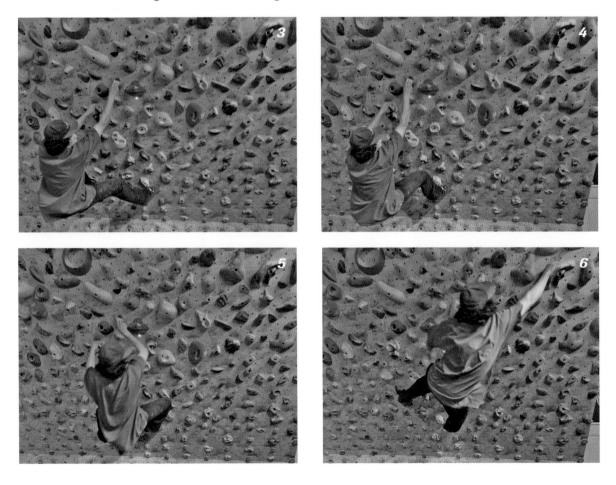

may take another pump or two, each time increasing the length of the arc. Sometimes a toe hook can pull you into the crouched position, eliminating the need for the extra pump but forcing you to push off from one foot alone.

Case four happens when dynoing sideways where you can't position your feet to push in the direction you want to go. For example, your hands are matched on a jug and you want to dyno 5 feet straight right for another jug. You wish there were footholds to your left to push off from, but the only footholds are directly beneath your hands. To get the momentum to reach right, swing your body from side to side (right to left and back) several times until you generate enough momentum to reach the next hold.

Double Dynos

Double dynos are dynamic moves where both hands (and usually both feet) come off the rock. This usually happens when the handholds are spaced more than an arm span apart. It's sure to generate beaucoup style points. As with other dynos, provide most of the thrust with the legs and use the arms more as pivot points. Often one hand leaves the starting hold before the other and is first to the target hold, quickly followed by the other hand to control any subsequent swing. Other times both hands will move in unison. Commitment is the key to double dynos, as you cannot reverse such a move.

Sandra Stuckey (5 feet 5 inches) blasts 7 feet worth of roof dyno in Rocklands, South Africa. Too bad the target is 7.5 feet away. Another day.

Swing Starts

There is no rule stating that you cannot jump for the first holds on a problem. Sometimes this is as simple as just crouching down and jumping up to the first holds. When those holds are too small or far away to grab this way, a swing start or a levered spring comes into play.

Swing starts were a John Gill favorite and a technique I like a lot too. The move consists of putting one hand on the rock, then dynoing from the ground to a hold high up the wall. Both feet can push off the ground, or one foot can push off the ground and the other off the rock. Use the handhold as a barely weighted pivot point to help direct the dyno, or if big enough, pull on it to help launch the body up. A lot of my friends pooh-pooh swing starts, saying you must start all problems with both feet on the rock. Had I held this belief myself, I would have missed out on many excellent problems. I find that the climbers who denigrate this technique are invariably piss poor at it. It's not as easy as it sounds.

Like any dyno, the thrust for a swing start should come mainly from the legs. Use the hand on the rock mostly as a pivot. Crouch down and explode up. Only crouch once—no "pumping doubt." To gain added height on a swing start, drop your free hand low as you crouch. When you dyno, swing that arm upward toward the high hold. This arm swing will provide more upward momentum. (To check this at home, do a vertical leap starting with your hands above your head. Now try it starting with both hands low and swinging them up as you leap. Much farther, eh?)

Because you only have one hand and one or no feet on the rock during a swing start, barndooring can easily happen. The trick to swing starts is to control or eliminate the barndoor. To do this, pick the launch spot for your foot or feet carefully; sometimes moving your foot just an inch to the side can make a dramatic difference. Often one must try several different launch spots to find the best one. Before you blast off, mark the spot you took off from by scratching a line with the tip of your toe in the dirt or by positioning your carpet so you take off from one corner. If you launch with success but fail higher on the problem, you can easily find the successful take-off spot again.

Sometimes barndooring can't be eliminated. When barndooring is a problem, it's usually because the climber's body barndoors away from the rock at the moment the climber grasps the high hold. To fight this tendency you can start with your feet positioned to initiate a subtle barndooring into the rock. This usually involves positioning your feet farther away from the base. These moves often feel awkward when one sets up, but halfway through the move the body ends up taking a more favorable trajectory, ending with a soft landing on the target hold. If your body is still swinging in when you latch the hold, you stand a better chance of hanging on than if your body were swinging out at that moment. If you overdo this, however, your body will swing back out after you've latched the hold and could pull you off. The key is to make this inward barndoor very subtle so that it cancels itself at the top of the move.

Another way to control barndooring is to vary the angle of your arm swing. This can cause your body to barndoor one way or the other, even if your feet take off from the same spot. You can change the angle of your arm swing to adjust how much you barndoor. Practice with different angles of arm swing. Practicing swing starts can be a great way to learn how your body moves during dynos. This knowledge can then be used on all dynos, whether they start from the ground or higher, off the deck.

Swing starts take a lot of practice to get good at. No matter how good you are at other starts, there will always be a problem out there you can start no other way. When you stick one there is an instant feeling of kinesthetic awareness that is a wonderful way to start a problem. Some people would rather use cheater stones than do a swing start. These poor

*By default, any **John Gill** problem is a classic, but some, like **Pinch Overhang (V5)**, **Horsetooth Reservoir, Colorado**, have gone beyond classic to become iconic. Andy Johnson squeezing the most famous pinch hold in bouldering with his right hand, then launching a swing start to nail the lip.*

chumps are missing out on some of the coolest moves out there. Furthermore, the same arm-swing technique used for swing starts can sometimes be utilized for extra distance on dynos partway up a problem (this obviously requires a good enough handhold for your pivot arm).

A levered spring is similar to a swing start, but utilizes a strong push downward on (as opposed to a pivot around) the starting handhold to add to upward momentum.

Veronica Lee uses a double arm swing start to begin **Harry Spotter (6c)**, Cresciano, Switzerland. She uses the momentum generated by her arm swings (and pushing off the right leg) to shift forward onto her left foot, then presses up on her left leg to catch the hold she wants.

John Gill uses a levered spring to climb this nearly blank wall at Pennyrile Forest, Kentucky, 1965.
JOHN GILL COLLECTION

Linked Dynamics

Just as a gymnast can use the momentum from one dynamic move to initiate the next dynamic move, so can a boulderer. Gill once wrote about this as being a potential future direction for bouldering. He was doubtless influenced by his rope climbing (a former event in gymnastics meets), in which the momentum of a powerful start could be maintained to the top of the 20-foot rope. (From a sit-down start, Gill could climb the rope in 3.4 seconds.) Because speed is rarely pursued in bouldering and it is rarely necessary to climb problems fast (other than forearm-melting traverses), the concept of

linked dynamics has not been carried very far. I can think of three situations where this conservation of momentum comes in useful.

The first is dynamics in which the feet start from greatly differing heights. A common example is a swing start with one foot on the ground and one foot high on the rock, say about waist level. Initially the foot on the rock is too high to push off of. Hence the foot on the ground provides the initial momentum. When the body rises high enough, the foot on the rock starts pushing, propelling the body much farther up the rock than if both feet had started on the ground. Less common are dynos starting with both feet on the rock but at greatly

*Dale Fox on **Saturday Night Live** (V4). His feet are at greatly different levels. Here he drops his right arm low so he can swing it toward the lip to generate the momentum and trajectory to shift his weight onto his right leg, which then provides the bulk of the thrust to launch him to the lip.*

Joshua Tree is famous for run-and-jump problems. Here Pat Goodman leaves some skin on the lip of Jump Chump *(J1).*

differing heights. In reality, any dyno starting without the legs evenly extended will apply this conservation of momentum principle when the weight shifts from one leg to the other. However, it is most noticeable when the leg thrusts are spaced farther apart.

The second linked-dynamic situation is on no-foot traverses: for example, traversing the lip of a roof. If one's hands shuffle so quickly along the lip that one's body trails the hands, the momentum of the body trying to swing and catch up with the hands can propel the climber across the traverse. To experience this, find a steel I-beam beneath a ceiling, a fat doorjamb across a garage door, or the continuous horizontal rail on a jungle-gym ladder. Traverse as fast as you can with your legs dangling. As long as your feet trail your hands, you will fly across. As soon as your legs start swinging back and forth, you will slow down. If you're strong enough, most problems suited to linked-dynamic traversing will succumb without this technique. However, linked dynamics give tremendous kinesthetic pleasure. The classic *Nat's Traverse* at Mortar Rock in Berkeley has a 10-foot-long leg-dangling section that is much more fun when done in one uninterrupted linked-dynamic flow.

The third variation on the linked-dynamic theme is the run-and-jump. This consists of running up to a boulder, jumping off the ground, kicking off the rock with one foot, and latching the target hold—all in one uninterrupted sequence. These problems can be great fun and can sometimes consist of several kicks up a face before the hands ever touch. Joshua Tree National Park is famous for its run-and-jumps. Locals have even devised a ratings scheme (J ratings) to compare the difficulty of the jump problems there.

Theoretically one could dyno upward, catch a hold, pull on it immediately, and keep dynoing upward, utilizing the momentum from the first move. While this sounds appealing, in practice it is nearly impossible to find a problem that can only be done that way.

Other Body Part Swings

In most dynos the momentum comes from the legs pushing down on holds. We have already mentioned using arm swings to create and direct momentum.

The same can be done with a free leg. A swing of the head forward can help keep the body close to the rock on some deadpoint moves.

Paul Robinson's arms are locked out wide and his feet sucked way back under the overhang—a very difficult position from which to generate any momentum for the stab to the lip. Paul brings his left leg out and behind him, then swings that leg to the left to generate momentum. He snags the lip, then hangs on tight to control the swing caused by his right foot coming off the back wall. Amber (V12), Ticino, Switzerland.

Feet-Off Dynos (aka Campus Moves)

At some point you might find yourself dangling from holds, unable to get your feet on the rock. If you hadn't kicked everyone's butt in a one-arm pull-up contest that morning, you'd just lock the next move off.

Unfortunately, locking off at your nipple ain't happening, so you're forced to lunge. No doubt about it, big guns help here, but you can still get help from your legs by kipping. Kipping is a quick raising of the legs, usually into a sitting or L position. For an instant, the momentum from the kip takes some of the weight off your arms. At this instant, pull up for all you're worth and snag the next hold. The resultant bend at your waist also makes more muscle groups available to help the

A no-foot finger traverse got me to this point where I have to bust a campus move to the lip. Two chalk bags and a mullet are weighing me down, so I need to kip my legs to generate momentum.

arms pull up. You can also swing your body back and forth like a pendulum and at the high point of the arc add a kip and fire. Practice these moves on a pull-up bar.

On no-foot traverse moves you can sometimes find yourself stuck in an iron-cross position, unable to let go to match on the hold you just grabbed. Your feet are dangling straight below you, and you feel that if you let go with one hand you'll drop on the other arm and rip it from your shoulder like a weed being pulled. To get out of this situation, swing your legs from side to side. As your feet come up under the hand you want to release, you will feel the weight come off that hand. At this momentary "deadpoint," let go of the hold and match hands. Hang on tight when your legs swing back down. This is easily practiced on a wide pull-up bar.

Mid-Path Trajectory Alterations and Counterbalancing

This concept is hard to describe in words. Some dynos will propel you away from the rock and/or target hold. Usually there's a barndoor in effect. Done with standard dyno technique, you will just swing off. Time to find some counterbalancing moves. This can be dynoing with your body to one side but swinging your arm sideways at the last moment to catch a hold. The initial sideways dyno kills your barndoor, then the last-second course correction snags the target hold. The permutations are infinite, but what we're talking about is swinging an arm or leg or hips in a different direction than the target hold to maintain contact with the launch holds, kill a barndoor, etc. We use momentum in one direction to align forces in the right direction to the holds we're pulling on, then when we get our upward/forward movement going, we use our reach to snag our target hold, which is hopefully positive enough to kill the subsequent swing we'll experience. Each situation is unique, and this is a wild and fun technique to play with.

Flashback to the early 1990s and the author rolling laps on Bachar Cracker, one of the most famous boulder problems in Yosemite. This line checks in at a "mere V4" but has a reputation of slapping down hordes of V-double-digit boulderers who never learned the fine art of jamming. Simply put, the climber who can't jam is only half a climber at best.

Jamming

Most boulders are solid chunks of stone devoid of cracks. Compared to face problems, crack problems are a rarity in bouldering, so why devote a chapter to jamming? Because crack problems are some of the coolest climbs out there. Just check out the splitter lines pictured in this chapter.

Crack climbs on cliffs are usually hard because they're long and continuous and you have to hang on to place gear. Cracks in boulders are usually short and are only hard if they are a bad size, greatly flared, or super steep. In crack climbing, every ounce of technique is worth a ton of strength. The climber who learns to jam efficiently is at a huge advantage. Jams present great rest opportunities and often allow one to do huge reaches with little effort. Jamming technique can often be employed on problems without cracks, as well—for instance, a toe jam between knobs or maybe a fist jam in a hueco. Get used to climbing with both sides of your hands and feet.

Basic Jamming Technique

The plethora of jamming techniques is worthy of a book in its own right. Here we'll just hit on the basics progressing from thin cracks to wide ones, starting with hand technique, then feet.

Fingerlocks

Fingerlocks are the easiest jam to learn—just find the right finger-size constriction in the crack, stuff the fingers in, and pull down to lock them against the constriction. In a vertical crack, aligning the thumb down will give more torque, making it

Mount Woodson, northeast of San Diego, California, deservedly has the reputation as the crack bouldering capital of America. Sheer splitters in bullet granite abound in all sizes. Here the author sends the classic off-finger testpiece Jaws. *A pad won't help on this landing, but one can stem back to the wall behind to back off until the final few committing moves. Elbows are dropped low to maximize torquing action.*

121

easier to hold the jam. However, the thumbs-down position limits how far you can move off the jam—lock the jam off too low and you'll have so much torque on your fingers they can be impossible to pull out of the jam. Thumbs up works best if you want to lock off low and move upward as far as possible. In horizontal cracks, pull sideways against the constriction to maintain the lock.

Chad Foti spent years in the gym developing the lock-off power to make reaches like this one at Rocklands, South Africa. While he was doing that, I was climbing and partying like a sailor on shore leave. Because I learned how to jam, I can fire this move without even bending my arm or breaking a sweat. I feel real solid on this thin hands–size crack, but just in case my jam slips, I've got my brain bucket on because there's a real abrupt lip on the boulder behind my head and I don't relish the idea of a hospital stay in rural Africa.

Jessa Goebbel reaches for the next fingerlock constriction on **Driving South,** *Mount Woodson, California.*

Jessa again on **Driving South,** *this time going thumbs down with her lower right hand and thumbs up with her left hand. At this point the left side of the crack is offset 1 to 2 inches, making it hard to go thumbs down with the left hand and still be able to rotate the left elbow down to increase torque. To get a solid thumbs-up fingerlock, Jessa picks a good constriction that the fingers can slot into and lock with minimal torque. Note how she keeps her arms straight to conserve strength while setting a thin toe jam.*

Finger Jams

Finger jams differ from fingerlocks in that the crack is finger width yet has no constrictions; hence a lot of torque needs to be exerted to maintain the jam. Go thumbs down in this situation—drop the elbow below the lock to increase torque and relish the pain.

Fingerstacks

Off-fingers is one of the tougher sizes to get comfortable with. Too wide for a finger jam, too narrow to get the big knuckles into the crack. It's time to fingerstack by inserting the thumb into the crack, forming a constriction between the back of the small knuckle on the thumb and the wall of the crack, then curling the fingers over the thumb and torquing. This is done in the thumbs-down position. Fingerstacks put a lot of pressure on the tip of the thumb.

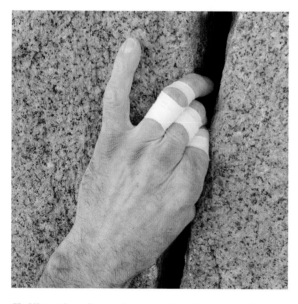

Unlike other finger jams, with a fingerstack the thumb goes in the crack, forming a platform to stack fingers on top of. Unless you have a proportionally long pinky, this orientation makes it preferable to leave the pinky out of the crack.

Thin Hands

Thin hands are when you can get the big knuckles of the hand in the crack, but not the wrist. In this case stuff as much of your hand in the crack as possible and focus on trying to squeeze your thumb across your palm. Some climbers exhaust themselves trying to cup their fingers and press hard on the fingertips and back of the big knuckles, but this is unnecessary—most, if not all, of the jamming force should

A lot of climbers freak when confronted with flared cracks or rounded lips. In reality both are usually your friend. Here a flared slot gives a great thin hands jam opportunity—notice how the flare matches the taper of the hand and fingers, allowing more skin contact than one would get in a parallel-sided crack. The thumb is squeezing as if it were trying to cup inside the palm—compare this with the thumb position in the other hand jamming close-ups.

come from the thumb squeeze. Thumbs down helps when you need extra torque, but as with finger jams this limits how low you can lock off the jam.

Don't let the angle of shadow fool you—Robbins' Crack, Mount Woodson, California, is 1¼ to 1½ inches wide for its full length. Climbers with small hands eat this stuff up, but those with average to big hands find it squarely in the thin hands realm.

Falling asleep on Robbins' Crack? Then book a tour to Hueco Tanks East Spur and give Mother of the Future (V9) a whirl—30 feet of fingers and thin hands out a horizontal roof. Check out the author's old-school footwear—full toe boxes with no sticky rands—this problem dropped a couple grades with the introduction of slippers, yet still has had only a handful of ascents. For added points, do the Hueco Triple Crown—Mother of the Future, Terminator, and The Morgue—the same day for 100 feet of horizontal jamming fun.

Hand Jams

Hand jams are when you can get a full hand in the crack, wrist and all. These are some of the easiest jams to master. Use the same thumb-squeeze technique as employed in thin hands, only now your thumb can squeeze farther across your palm, exerting even greater force. Same rules as to thumbs up or down.

The common rookie mistake is to try and cup the fingers to exert jamming force and just let the thumb wander wherever.

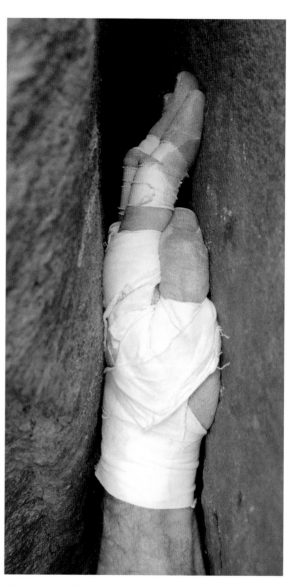

Proper hand jam technique with the thumb squeezing as far across the palm as the crack allows.

A meat and potatoes hand crack at Cresciano, Switzerland.

Off-Hands

Off-hands are used when you're squeezing the thumb as far as it will go across the palm, but the hand jam still rattles in the crack; however, the crack is too narrow to fit a fist in. Time to cup your hands and torque thumbs down. The pressure will be primarily on the back of the big knuckle of the index finger and along the pinky finger side of your palm. With roofs, because you're pulling straight out on the jams, it helps to bend the wrist toward the thumb side and set the jam sideways in the crack with thumbs pointing toward each other. You can then torque the hands in opposite directions to help them stay in.

Thumbs-up cupped hand jam. The thumb is squeezed to its full range of motion across the palm to expand the hand as wide as possible in this orientation.

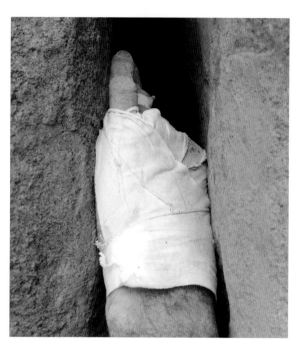

Cupped hand turned thumb down for maximum torque in an off-hand jam.

Right—Rockland regulars told me this stellar double-overhanging hand-to-fist number had never been climbed. Man was I psyched to try it. The first bulge was nice flared hands, but now I'm confronted with an off-hands-to-flared-fist jamming crux through the upper bulge. Time to reconsider my risk/reward calculations. I was a bit pumped and a lot nervous—not the right combination to forge ahead, so I used some energy to check out the next move, then downclimbed until I could safely jump off. Make no mistake, downclimbing is a big part of bouldering, especially higher problems on virgin terrain. After a long rest (and a couple easier first ascents) I went back up and finished 51's The New Dead.

Fist Jams

Fist jams are done by relaxing the hand and cupping it, then sliding it in the crack width-wise and squeezing to make a fist. Thumbs can be up or down, but because the hand is oriented 90 degrees away from the position of hand and finger jams, there is less additional torque to be gained in a vertical crack. You can lock off a thumbs-down fist jam and still pull it out easily. When it gets slightly too wide for your fist, you can position your thumb on the outside of your fist to expand the range—usually painful and not that secure, but of use if your feet are taking most of the load as they should.

*Poppy Coulter ain't afraid of no meat-grinding fist crack. She's spending her Christmas Day working the wicked finishing stretch of **Big Bob's Big Wedge (V5)**, Joshua Tree National Park, California. Most suitors find the lip crux easier if they invert and lead with a foot jam above their hands.*

Textbook juicy fist jams on Big Bob's Big Wedge.

Off-Widths

Off-width cracks are too big for fist jams but too small to fit the entire body in—pretty rare in bouldering and requiring such a panoply of techniques such as arm bars, chickenwings, hand stacks, and leavittation (named after developer Randy Leavitt) that we don't have space to dwell on them here. Off-width masters are a rare breed indeed—you probably don't want your sister dating one.

The author improvising on Beer Factor, High Valley, northern Mexico. Most off-widths in corners are best attacked with one's entire back against the main wall (in this case the left wall). Here I liebacked a couple moves down low, then shoved my shoulder in to continue up with arm bars and right foot heel-toe jams. If I fell now I'd drop straight down to the pad—if I had stayed in lieback mode and my hands gave out I'd hurtle into the prickly pear in the lower right corner of the picture. A few moves higher I false-gripped the outer edge above the jog and then twisted around into left-side-in (standard-style) technique to finish up.

A hand-fist stack employed in leavittation technique.

Chimneys

Chimneys are cracks big enough to accept your whole body. Pure chimney boulder problems are rare, but chimneying is often used to descend between boulders. Because it is often impossible to protect chimneys on roped climbs, it doesn't hurt polishing one's chimney technique on the boulders so those runouts don't feel as scary.

Chris Hill squirms up into a bombay knee-back chimney. Until he gets his knees up into the chimney, his arms are working overtime providing the pressure to stay put.

Standard foot-back chimney technique.

Toe Jams

To toe jam, align your foot with boot sole against one side of the crack and top of toes against the other and stuff as much of the toe of the boot in the crack as you can, then torque the foot by rotating the lower leg in line with the crack. Sound painful? It can be, especially in flimsier boots. Sometimes the crack is so thin, as with finger cracks, that one must drop the heel low and run the outside edge of the sole of the boot (next to the smaller toes) into the crack and try to torque. When the crack gets wide enough to stuff more than just toes in, resist the temptation to just toe-in straight at the crack with the sole facing down—instead stuff and torque. Fully extending the leg when torqued solidly in a foot jam will make it hard to remove—leave some bend in the knee when

Stuff the toe deep, then rotate the knee in line with the crack to apply torque.

moving off foot jams. Foot jams come in handy whenever there's a groove your toe can fit in. They can be used in flares that are too wide open to jam with the hands. Often you can find a foot jam on a problem with no other jams.

Jamming Practice

A good way to practice jamming technique on boulders is to walk your hands up the crack as you climb, placing each jam immediately above the previous jam. In this fashion you can get as many moves from a 15-foot-long crack as from an 80-foot-long crack jammed with long reaches. By walking your hands, you don't reach past the awkward sizes and are forced to jam all the bad sizes a crack has to offer. This does wonders for your technique. It was practice like this on *Bachar Cracker* that allowed me to put up problems like *Mother of the Future* in Hueco Tanks, a 30-foot horizontal roof split by a finger and thin hands crack.

Jamming Drills

Even more so than with handholds, it's instructive to get on a slightly overhanging crack, set your jams, and get in good posture, then gradually relax your jams until your hands start to slip. At first you may find no matter how hard you're squeezing you seem to be slipping—this is because you haven't refined your technique. Whereas face climbing comes naturally, jamming doesn't. Put in the miles (yes, miles—it helps if you can climb a bunch of lower-angled roped crack pitches to get this experience) and you'll be rewarded. On my recent trip to Rocklands, I was putting up V2 jamming problems that completely baffled my compatriots cranking V13 faces.

Not all cracks are most easily scaled with jamming technique. Cody Roth bloodied his hand trying to jam this fist/off-width, then found an easier solution shuffling underclings and double heel-toe locks.

More Bouldering Tricks

Sizing Up a Move

Lots of moves can be harder or easier depending on how they fit your body. Before wasting energy trying a body size–dependent sequence that may or may not work for you, measure the rock to see if you will fit. Here are three examples.

Knee bars can be great energy savers, especially on really steep problems—like those at Hueco Tanks. On my body the distance from my fingertips to my elbow is the same as from my toes to my knee. I can hold my forearm up against a potential knee bar and know instantly if my lower leg will be too long, too short, or just right to try a knee bar. If there are several foot placements on a potential knee bar, I can find the best one with this trick. If I can't reach the area I'm sizing up, I can measure with a long stick marked with my toe-to-knee distance.

On dynos, I like to know if I can hit the target hold with my feet still on the holds they're pushing from, or if my feet will have to come off the starter holds. (Keeping my feet on can help tremendously with my balance when I hit the target. Also, if your feet come off, it will be nearly impossible to reverse the move if you miss the target hold. On feet-off lunges you generally fall farther out from the face

as well.) My bubbabrush, from the end of the blow tube to the tip of the toothbrush, is the same distance as from my knees to my fingers (held above my head). I reach my bubbabrush up to the target hold (and clean it off, of course), then hold the shaft against the rock. I make a mental note where the end of the blow tube reaches. I put my fingertips at that point, then check if my elbow reaches the foothold as if measuring for a knee bar. If so, I can count on hitting the target hold with my foot still on. If not, I will plan to lunge with my feet coming off or I will pick a higher foothold, if available, to lunge from.

For heel-toe jams, I can take my boot off and check the fit. Your foot will bend in most heel-toe jams (especially with softer shoes), so if the jam is a half inch or inch shorter than your boot, it will probably work.

In some situations it's hard to keep your eyes on the target. It helps to know where another part of your body, say your elbow or your eyes, will be in relation to the rock when the target hold is reached. For instance, there may be a distinct point of rock 18 inches shy of the target hold and in line with the move—focus on getting the elbow to that point and the hand will fall on the target.

Well, he's good for something . . . Why carry your chalk bag when you can make your boyfriend caddy? Sandra Stuckey and Yves Hangi at the Eight Day Rain sector, Rocklands, South Africa.

My fingertip to elbow length is just a bit longer than the long axis of this hueco—I won't be able to get a knee bar deep in it, but I spy a small toe dish just outside the hueco that will work.

Using Chalk

The use of chalk to keep hands dry is acceptable in most bouldering areas in America. Nevertheless, there are some areas in which it is not allowed, either through local consensus or statute. Before you reach into your chalk bag, be sure chalk use is acceptable where you are climbing. That said, let's dip into this subject further.

For the most part there's nothing more to chalk use than dipping into your chalk bag whenever your hands feel moist. Occasionally a bizarre move will be easier if you chalk up body parts other than your hands. For instance, if you're palming a rounded ledge shaped like a car fender, it may help to chalk your forearms for added friction. Or say you're smearing your calf around an arête to stay in balance—go ahead and chalk your calf if it will help.

On really long problems on really hot days, you may want to put on a "primer coat." Liquid chalk works best for this. If you only have powder or block chalk, rub your hands together with the chalk, being sure to get a good even coat, not just on the inside of the fingers, but also between the fingers, across the palm, and even along the backs (tops) of the fingers. I feel this chalk layer helps keep perspiration from creeping between the fingers and onto the inside where they contact the rock. After applying the primer coat, I sometimes chalk my tips one more time before getting on the rock. This is necessary only when you are sweating profusely and on a problem that will take several minutes or more to climb.

On cold days chalk sometimes seems to just roll off your fingers—to get it to stick, wet your fingers a bit and then chalk up.

Gauge your chalk use according to conditions. Don't use more chalk than you need. You'll just be pissing away your money and creating a mess to boot. Be sure to brush off the problem before you leave. Be sure to brush off the problem before you leave. (No, that isn't a typo—just a point that deserves repeating.)

What to Do When You Can't Chalk Up

Let's say you're on a problem that is long enough to exhaust the chalk you put on at the base. The climb is so hard that you're about to have an aneurysm while you desperately hang on with one hand and try to chalk up the other. Problem is you're playing hide-and-go-seek with your chalk bag that has slid around your belt and is just out of reach. Meanwhile your fingers are dripping off the holds like fudge rolling down a sundae. What do you do? Below are several strategies.

Plan A

Wear double chalk bags—one on each hip. You can dip very fast this way because you aren't fishing around for a bag dangling somewhere behind your butt.

Plan B

Wipe your fingers quickly across your shirt, shorts, or pants and gain some relief that way. This is much quicker than reaching into a chalk bag, even double bags, but does not have as great a drying effect unless you utilize Plan C.

Matt Segal fishing for his chalk bag on **The Chube** *(V3), Joshua Tree National Park, California.*

Plan C

Just prior to the attempt, rub a block of chalk on your shirt, arm, or back of your hand, leaving a deposit of chalk. You can quickly slap this chalky patch to dry your hands. If you have hairy arms you can store quite a bit of chalk this way. If you sweat enough to soak up the deposit of reserve chalk, or if you have the verve to shave your arms to accentuate your muscle definition, this trick may backfire. In this case, try Plan D.

Plan D

Seed some of the bigger holds on the problem with sprinkled-on chalk. When you grab these holds,

Ego-Swelling Combat Tale #4: The First Flash of Autobahn

I include this story not just to pump up my ego—my head will probably not fit through a standard doorway after I write this—but also to give an example of the worst-case scenario when it comes to battling sweat.

Spanning 850 feet, the *Autobahn* is the longest bouldering traverse I know of in the United States. It's situated in Chandler Park, overlooking Tulsa, Oklahoma. The first time I visited Chandler, the *Autobahn* was soaking wet in several sections. Locals told me nobody had ever flashed it. Into my mind seeped thoughts of all the free beers and notoriety I would receive should I pull off this feat. Since the route was out of condition, I stayed off all of it, saving it for a later flash attempt.

My chance came over a year later when I visited Tulsa one July to give a slide show. As is typical in Tulsa in midsummer, the temperature was in the mid-90s and the Weather Channel reported 1,000 percent [sic] humidity. Just stepping out of an air-conditioned car would cause sweat to instantly bead up on your skin. These were less than ideal conditions, but this time the route was dry and I had no idea when I would be through Tulsa again. Had I read my own book, *Stone Crusade,* I would have been reminded that the Tulsa hard cores (namely, anyone crazy enough to go bouldering there in the summer) wore dishtowels tucked into their shorts to dry their hands on and terry cloth tennis wristbands to intercept the streams of sweat running along their arms. Stupidly, I got on the *Autobahn* armed only with my standard western U.S. summer wear: double chalk bags, shoes, shorts, and a tank top. At least I had the foresight to top off my chalk bags before I started.

The first 200 feet went well and quickly. By dipping into my chalk bag every few moves, I could stem the tide of sweat pouring out of my hands. The hint of a pump was creeping in, however, so my pace slowed to take advantage of the periodic rests. This slower pace, though, meant that mere dips into the chalk bag could not keep up with the sweat. As I watched my feet step from toehold to toehold, I could see a dark line of sweat-soaked leather gradually migrate down from the top of my boots. Likewise, the sweat pouring along my arms rolled down to my hands whenever I lowered them to shake out or chalk up. For the next 100 to 200 feet I could wipe my arms on my shirt to dry them, but soon it became satu-

your fingers will get a free chalk-up. Unfortunately, by sprinkling chalk on the holds, you will make them harder to hang on to (you have just defeated the purpose of cleaning them off). This is why it is best to only seed holds that are big enough that you will have no trouble hanging on whether they are clean or not.

Plan E

Wait for a drier day, or colder temperatures, or until you are stronger.

rated, clinging wet and heavy on my body. At around the halfway point I was rubbing my entire arms with chalk, trying to get enough chalk in the hair to dam up the rivers of sweat coursing along them. Had it not been for several good stem rests I could not have let go to do this. Soon, however, it became apparent that two full chalk bags would not last me until the end of the traverse.

Between figuring out the moves, resting, and pacing myself for such a long problem, I had chewed up two hours by the time I reached the 500-foot mark. My spotters, who had enthusiastically followed my attempt for the first few hundred feet, had long ago moved on to problems of their own. Where the wall reached its tallest, I followed a high line with my hands 20 feet up. At this point my hands started to open up and my feet were moonwalking across the polished limestone. The fear of breaking both my legs on the uneven landing below saw me through to the next big holds where I could hang on and call for help. My friend Damien came over and, as requested, placed my supply bag of chalk on the next ledge where I could drop both hands and manipulate it. There I restocked my chalk bags and shook fresh blood into my arms. The sweat line on my shoes had nearly reached my toes. Soaked to capacity, my light cotton shorts were doing battle with the elastic holding them up. I thought better of taking my shirt off, figuring it might keep my shorts and the rock drier.

After another hour of pushing, pulling, stemming, shuffling, swinging, and sweating, I came to a ledge where I could sit down. The water line on my shoes had by this time disappeared below the rands. My friends rejoined me—they had finished their bouldering session while I was still on my first problem. By this time my arms were rubbery and I feared blowing the flash on the last section. I took a long rest, peeling my shoes off and drinking from a water bottle tossed up to me. My friends were getting antsy. The encouragement for me to flash the route had turned into: "Hurry up so we can get some cold ones."

On the home stretch I made some route-finding blunders but pulled through several times on moves when I thought my fingers would surely peel open. The end came sooner than I thought, but none too soon for my friends, who told me I'd been on the same problem for three and a half hours.

The morals of this story? (1) Prepare before you take off—heed the example of others, particularly locals who have conditions figured out; (2) have good friends along; (3) determination, if strong enough, can substitute for strength; and (4) don't tell your partners where the car keys are until you're ready to leave.

Hold Cleaning

Dirty holds are harder to pull and stand on than clean holds. Unless you're stepping up to a virgin problem, odds are you'll only be brushing off chalk and possibly some dirt or fallen leaves. Climbing chalk loves to bond with moisture. That is why it sucks the sweat and wetness off your fingertips. Unfortunately, it has a limit to how much moisture it can absorb. The more moisture it absorbs, the greasier it feels. Hence we have to continually use fresh chalk to dry our fingers. The used-up chalk ends up caked to the handholds and will make them feel greasy if not cleaned off.

Brush dirty holds gently with a toothbrush to loosen dirt and greasy, used-up chalk. Blow the loosened dirt and chalk off the holds by mouth or with a blow tube attached to your bubbabrush. On some problems you may have to climb partway up, hang on, and clean off a key hold.

Many Europeans and some Americans like to clean holds by whacking them with a towel. Other than for sweeping off leaves or pine needles, I find this to be fairly ineffective. It removes loose detritus but does little for packed-on chalk. In some cases it even packs the chalk on thicker, making it harder to work with the true texture of the hold. Because the boulders have been good to me, I treat them as my friends. Towel-whacking seems to be a negative use of energy, promoting the "at war" with the boulders approach instead of being "at one" with the boulders.

For out-of-reach holds, use a bubbabrush or reach over from the top of the problem or a nearby tree if possible. For cleaning while on a problem, use a brush attached to you with a string or Gammon Reel.

Don't forget to brush your footholds. This sounds simple, but you wouldn't believe how many climbers overlook this. Brushing footholds makes you attentive to where your feet will be placed, and this pays dividends when you get on the problem.

After you finish trying a problem, brush the

You will stick to the holds better if you brush all the caked-on chalk off the holds.

holds before you leave. This is a courtesy to the next climber, who just might be you, and gives the holds time to "breathe." It may be my imagination, but holds seem easier to grab when they haven't been basting in greasy, used-up chalk for several days. You might as well have everything going in your favor.

Certain holds, particularly very polished ones, can be easier to grip after they have been cleaned, then patted with fresh chalk. A thin residue of fresh, but not loose, chalk can impart a "grippier" texture. On very greasy holds it sometimes pays to brush them clean, dab some fresh chalk on them to soak up any additional grease, then brush them clean again.

How to Make Friends and Influence Boulders and People

Want to be the most popular boulderer at your home area? Get the permission of the area's owner or administrators, then give the chalk-choked boulders a good water wash. Chalk is water soluble; with enough water even the most caked problems will come clean. First, remove as much dry chalk as possible with standard brush and blow techniques. Then, if taps are available, spray with a hose. Otherwise, get a bug sprayer or a firefighter's water backpack pump unit to wash the holds. You may need to brush the holds while spraying them to get all the chalk off. This job is obviously easier if you have the help of several other boulderers or the local climbing club.

Warning #1

If you use too little water, you will end up with drippy white stains descending from all the holds. You will have created an ugly mess.

Warning #2

In areas with rock art (such as Hueco Tanks), don't wash holds where the runoff will run over artwork.

Warning #3

In many areas the rock becomes more friable when wet—plan your washing so there will be adequate time for the holds to dry to maximum strength before climbing resumes. For example, don't wash them off the day before the weekend rush or the big bouldering contest.

Warning #4

Most areas will benefit from this treatment, but some might not. Obtain the advice and approval of the locals before acting. They might know some reason why water washing might be detrimental.

Hold Drying

If you're dying to try a problem with wet holds but can't wait for it to dry naturally, there are several strategies, depending on how wet the holds are. First off, however, determine if the rock type is one that becomes fragile when wet, such as soft sandstone or volcanic rock. If so, stay off the problem until it dries thoroughly on its own and the holds regain their maximum strength. This usually takes at least twenty-four hours. On certain rock types, like most granite or quartzite, this is not a problem. When in doubt as to the solidity of the rock, ask for local advice or err on the side of caution. Breaking a key hold off a classic problem is not something you want to live with.

Assuming a strong rock type, the first step is to sponge up as much moisture as you can with a towel, rag, T-shirt, etc. If there's a breeze (or if you fan the hold), the remaining moisture may then escape to the air in a minute or two. This is the ideal scenario, as it leaves the hold superclean and chalk-free. If the hold remains moist, then dab some chalk on it to soak up the moisture. It's important to sponge off the hold first or you will end up with a pasty mess of wet chalk on the hold and a resulting prolonged clean-up. (When a hold is in this condition, you need to wipe and/or scrape the paste out, then repeatedly apply chalk and remove the paste until the paste becomes dry enough to brush off.) Even if you sponge the hold well, you will probably need to go through the chalking process several times to dry it completely.

Rosin

Also known as pof (rhymes with hoof), rosin is used at a few European areas, most notably the famed boulderfields of Fontainebleau, in France. It is a tacky drying agent used on hands and boots that is wrapped into a fist-size ball in a dishtowel or old T-shirt, forming what looks like a Halloween ghost decoration. It is not water soluble, therefore is very hard to clean off the rock. Rosin users whack the rock with their pof rags to prepare the holds. Repeated applications of rosin eventually cover up the texture of the natural stone and impart a slick, greasy texture that is jingus to hang onto without more rosin. Starting to sound a lot like heroin, right? Because of its deleterious effects, rosin use has not been accepted at any bouldering area in America. If you see climbers using rosin anywhere in the United States, kindly ask them to refrain. If they refuse, tell them where they can shove their pof ball. Better yet, do your boulders a favor and confiscate it. I had to do this with a famous German sport climbing legend who was using pof at Yosemite's fabled Camp 4 boulders. "Hey can I see your pof bag? Oops, I dropped it in the bear-proof Dumpster." Despite looking strong as a bear, he didn't chase his pof or me.

Cleaning Your Boots

Clean boot soles stick better to holds than dirty soles. Pit a pair of clean $20 hand-me-downs against a pair of dirty $140 super slippers with the latest sticky rubber—the cheap clodhoppers will win every time. Sticky rubber loves to stick to dirt just as much as it does to rock.

For Good Performance

The easiest way to clean your soles is to wipe your feet on a clean carpet patch at the base of the problem on each attempt. Frequently beat the dirt out of your carpet to keep it clean—there's no use wiping your feet on a dirty rug. (This is why fixed

A half-assed effort at cleaning this boot left a lot of sand on the sole. Not only will the sand act as little ball bearings under the climber's foot, it also will harmfully abrade the footholds, making them just that much more polished.

rugs don't work—99 percent of the time they are dirty pieces of trash. It's a safe bet that climbers who are too lazy to carry their own rugs are too lazy to maintain those they've left behind.) Also be sure the footholds are clean on the problem. There's no sense in cleaning your boots, only to dirty them on the first footholds.

If you forget your rug you can use a sweatshirt or T-shirt, or wipe your feet on your trouser legs, socks (if you're wearing them), or across the suede leather uppers of your boots. To keep one foot clean while wiping the other this way, stand on your heel and keep your toes raised above the ground. This will get the heel dirty, but as one is usually climbing on his or her toes, this is seldom a concern.

For Better Performance

For increased performance on difficult problems, it's worth washing the soles of your boots. I usually spit some clean saliva (no gooey, candy-striped hawkers, just the clear, watery stuff) into the palm of my hand and rub the toe of my boot until it is clean.

Eric Decaria giving a spit-shine to his boots prior to sending the stemming nightmare **Streetcar Named Desire,** *Joshua Tree National Park, California.*

You can also use water and a rag, or if you're feeling really anal, rubbing alcohol. To start a spit-shine, I first pat the excess chalk off my hands. I may even spit-wash my hands first, so that when I work on my boots I will not be rubbing a chalk/saliva mixture onto them. When spit-shining your soles you can actually feel the friction of the rubber gradually increase. When the sole is clean it should make a squeaky sound when you rub it, and/or your hand

will chatter across the sole instead of sliding across it. If you need the heel clean for a tough heel hook or the instep clean for a rand smear, clean those areas too.

For Utmost Performance

For utmost performance on the most desperate of problems—those you'd give a tooth or testicle to make it up—it's time to scrape the old, oxidized rubber off the soles. Rubber, no matter how clean it is, sticks better if it is unoxidized. Rub the soles of your boots together until a small layer of rubber comes off—it will look like the debris from a pencil eraser. Be sure to brush this debris off. Left behind will be a fresh layer of clean rubber with that dark black, "just out of the box" look. If I'm trying a problem with really dinky toeholds and I only need the tip of my shoe clean, I will rub the toe of my shoe across the rand of my other shoe until I see that fresh black color appear. I do this after I have wiped my feet off on my rug, but before I step onto the problem. Quite obviously, repeated rubbing of your soles will wear them out more quickly. Unless you have money to blow or get your shoes for free, I would use this method sparingly.

Often when you wash your soles or rub to a fresh rubber layer, you will be sitting somewhere other than at the base of the problem. Be careful not to get your freshly cleaned soles dirty when walking to the problem. Walk on your heels, keeping your toes out of the dirt. If it is muddy, make a path of stepping-stones to the base, taking care to position them where you won't fall on them. Some boulderers put their feet into plastic grocery bags and walk to the problem, not taking the bags off until they step onto the rock. Others, who frequently climb in muddy areas, get a pair of oversize galoshes for this purpose.

Beware: It is very easy to spend five minutes cleaning your boots, cautiously walk over to the problem, then, just as you step onto the rock, roll your toe into the dirt as you push off the ground,

Kiss it goodbye if your boots aren't impeccably clean on this river-polished sandstone. Highball master Jeff Johnson hiking the crux on Entrée, Ojai, California.

negating all that time-consuming prep work. To prevent this common mishap, you can position a small, clean stick or stone under your toe while you are standing on your heels. When you take off, your toe will roll up onto the stick or stone and not touch the dirt. (If you are ethically opposed to cheater stones, as I am, you will want to make sure the stick or stone does not give you an unsporting reach advantage on the first move.) Do not fall into the trap of thinking that you can walk over to a carpet patch at the base of the problem, then let your toes down once they are on the carpet. Unless you bought the carpet brand-new that day and had never wiped your feet on it, it will contain enough dirt to reduce the efficacy of your cleaning job.

If your shoes become dirty during the course of a problem, say from a dirty or crumbling foothold, wipe them off on your opposite pant leg. If you are wearing shorts you can wipe across the upper of your other shoe (sometimes awkward or impossible) or, if it's not too sweaty, the inside of your calf. If you can't get in balance for these tricks, you can wipe your foot across a clean patch of rock to knock grit off or tap or kick the rock to dislodge grit. Sticky rubber, however, is tenacious, and these last two tricks don't always work.

Hard-to-See Holds

Sometimes problems require blind reaches to out-of-sight holds. To dial in to such a hold, make a mental note of visible features in line with the hold—examples are distinctive lichen patches, a water streak, a hairline seam, a ripple in the stone, even the edge of a shadow (though the latter is obviously ephemeral). When reaching for the hold, follow the line of these natural markers. Sometimes the line might not follow any markers, but you might know to reach around the corner 6 inches above the dime-size blob of moss. This takes practice to get good at, but proficiency in this skill generates beaucoup style points.

Style is a very personal matter. This sassy blade is rocking foot-long tick marks, stacked pads, and matching Kid Castro bunhuggers on a misty 55-degree November day. He's whacking those naughty holds a good one with his pof rag, and some day (not this one) he might get more than one move off the ground.

Many boulderers opt for the easy way out and just draw a chalk line pointing to the hold. This is called a tick mark or rookie stripe or worse. Unfortunately this tactic has gotten out of hand at many areas, to the point that some climbers will draw tick marks toward every hold no matter how big it is, or whether it is visible or not. Furthermore, a tick mark need only be visible from 6 feet away at most, not 200 yards away. Ticking reeks of amateurism and laziness and does nothing to improve one's technique, especially for on-sighting. The current epidemic of tick fever has its roots in gym climbing, where by necessity every hold is marked to delineate a problem. This isn't the case outdoors, so it's time to take off the training wheels and learn to climb like a big boy or girl.

Tick marks create a mess. Whereas chalked holds are often mistaken by nonclimbers to be some kind of water stain, natural precipitate, or guano blotch, tick marks are obviously unnatural and amount to little more than climbers' graffiti. Viewed as graffiti, tick marks quickly become a threat to access. No access, no bouldering, you don't get better. Ten out of ten boulderers will swear they brush their ticks off after "they're done." Nine out of ten are liars; otherwise I wouldn't have been able to set the current record of 265 ticks brushed off in one hour at Switzerland's famous Magic Wood boulders. Can you beat that?

A sign put up by landowners in Rocklands, South Africa.

The Boulderer Who Never Saw a Tick Mark

I started climbing at Indian Rock in Berkeley back in the mid-1970s. At that time there was a boulderer named Dennis who frequented the area. Dennis was completely blind, so handholds and footholds were impossible for him to see. He'd walk toward the wall until his white cane hit it. Then he'd lean his cane against the wall and feel the wall with his hands until he was oriented with the problem he wanted to try. While climbing, Dennis would have to sweep the wall with his hand to find the footholds. When he found a good spot for his foot, he'd register in his mind where it was, move his hand back to a handhold, then bring his foot exactly to the foothold he'd picked. Because he wasn't dependent on tick marks, or even sight, he'd developed amazing powers of kinesthetic awareness. Imagine how much your bouldering would improve if you had that kind of body awareness. Now stop imagining, put on a blindfold, and start practicing. Pretty soon tick marks will look embarrassing.

When I see climbers smear chalk on footholds to mark them, I wonder if their moms drank a lot when they were pregnant. These climbers might as well have wiped dirt on their shoes before they stepped on the problem. Chalk sticks to rubber just like dirt does and reduces the rubber's stickiness (lower coefficient of friction). Of course, if a problem is too easy for you, you might try this trick to make it harder for you and everyone else.

If you can't find any natural markers and you can't dial into a hold without help, have a partner point to it with a hand, an extendobrush, a stick, or a shadow. Hell, if it's dark, have him or her use a laser pointer. If none of this works and you feel you must mark a hold, don't draw on the rock with a block of chalk, just use a faint thumbprint. (With footholds, put the fingerprint next to them, not on them.) Your eye will be drawn to the hold just as well and you will have an easier time brushing it off when your session is over. As they say, "the longer the tick, the shorter the . . ."

Number 10 *(6c) on the white circuit at Franchard Isatis, Fontainebleau, France. Many climbers slap the beach ball top-out, but most don't hit the shallow dish that is key to hanging on. Here one partner points out the dish so his buddy can send.*

Cheater Stones

Cheater stones are objects, usually rocks or a stack of several bouldering pads, located underneath a problem so climbers can reach holds they couldn't reach by standing on the ground. I believe that getting to the first holds is a part of every problem, and I strongly disapprove of using cheater stones for this purpose. To be more blunt, for me to give advice on how to use them would be like the Pope giving advice on using condoms. Still, in the interest of completeness, objectivity, and curbing overpopulation, I will strike a deal. I will tell you what I know about their use, if Pope Benedict will preach some birth control. I'll go first.

- By placing a cheater stone at the base of a route, a climber instantly creates a bad landing. Falls onto cheater stones have sprained or broken more than a few ankles. If possible, have a partner remove the stone the instant you pull onto the rock or kick it away yourself. Take care not to fall on your partner. Some cheater stones will be too big to move quickly enough and are best left in place so the climber knows where the danger zone is.
- Take the time to make a stable stack. Climbers will often stack several rocks to gain the height they desire. Toppling off a shifting cheater stone before getting on the rock is a quick path to embarrassment and rolled ankles. Occasionally a

Bryant Fehlman using a three-pad stack atop a mountain of cheater stones to pull onto Evilution, Grandpa Peabody Boulder, Buttermilks, California. Knowing such tactics would condemn his soul to eternal damnation, Bryant figured, "What the hell, toss in a power spot."

Nowhere in the Ten Commandments does it state "Thou shalt not jump for the first holds." Instead of resorting to stacked pads or cheater stones, Olivier Charles fires a proud jump start on Sgarbamella *(6c)*, Cresciano, Switzerland.

climber will start off an unstable stone to make it easier to kick it away as soon as he or she steps off it.

- Remove cheater stones after your attempt.
- Remember the words attributed to Britain's legendary Joe Brown (5 feet 4 inches). When asked how he reached the first holds on some notoriously reachy gritstone problems, Brown responded, "I climb up to them."

If you can't reach the first holds, there is no rule that says you can't jump off the ground to get to them. Some fabulous problems begin this way.

Taking the idea behind cheater stones a step further, some boulderers have used ladders to partially ascend a wall before they start climbing. This is done to facilitate working on moves higher on the problem by not expending energy climbing up to them. I dislike this idea even more than cheater stones. For me to advise on the use of ladders would be like the Pope endorsing abortion. I'll just say I wouldn't want to fall on one. You can't ascend to nirvana on a ladder.

Okay, I'm done talking about this. Benedict, it's your turn. (Going-to-print news flash! Pope Benedict just kind of endorsed condom use for male prostitutes. He must have read my books and heeded my pleas.)

Power Spots

Power spotting is the practice of having a spotter push a climber up or along a problem, taking a portion of the climber's weight so the climber can rehearse moves he or she couldn't do otherwise. This process is then repeated with the spotter taking less and less weight off the climber, until eventually the climber does the problem without the spotter's assistance.

Proponents of power spotting say it allows one to get stronger and do any given problem quicker. Personally, I'd rather spend that same time climbing problems I can do on my own and getting stronger and better that way. I'll gain more experience by climbing more problems and I'll have more fun. When I'm ready to go back to the original problem I couldn't do before, I'll have that many more ticks under my belt and the confidence that comes with that.

Power spots, cheater stones, and tick marks are gambits to bring a problem down to a lower common denominator. I recommend eschewing these tricks and bringing one's abilities in line with the true difficulty of the problem. The extra strength and technique gained working a problem in the latter style will benefit you on all subsequent problems. As always, the reward received is proportionate to the effort expended.

A power spot in action— yo Bro, umm, that tickles, but not in a good way . . .

The Mental Game

Ninety percent of bouldering is mental, yet most climbers spend 90 percent of their time trying to get their muscles strong. If that time were spent training their brain, they would be much better off. When used to capacity, the mind becomes a Saturn booster, ready to lift you to new heights. When allowed to languish, the mind becomes a big fat sea anchor, holding you back until you reel it in.

Falling is Not Failing

The first thing to get straight in your mind is that falling is an integral part of bouldering. It's how we learn what works and what doesn't, how we decipher sequences, and how we learn what we need to work harder on. Falling is only a failure if you don't view it as your teacher. (The only exception to this rule is when a fall in a "no fall" scenario causes injury or death. Falling in that case is a failure to properly evaluate your skills versus the risk and difficulty involved. Few climbers put themselves into this scenario. Still, if you survive, it will doubtless teach you something.)

What Your Brain Is Up to While You Climb—Muscle Memory

Every climbing move starts in the brain. The brain tells the muscles to contract and your body moves. As your body moves, it sends sensory signals back to the brain reporting on how the movement is going. Every move causes countless neurons to fire in the brain. Linking the neurons to make it all happen are synapses. The more one repeats a movement, the more synapses that are built between neurons, wiring in the brain's ability to repeat the movement—the phenomenon known as "muscle memory." If the movement is successful, say a smooth long dyno, you end up with good muscle memory. However, if the movement is self-defeating, say yanking your foot off a key hold each time you try the same move, then you have created bad muscle memory.

As boulderers we obviously want to create as much positive muscle memory as possible. To accomplish this, it's useful to spend time climbing problems well within one's ability and focusing on climbing them with the utmost technical precision—good posture, flawless weight shifts, no overgripping, and so forth. The more repetitions, the stronger ingrained the good muscle memory will become. Do this with all kinds of moves. A primary reason most of us excel at one style of move and not at another is that we tend to gravitate

Cool calculation or burning desire?
Shadow Ayala has both.

toward problems that show off our strengths, not expose our weaknesses. We put in more reps on those problems, hence build better muscle memory (and positive emotional associations of success) for that style of climbing. Meanwhile, we put in fewer reps addressing our weaknesses, hence have reduced muscle memory (and likely negative emotional associations) for that style of climbing.

Think of the mind as housing a "library of moves." Whenever we get on a climb, we can just go to the library and check out the moves we need one by one until we reach the top. When we are beginners our library is small. As we gain experience the library gets bigger and bigger and thus the odds we will have the right move to check out increases. Experts will be able to try a move during a climb and if it feels wrong, go right to their Plan B. If that doesn't work and they don't have a Plan C already in place, they can instantly check another move out of the library to try and another if that doesn't work. They can do this all in the course of one attempt, a key component to on-sight success on the rock and in competitions.

A large library of moves makes reading the rock easier before one tries a problem. You can look at the holds and imagine the sequence, trying out different moves from the library and seeing which "feel" right. The "feeling right" part is not just saying, "looks like a gaston will work," but is thinking about that gaston, then instinctively feeling how that move would shift the weight and change angles of pull on the holds, how the resulting body position would affect the next move and the one after that. If you're just getting started climbing, you may feel you don't possess such instincts; however this is something that gets wired into your brain as well with repetition and experience until it becomes second nature.

Experimenting with as many styles of moves and types of rock as we can is the quickest path to building our library of moves. Don't be afraid to try new moves and build more muscle memory. If you

have never climbed outside a gym before, make the effort to get outside. Gyms rarely feature slabs, mantels, cracks, and such; therefore they can only build one's library of moves so much. In addition, going bouldering with more experienced boulderers can be invaluable. Don't confuse strength and experience. The person cranking hardest at the gym may have unnatural genetic strength making up for lousy technique and a slim library. Who is the person you see at the boulders who appears weak but climbs smooth and hard? That's the person who's packing the Library of Congress between his or her ears.

To avoid matching in the finger pocket on this traverse problem, Dave Winthrop digs into his library of moves and busts a "rose move" (so named because this outward-facing cross-through move was key to solving the famous 1980s French sport climb Rose and the Vampire). *Rocher Fin sector, Fontainebleau, France.*

Retraining Bad Muscle Memory

In 1982 I broke my pelvis in four places and totally jacked up the cartilage in my hip sockets. Over the next twenty-four years I lost more and more cartilage until I had none left and was grinding away bone on bone. This hurts. A lot. During those decades, the arthritis robbed me of more and more hip flexibility to the point where one bouncer wouldn't let me in a bar because I walked so crooked. My friends told him, "It's okay, he's not sloshed, he always walks like Frankenstein." By the time I had my hips replaced, my left leg high step was all of 4.5 inches and by necessity I climbed stairs on all fours. To accommodate this disability I developed a very stiff style of climbing: moving sideways to the rock to keep my hips in, propelling upward with my right leg, and posting with my left to get up problems. After getting slick new chromium cobalt steel hip joints I regained a bunch of flexibility, but I was dogged with decades of ingrained bad muscle memory telling me my left leg would never make this high step or that stem. It takes a real conscious effort on my part to talk my leg into lifting to make such moves when the brain says "Uh uh, you don't do that anymore." It's a battle I face every time out.

The above is an extreme case of bad muscle memory. The best way to retrain such a condition is to do lots of practice climbing on easy problems, say during your warm-up or at the end of a session, and force yourself to do moves the right way, not the memorized way. For me that means doing these warm-up problems and trying to high step as many of the moves as possible. Repetition of such moves gets the brain to start building positive muscle memory.

Emotional Wiring

In addition to good muscle memory, we want to develop positive emotional connections to proper movements. When we bust a torso twist just right and feel superpowerful doing it, we want to create the association between "move executed well" and "damn that felt strong." This can be done by just thinking back on your best moves and how they felt. Attaching a label to the feeling helps create the association. Say you set a toe just right and really drive on it—you could label that feeling "drive." Or you land on a small crimp just perfectly after a deadpoint, bearing down with intent and feeling

Kayla Dempsey is stoked after staying cool and persevering through a necky topout on this boulder at the Cul de Chien sector, Fontainebleau, France. The problem she just climbed is quite delicate at the top, so smooth execution is required—if you thrash you're off. She can take her positive feelings of success, associate them with her proper execution of the moves, and use this to her advantage in the future.

glued to the rock—you might label that "stick." Then, when psyching for a problem you can previsualize doing the moves well and throw your labels on them. "Right undercling, hips in, precise with the right toe, now 'drive' and 'stick,' cross through, grab summit jug." If you've already worked the moves successfully and are ready to link, focus on the times the moves felt just right and put those images/feelings into your pre-send previsualization.

If you send your mega-project but just barely grovel through it, consider repeating it until you can do it flawlessly, wiring in good muscle memory, not wiring in groveling as something associated with success (both bad muscle memory and emotional association). Too often one will hear cheers of "good job" when a climber just barely thrashed up a problem—you know better. Don't let the cries of "good job" become mentally associated with inferior performance.

Previsualization

Climb the problem in your head before you get on the rock. Run through all the moves, not just the crux. Think in real time, feeling every weight switch, every sharp hold, each muscle stretching and contracting. Don't forget the footwork and breathing. Hear the slap of the hand on a jug, the crowd

Sandra Stuckey previsualizing her sequence for a rising traverse in the Eight Day Rain sector, Rocklands, South Africa.

at the base chanting "C'mon Dude." Think of how you will feel standing on top. Don't just "visualize" the moves as if watching yourself climb, but really "feel" the moves from the perspective you'll have while on the rock. Run through the whole experience in your head, then do it.

Relaxation

Don't waste energy prior to getting on the rock. Save your energy for doing the moves. Let your mind tell your muscles to relax. Run through a mental checklist of body parts from toes to head. Do they all feel loose? Are you tensing any muscles in anticipation of the problem? Focus on relaxing the tense muscles. Feel the tension drain from your body at the base of the boulder. Breathe deeply through your nose, filling your lungs from the bottom up, then feel your body loosen as you exhale through your mouth. Relaxing is both a mental and physical technique. Practice it at home and at work so it becomes second nature when you step up to your next challenge.

Frame of Mind

Most climbers benefit from keeping a calm demeanor on delicate problems. For thuggy problems you may find a mindset of controlled aggression beneficial. But there's no need to get aggro before breakfast. Save your energy and relax, then with your last few breaths before you start up the problem, flip the switch and crank. Some problems have both thuggy and delicate sections, say an overhang followed by a dicey slab. For these you want the ability to flip the aggro switch on and off at your command. Easier said than done, but one trick is using breathing to help trigger the on or off. Deep breathing often has a calming effect, sharper breaths can amp you up.

Focus

Bouldering is wonderful mind detergent, just waiting to wash your brain clear of all thoughts about your job, money, significant other, etc. John Gill called it "moving meditation." Focusing is as easy as getting on the rock and thinking about nothing but executing each move flawlessly. Difficult problems are particularly good for bringing focus. So are risky "no falls allowed" problems that require full attention. That said, if you find yourself unable to focus on a risky problem, climb back down and return when your head is clear. Don't get injured forcing the issue if the mind isn't focused on the task.

Thinking Positive and Trying Hard

Feed on previous successes, large and small, recent or in the distant past. Think back to how you felt with each success, then take that feeling of success and use it to create a positive mindset in the present moment. When I think about how I felt on top of *The Thimble* (John Gill's elite highball testpiece), I feel proud and enthused. Reliving that memory makes me feel flat-out better and makes any session seem full of possibility.

Success isn't dependent upon reaching the top of a problem. Some days I do zero problems, but they are successful outings because I had fun and learned from my mistakes, thereby improving my knowledge base. Any improvement, physical or mental, is a success. Next time out I know I've got better knowledge and a better chance to send.

A small percentage of people psych up better by adopting a "I might as well try it even though I can't do it attitude." Whether you prefer to set lofty goals and aim high, or "aim low and overachieve," when you get on the rock, try hard. No, I said *try hard*. I don't care how pumped you are, don't let go until they pry the holds from your cold, dead fingers. What do you have to lose? If you fall you're no worse than you were before you got on the problem—you still haven't done it. But you may gain valuable knowledge in the attempt that you would never gain by staying on the ground.

John Tollefsrud trying hard enough to win a tractor pull against an F350. Mr. Witty (V6), Happy Boulders, Bishop, California.

Dealing with Fear of Falling and Fear of Failure

To successfully deal with fear, you must first figure out if the fear is rational or irrational. Rational fears are fears about events or actions that will cause concrete adverse outcomes, such as injury. When it comes to bouldering, rational fears are things like "If I fall off the top of this, I'll hit that block and break my ankle," or "That flake sounds hollow, it might break." In cases of rational fear you need to listen to your mind, assess the situation, then apply proper risk management. Examples of risk management are discussing fall angles with your spotter, proper pad placement, helmet use, and backing off.

Irrational fears are fears about events or actions that, if they occur, will only create a negative outcome if you view the outcome as negative. Examples of irrational bouldering fears are the fear of falling when you have a trusty spotter and well-placed pads or the thought that "If I fail on this V1, everybody will laugh." In the first scenario, it can help to take a practice fall into the hands of your spotter to clear your head. In the case of fear of embarrassment, you just need to talk some sense into your own head.

When a botched elbow surgery left my left hand partially paralyzed, I was paranoid that my friends wouldn't like me as much if I didn't climb as hard as before. Boy was my head up my ass. Turned out my friends couldn't care less how hard I climbed; they just liked bouldering with me because of the passion and drive I brought to the boulders each time out. Most of us think those around us spend loads of time obsessing about our performance—wow, are we really that self-centered? Other people, even the critics on 8a.nu, spend far less time thinking about us than we care to admit—they've got their own problems and ego to deal with. Once you realize that, you can relax and enjoy bouldering each time out whether you flail or crush it. When you rid your mind of concerns about what others think of you, you'll find

Ariel Atkins is "bivering" above the Colorado River near Moab, Utah. She's launched this huge huck from the rail behind the guy's head on the right. Nice dyno form as her body is flying parallel to the wall. If Ariel fails to latch the target she knows she won't get hurt, just wet. Therefore she realized any fear of falling on this move is irrational, dismissed the thought, and blasted for it.
LISA HATHAWAY

your new relaxed mindset allows you to attain the success that may have eluded you before.

If you're afraid of failure, ask yourself if you're more concerned with how others view you than how you actually climb. I can't guarantee everyone feels this way, but I'm way more impressed by the climber who tries real hard every time up, refusing to give in, than I am by the climber who smooths

every problem but is obviously climbing below his or her level to avoid embarrassment or just show off. Remember, failure is just an experience you fail to learn from. Focus on the moves and the kinesthetic pleasure of the experience and there won't be room in your head for fear of failure. Alternatively, make the fear of failure work for you by forcing yourself to get on something you're scared to fail

As experienced boulderers, both Paul Robinson and Sandra Stuckey understand that falling is part of the bouldering process. However, both climbers have differing demeanors thus different ways of dealing with setbacks. Paul is very even-keeled. Here he is on day gazillion trying to bag the second ascent of Monkey Wedding (V14), Rocklands, South Africa. Moments earlier he took his umpteenth fall. He calmly rests beneath the problem, analyzing the condition of his tips and what he could do better on the next attempt. He sent the problem a few sessions later. Sandra was hugely motivated to climb the iconic V7 Rhino problem at Rocklands. Sandra is more emotional than Paul. She is distraught at having cruised out the belly of the beast, only to fall off the toss to the finishing hold. She lets her frustration gush out, thus clearing her mind to get on with the psyching-up process. She sent the next try.

on—once you've pulled off the ground it's succeed or fail, and you may find your fear of failure gets you to hold on that much longer and see you to the top. I've been on plenty of problems where I thought, "Dude, you know you can do this move—if you back off now you'll be a chickenshit for life." So I kept cranking and I sent.

The biggest failure is not trying at all.

When you venture farther up off the deck, the natural fear of falling can hold you back from doing a move you know is within your ability. This is a combination of rational fear (long fall could cause injury) and irrational fear (I'll fall on a move I'd never fall on right off the ground). Apply every risk management strategy at your disposal, then replace the thoughts of falling with the thought that you've done similar moves hundreds of times before—just do it again like you're only one move off the ground. When you come to the move in question, the only thought in your mind should be to execute the move well. If you are still thinking about falling, it's time to climb back down and re-psyche.

Boulder problems with many moves can give an illusion of height. You may have done a dozen moves and thereby feel like you've climbed above your comfort zone, but in reality the moves were short or it was an extended sit-down start and your feet are only 7 or 8 feet off the ground. Step back and check just how high your feet were when you were feeling scared—you may be surprised how close you were to the ground. With this new perspective you can try again with confidence.

Chronic Excuse Syndrome

Do you suffer from Chronic Excuse Syndrome? Do you blame your failures on gear or physical weakness? Unless you recently lost a limb or you're wearing Rollerblades instead of rock boots, these are lame excuses. Look for the real cause. Do you need to improve your technique? Concentrate more? Readjust your goals? Next time you're tempted to say "I'm too short" or "My fingers are too fat," think of Pete Davis, pictured here. I've never heard him say, "If I just had two hands." (Okay, once Pete did complain about the skin splitting on his stump, but we'll grant him a mulligan on that.) Chronic Excuse Syndrome is indicative of a negative mindset. Instead of wasting your time and your partners' patience spewing excuses, use that energy to concoct a strategy to address the issue. Create a positive mindset that each unsuccessful attempt is an opportunity to learn and get better.

Pete Davis pulling over an overhang at Turtle Rock, Durango, Colorado.

Be Honest with Yourself

Are you pushing yourself or just coasting? Are your goals realistic? Remember there can only be one best boulderer in the world. I personally know that she's a Nubian grandmother who fires V21 in bare feet to get grain from a storage hut located atop a boulder in the sweltering Sudanese desert. So where does that leave the rest of us? Free to become the best we can be. If you concentrate on that goal, then everything else—fame, fortune, inner peace, acne—will take care of itself. A good way to focus on this goal is to climb problems you want to do, not those that others want you to do.

Goal Setting

Having a concrete goal, say climbing *See Spot Run,* will help you stay focused better than saying "I want to be a highball king." What is it that you want from your bouldering, and from your life for that matter? If you can't answer the former in a few seconds, maybe it's time to pause and think it over. Do you want to climb a certain grade or an iconic problem? Do you want to travel the world's classic boulder gardens? Win the local gym comp? Spot hot girls on really hard problems? Identify your goal and write it down. Post it on the bathroom mirror so you see it every night and every morning. Make a plan to achieve it.

Break up your goals into smaller goals. Say a problem is taking you several tries, days, or even weeks to figure out. Set a goal each time out to make it an inch farther up, or to figure out a better way to do a certain move. Every time you learn something, you become a better boulderer. I recall being psyched to flapper a fingertip when working on the *Upper Meathook* at Colorado's Horsetooth Reservoir. My goal for that day had been to put more weight on the tiny hold I was dynoing for than the last time out. That flapper was proof of progress. The next time out I set the goal to stall on that hold before falling. Eventually I did the problem.

Your bouldering goals don't have to be number related. On this trip, New Jersey climber Marcie Puskarik wanted to experience the classic routes at Fontainebleau, such as this pocket line at Bas Cuvier. It appears Tony Encinas's goal is to rush in and spot hot girls, but he's aiming higher than that. Later this trip he'll ask Marcie to marry him. Marcie fired the problem. And Tony? Hell yeah, Dude!

Alternatively, you can put that problem on hold and form a ladder of similar but easier problems to work on. Say you want to do a certain V6 with a crux mantel. Compile a list of similar V3 to V5 mantel problems and knock them off in ascending difficulty, in the process building the strength and skill to go back to your project and send.

The same approach can be used for a bigger goal, such as climbing consistent V10. Break it down into achievable steps so you can experience repeated success to keep the positive vibes flowing. For instance, set a goal to climb solid V7 by the end of this season, V8 midway through next season, V9 the end of the following season, and so forth. Unless you want to be known as a poser, avoid the temptation to look for the softest V10 you can find, tick it, and declare "mission accomplished." The true V10 climber (or V3 climber or V14 climber) is the one who can walk up and send 90 percent of the problems in that grade. Strive to be a master of the grade, not a slave to it.

Role Models

When I started bouldering we all pretty much had the same role model—John Gill, the Master of Rock. Gill was the only boulderer with national recognition, and his exploits seemed mythical in proportion. We all wanted to be able to do one-arm front levers and pinch grip chin-ups like Gill. Few of us ever repeated Gill's repertoire of strength tricks, but we got stronger trying. Some of us, myself included, traveled the country trying to repeat as many of Gill's problems as we could. This made us better too.

Nowadays there are loads of tremendous Big Name boulderers for one to choose as a role model. Or your role model might be the soft-spoken person at the local rock pile who seems so at home on the rock you could swear he came out of the womb bouldering. Maybe your role model isn't even a boulderer. I remember when I aspired to climb boulders as well as Michael Jordan played basketball. Jordan was confident and dynamic and inventive, creating new moves in midair that left everyone shaking their heads. I strove for those attributes in my bouldering. The point is to pick a role model who climbs the way you wish you climbed. Do you value precision, confidence, power, fearlessness, an adventuresome spirit? What about humor in the face of failure or determination coming back from setbacks? Or do you just value the ability to crank 5.15 after smoking bowls all day?

Unless your role model is your identical twin, chances are you won't be able to climb just like he or she does. Instead of trying to mimic great climbers' actions, incorporate their approach. That's what got them to the level they're at, not the moves they pull off. Do they train religiously? Meditate? Sacrifice basic comforts (fixed address, steady job, yummy food)? Are they out at the boulders long after everyone else has gone home? Go meet your role model and pick his or her brain. Ask about their approach and philosophy as it pertains to bouldering. He or she will be flattered. Ask yourself how your role model would climb and work to improve if he or she was given your mind and body. How would you climb if given your role model's mind and body?

Remember that role models are human just like you. What they have achieved came through hard work, not superhuman powers. Any of us can put hard work into our bouldering if we so choose. Over the years I became friends with my role model, John Gill. He's such an independent thinker that he seems on a different plane than the rest of us and I often had trouble thinking of him as just a boulderer like you or me. One day when he was pushing seventy, he remarked to me that he was pissed off because one-arm pull-ups were getting difficult. I know how you feel, John.

Comfort Zone

We all have a comfort zone inside which we will fearlessly walk up to any problem and try it. Outside that zone we are crippled with fear—fear of falling, fear of embarrassment, or fear of failure. Consequently, we are reluctant to try climbs we feel are outside our comfort zone. Staying inside your comfort zone, however, is a recipe for stagnation—improvement is unlikely. Better boulderers have a wider comfort zone than most—that's because they have confronted their fears and risked climbing outside their comfort zone. Every time you venture outside your comfort zone (assuming you don't get injured), you help to expand it. The more you expand it, the more problems become available for you to improve on, the more confidence you gain, and the easier it is to step beyond your comfort zone again. You aren't training, mentally or physically, unless you are pushing yourself to do stuff you couldn't before.

One of my favorite bouldering partners is Mark Wilford. Mark has an absurdly huge comfort zone, like first-American-to-solo-the-Eiger-North-Face huge. It's nearly impossible to get the guy rattled, but whenever we go out highballing I try, and he does the same to me. Feeding on this friendly, albeit risky, competition, we have both pushed ourselves beyond our comfort zones and in the process expanded them. So competition is one way to get yourself to step outside your comfort zone. Other ways are going to a new set of boulders, a different rock type, or out with a new partner and pushing yourself. Identify your fear—falling, embarrassment, failure, being caught in last year's fashions—then sack up and step out of your comfort zone and see how it feels. It doesn't have to be a big step. Each time you step beyond and feel success, you will be driven to try again. It gets addictive. Oh yeah.

*Adam Strong on **Moonraker (V9), Buttermilks, California.***
DAWN KISH

Commitment

If you want to get better at bouldering, you need to commit to that goal. This will likely mean you have to sacrifice in some other area of life to make time for bouldering. Maybe you have to skip poker night with the boys to go to the gym. Think of what your priorities in life are and spend your time pursuing those. If surfing the web is not a life priority, maybe your time would be better spent at the bouldering wall. As the saying goes, "No Commitment, Sell Equipment."

Burnout

Nonstop pursuit of any activity can lead to burnout. If you find the joy is missing from your bouldering sessions, go ahead and take some time off. Tick some of the other things on your bucket list, like that trip to Hawaii. (Say what? There's bouldering at Waimea Bay? Noooo!) After some time off you'll probably find you return to bouldering with enough fresh energy to make up for any strength losses.

Results

Developing mental strength for bouldering (or most any endeavor) is a process that takes practice. You can't just flip a switch and overnight become fearless and focused. It takes practice. The good thing is the practice is fun. Like getting on a roller coaster, it may seem freaky to let go of absolute control, but after the ride you're energized.

You've gotta have heart—well at least for **The Heart** *at* **The Elephant** *sector, Fontainebleau, France. Dave Winthrop climbing.*

Ego on the Rampage, Part 500:
The Most Famous Boulder Problem in the World

Due to its difficulty, aesthetics, and position center stage in Yosemite's notorious Camp 4, *Midnight Lightning* has become the most famous boulder problem in the world. Time and again climbers would accost me and say, "You're such a big boulderer. Have you ever done *Midnight Lightning*?" I could have replied, "No, but I've done scores of harder problems," but I knew this answer wouldn't cut it. Never mind that neither Gill, Holloway, or Murray had ever sent it; back in the 80s and 90s, in many climbers' eyes, climbing *Midnight Lightning* was tantamount to a baptism into the boulderers' Hall of Fame. Rather than try to convince them otherwise, I felt obliged to make the pilgrimage and come to grips with this "problem of problems." At the end of a very successful winter at Hueco Tanks, I was feeling strong and ready. I was also feeling a lot of pressure to prove myself. I put the rest of my life on hold and drove to Yosemite.

Whenever anyone steps up to *Midnight Lightning*, a crowd of spectators thickens around the base like iron filings drawn to a magnet. Stories abounded of locals chasing wannabes away from the problem so that they wouldn't grease up the holds for the "real climbers." It was as if each successful ascent of this testpiece served to diminish its formidable reputation. I felt like a boxer entering the ring intent on taking away the hometown champ's title belt. I thought the crowd wanted to see me fail. In retrospect I'm sure that most of this negative energy was of my own making. Doubtless most of the crowd that day wanted to see somebody pull off the testpiece.

Utilizing my strength and maximizing my reach, I made it to the lip several times with no great difficulty. Getting over the lip was another story. My lanky limbs felt ill-suited for a straight mantel, so I tried planting my right foot on the lip and laying away with my left fingers placed high on a terribly sloping bump. I climbed up to this position a few times before I felt comfortable letting go of the right hand undercling at the lip and committing to the move. I was pushing the move out. With every inch my body rose, the layaway bump felt greasier and greasier. My face was plastered against the wall, so I couldn't see the finishing thank-god hold. My right arm was waving above me searching for that hold. I asked the crowd, "How far?" but heard no reply. I took the silence to mean I was still a foot away. Should my left hand pop, I would take a sideways fall and risk breaking my wrist like a friend had on this same move. Worse yet, I might land on my head. I jumped. I missed my 30 x 30 inch bouldering pad by several feet and felt a pain like a nail being driven into my heel. I sucked up the impact with my legs until my knee hit my chin and drove a canine tooth through my lip, nearly puncturing through both sides.

Compounding my anguish was the news that I had been just a few inches shy of the finishing hold. If the crowd had come looking for blood, they got it. I couldn't have fallen from any higher up. Knowing that, I felt success was only a try away. I could stand on my toes but certainly not on my heel. Since I wouldn't be weighting that heel while trying the problem, I hopped on one foot to the base. The pain drove some sense into me. I decided to go to the medical clinic and have my foot X-rayed. If it were only a bone bruise, I would try the problem again that afternoon. That way I would have plenty of rest.

As it turned out, my heel was fractured. After a long, miserable drive back to El Paso, I crutched out of my car to an unenthusiastic embrace from my soon to be ex-girlfriend. She couldn't have cared less whether I had climbed *Midnight Lightning* or not. I had been so obsessed with bouldering that I had been ignoring her.

A year later I drove back to Yosemite. I took a set of crutches with me, just in case. Camp 4 was closed, so no crowd flocked to watch. This was fortunate, because even though I was too scared to commit to the lip moves without a spot, I came to appreciate the problem for its beautiful moves and aesthetic line. I no longer wanted to climb *Midnight Lightning* to impress others; I just wanted to climb it.

Shortly thereafter I returned with a spotter. A small crowd formed but was not distracting like before. This time I bounced several sticks off the wall above the lip and positioned my bouldering pad where they landed. After a half-dozen sorties to the lip, I abandoned my previous sequence, made harder by a hold broken since my ill-fated visit. I still had enough gas to get to the lip. For want of any better strategy, I opted to try the mantel I had previously regarded as applicable only to short climbers. Halfway through my first mantel attempt, I felt a strange weight shift as my left palm lifted slightly from the sloping mantel shelf. My weight became distributed between my right foot on the lip and my left forearm, which was pressing against a steep, flared groove/ramp. My arm greased out and I went flying. This time I landed unscathed, save for a juicy raspberry on my forearm.

***The author celebrates
after* Midnight Lightning.**

Success seemed imminent. I chalked my forearm up and climbed to the lip once more. To get to this point I had put in a lot of work: I'd waited until I was strong enough, and called on years of experience. I'd cleaned all hand- and footholds meticulously between attempts and carefully primed my boots. I had waited patiently for cool temperatures. I had previsualized all the moves and ran them through my head as I relaxed before each attempt. I'd utilized tricks like the stick toss and chalking my forearm. I did everything right, but for the wrong reasons. Perhaps that's why I got slapped down on my initial attempts. This time though, my motives were purer. I felt no negative energy tugging down on me at the lip. All I felt was my weight shift from my palm to my forearm and then to the fingers of my right hand as they curled onto the final hold. A few minutes later I was back at my van. I reached into the cooler and pulled out a special bottle of beer on which I had drawn a lightning bolt. The bitter beverage tasted oh so sweet.

Strategy

Most of us have had the experience of being burned off on the boulders by physically weaker individuals. Their technique seemed no better than ours, and damned if they weren't wearing the same shoes we were. We wanted the problem even worse than them, so what's the deal? Why did they succeed where we floundered? Because they used good strategy and they didn't make mistakes.

Bouldering Strategy

Bouldering strategy consists of decisions made before you get on a problem, or between attempts. Good strategy should be used on all problems, not just ones that trouble you.

First off, find the descent. There's nothing quite so embarrassing to a boulderer as styling some problem to the top of a boulder, only to find out he or she can't get back down. This is jokingly called a Rule One Violation. Walk around the boulder first to find the easiest way down. If it looks tricky, it might pay to climb up the downclimb first to familiarize oneself with the moves.

Stand back from the problem and scope it from a distance. What look like great holds from the base of a problem often reveal themselves to be sloping butter dishes when you get a true perspective. This is especially important if you plan to dyno

to a specific hold. You may also discover that a key hold is dirty.

Check the topout from above. Is there a hidden hold? Are the final moves dirty? Covered in wet leaves? Will you bonk your head on a tree branch when you step up on the lip?

Previsualize a sequence. Look at the problem and imagine yourself doing it. Where will your hands go? Where will your feet go? Which way will your body shift? Where will you land if you fall? Feel yourself doing the moves. Feel how your weight shifts, how that sideways move will twist your fingers on that knob. Climb the entire problem in your head before you grab the first hold. A plethora of chalked holds make it easy to get suckered into just reading the hand moves. Don't forget to look for the footholds and memorize their positions.

Have a Plan B. Previsualize an alternate sequence before you attempt the problem. Suppose you climb halfway up the problem and find that your initial previsualized sequence doesn't work. You can either downclimb or jump off, or you can make use of your ascent to that point and try your alternate sequence. In this way you don't burn up extra gas getting to the same spot a second time to try a different sequence. Have a Plan B for your feet as well as your hands.

You don't want to make a mistake up here, so you can be sure Kevin Jorgenson has put a lot of thought into his strategy for this ascent of Mojo Risin' (V5), Hueco Tanks, Texas.
ANDY MANN

The descent from Classic Curl is an intimidating jump—a good thing to prepare for before you start up the boulder. Erin Fox, Joshua Tree National Park, California.

This boulderer may be young, but he's smart. He's checking the lip moves and brushing away the leaves in preparation for his attempt.

Anticipate your fall angles and discuss them with your spotter. Tell your spotter how you plan to try the problem and at which angles and on which moves you think you might fall. After this step, forget about falling and concentrate on succeeding.

Put everything in your favor. Clean handholds and footholds. Clean your boots. If you won't be chalking up en route, leave your chalk bag on the ground. Make sure the sun won't be in your eyes.

Be patient. Cold conditions can be great for bouldering. Your hands don't sweat, boots stick better, slopers feel grippy not greasy. On the minus side your fingers can get numb, your body is more prone to injury, and all those clothes hide your finely chiseled physique. A good warm-up is your best defense against injury. It also helps to warm up the fingers. When fingers get numb during a problem, you've got a real problem. Sometimes dipping into a warm chalk bag can help, if only to get them out of the wind. Putting hand warmers in chalk bags also is effective.

Make the most of suboptimal conditions. Use warm or humid days to work moves in trying conditions—when conditions are good, those moves will feel casual.

Develop a psyching-up routine. This can be anything from peaceful meditation to kicking a punching bag, from screaming at your partner to whispering to the boulder. Find what works for you. My routine goes like this: I think of similar problems I have done. I think of how smoothly I will do the moves. I think of how it will feel when I latch on to the crux crimper. I remember that feeling from other problems. I give that feeling a one-syllable name: I call it "stick." I think of the crux move and I think "stick." I imagine how good I will feel pulling over the top. While I'm doing all this, I am relaxing my muscles. I feel my arms get heavy as they relax. I feel them pull down on my shoulders and gently stretch my neck muscles. By this time I have dumped all extraneous thoughts—I feel light and focused. I concentrate on the moves

as I rub chalk into my fingers. I run through my previsualized sequence one more time, thinking "stick" on the hard moves and imagining my lip-stretching grin on the summit. Finally, if it's a really hard problem, I'll spit just before I step on. That extra five grams might hold me back, you know.

Rest long enough between attempts. The tendency to jump right back on a problem after you pop off is great, but your chances of success increase if you rest until you feel like new. Give a buddy a spot, clean the holds on your problem, spit shine your boots, do some relaxation exercises . . . anything to give your body adequate rest before the next attempt.

Don't wire in failure. If you are getting tired and falling off a move you've already done, it's time to get off that move. You may think you're getting stronger by working your muscles to exhaustion, but at the same time you are training your muscles to fail on that move. Even if you go back fresh, your muscles will say, "We don't have to contract as far to do this move," and you'll come up short again. It's a bitch trying to erase bad muscle memory.

Dial in all the moves, not just the crux. When you're too tired to work on the crux moves, work on the finishing moves. Get them wired while you're tired so they won't feel foreign when you finally do climb through the crux to them. Breaking a project up may mean working it in several distinct sections. But when it makes sense, say when working a sit-down start to a problem you've done before, don't work it in just the distinct sections, but practice overlapping the sections to build muscle memory for the linking moves. In short, use your mind to save your body.

Practice reading the rock. Reading the rock and sussing moves is an acquired skill. The more you practice, the better and faster you get at seeing indistinct holds and previsualizing tricky sequences. You can do this in the gym, but you'll get better at it outdoors where there are more options to consider. Gym routes are already mapped out, making the task easier—the same can be said of routes

Marcie Puskarik and Hillary Haakenson practice reading the rock on this boulder at The Elephant sector, Fontainebleau, France. Neither has done this particular line, and since Marcie and Hillary are of roughly the same height and reach, the beta they are discussing could potentially work for both of them.

outside where some lazy boulderer didn't brush off his or her tick marks. Practice reading the rock on problems with little or no chalk for maximum benefit. You needn't confine your practice to problems you're about to attempt. I enjoy seeing an incredible line and imagining how I would climb it if I could turn the injury clock back.

Evaluate the performance of yourself and others. If you can watch video of yourself, analyze your mistakes and make a plan to correct them. Are your hips too far from the wall? Are you overdynoing? Also take note of what you're doing right, and build a positive mental association with those moves. If you don't have access to video, ask others to evaluate your performance. In turn, watch others climb and see if you can clue into things they could do better (only offer your assessment if it is desired).

Avoiding Common Mistakes

Keep breathing. Your muscles are begging for that good old O_2, so don't forget to breathe while you're on a problem. This sounds obvious, but it happens all the time. Take deep breaths to calm yourself when the going gets scary. If you find yourself having trouble remembering to breathe on problems, it can help to start into a forced rhythmic deep breathing several breaths before pulling onto the problem, then maintain that breathing rhythm throughout the problem. Certain core strength–intensive moves make it hard to inhale during the moves—just as you previsualize a move sequence, you can also previsualize your breathing sequence for a problem and plan out which spots on the problem will allow you the best chance to inhale deeply and get oxygen to the muscles. Your spotter or other bouldering companions can remind you to breathe too. Practice deliberate breathing on easy problems and during your warm-ups.

Avoid shortcuts. Avoid shortcuts like not cleaning your shoes before warm-up problems. Clean them every time. Energy wasted on the warm-up won't be there for the send. Climb precisely and in good posture to the rock, and the energy savings will add up in your favor.

Don't just grab the top of a problem and then jump off. Go ahead and push out the mantels. Manteling may be out of vogue these days, but it works the triceps as few climbing moves do. Building up your antagonist muscles can help prevent tendon and joint injuries. It's no surprise that so many climbers have these injuries—they spend all day pulling and no time pushing.

They call him "Pufferfish."
Mason Daly will explode
if he doesn't breathe soon
here. **High Plains Drifter**
(V7), Buttermilks, California.

Don't be afraid to learn from "less-experienced" climbers. The second you think you know it all is the second you cease to learn and improve. I've learned plenty from old sages, but I've also picked up a lot from climbers who weren't even born by the time I'd cranked my 10,000th problem.

Rise above the ratings game. Time spent worrying about ratings or how somebody else is climbing is time wasted. Climb problems for their beauty, not for their numbers. Would you rather have someone call you by your name or a number? Climbers who chase numbers usually quit the sport as soon as they slip back a grade or formerly inferior climbers start outclimbing them.

Don't beg beta. Unless you are a newbie and at a complete loss, try figuring sequences out for yourself instead of just copying others' beta. Problem solving is one of the great joys of bouldering. Good problem-solving skills separate better boulderers from average boulderers. Begging beta from someone who has already done the problem will retard development of your problem-solving skills. One caveat: Working out beta with another climber of your skill level when neither of you have been exposed to the problem can be a good exercise.

Don't get stuck on bad beta. If your sequence isn't working, try something new. Rule out moves that won't work; for example, a reach you can't make or a knee bar you won't fit.

Don't rely on the sequences of others.

Unless that other climber is your identical twin, chances are your body is better suited to a different sequence. Go ahead and experiment.

Don't be afraid to fall. Falling is not failing. It is an integral part of the bouldering game

To surmount the sloping lip on U-Turn (7b), Cresciano, Switzerland, Olivier Charles has no choice but to toss his heel over and burl out the mantel.

True Combat Story #88: The Real Victory

I don't care if you're John Gill, Fred Nicole, or Lisa Rands—if you're a devoted boulderer, it's likely that your list of desperate problems you couldn't do is nearly as long as the list of desperates you did crank. The Brits call V0, V-naught. I jokingly rate any problem I can't do as V-not. Most of my V-nots were problems I'd give up on after a few days, planning to return to them when I was ready. When it came down to it, I always preferred climbing something I could do than flailing on something I couldn't. Nevertheless, I wanted one problem at Hueco Tanks so bad that I returned day after day. It was a beautiful sit-down start to *Lip Service.* I dubbed it *Full Service.*

Feeling territorial and insecure, I asked other climbers to stay off my prize. Some were stronger than me, and I was afraid they'd bogart the sequence I'd worked so hard to discover. Days stretched into weeks, winter gave way to spring, and still I could not link the first two moves with the rest of the problem. I was so obsessed that I would wake in the wee hours and watch the sun rise as I drove into the park. I would have an hour to try the problem before it got too hot. Every time out I felt sure I'd crank it. Every time I'd gag on the same micro-toe hook.

I returned the next season with *Full Service* at the top of my list. By this time the mental block was firmly in place. Every time I tried to link it, I'd yank my toe off. It was as if I needed this problem to fail on, to teach me some kind of lesson. I was plenty strong enough, but I'd tuned my muscle memory to fail on this one move. My frustration built, as did my conviction that I'd found the only sequence that would work—hence I didn't try new sequences. I was climbing stupidly in more ways than one. Bob Williams watched me fail time and again. He watched me practice failing. He warned me that "practice makes permanent," and he was right. He also bluntly added that being first to do a route is no big deal if nobody else is trying it. Harsh but true.

I started to hear rumors that someone else had climbed it and was staying mum so as not to blow my buzz. I wondered whether those rumors were true or merely made up *to* blow my buzz. Maybe both.

(unless you're high bouldering or cranking above a bad landing). If you aren't falling, you aren't pushing yourself. If you don't push yourself, you won't improve.

Remember the footholds. Tired of hearing about footwork? Well, I'm tired of writing about it, but it can't be stressed too much. If it were advantageous to climb with just our arms, we would walk on our arms too.

Avoid target fixation. Don't obsess on the hold you can't reach; concentrate on finding a new sequence.

Can the excuses. Too often, boulderers will tell themselves they'd crank the problem "if I was just a bit stronger" or "if I was five pounds lighter." This may or may not be true, but before telling yourself any of the above, consider if there are weaker or heavier climbers than you doing the problem you can't. If so, what's holding you back is not your strength to weight ratio, it's your technique to ego ratio. Identify the weak technique (footwork, posture, triple-pumping dynos, etc.) and find similar problems (or set some in the gym) to work on that weak link. Errors are cues for improvement.

I was ripped to the gills and down to 161 pounds, my lightest in ten years. Nevertheless, I had a ton of garbage in my head.

Later that season Dale Goddard climbed it, claimed it, and renamed it *Serves You Right*. The name was pointed but appropriate. Had I respected others' rights to try it too, perhaps they would have respected my desire to bag it first. What's more, Dale had found a much easier sequence. My own stupidity had cost me the first. Had I not been so pigheaded, I might have discovered that sequence or the even easier moves discovered later.

Though I didn't climb it, I learned more from *Full Service* than from any other problem. Perhaps that mental block existed for my own benefit. Perhaps it remains there for the same reason. Had I bagged the first, I might not have learned the fruitlessness of territoriality, the "practice makes permanent" principle, and the ugliness of disrespect. Scores of boulderers have climbed *Full Service* now. I doubt anybody gained as much from it as I did.

Sonny Trotter on* Full Service *(V10), Hueco Tanks, Texas.
ERIC ODENTHAL

Gym Bouldering and Competitions

By Paul Robinson

I thought bouldering gyms were just places to pick up dates with less than four legs—shows how much I know. Which is why I've turned to the 2008 American Bouldering Series National Champion Paul Robinson to tell us more.

—JS

Paul Robinson training at the CATS gym in Boulder, Colorado.
STEVE WOODS

Gym Climbing

I first began climbing at age eleven in a climbing gym. In the late 1990s climbing gyms were popping up everywhere. To climbers who started before me, it seems an odd place to begin climbing; to climbers after me, it is commonplace. Climbing indoors increased my ability enormously. Other climbers who grew up climbing plastic would probably agree.

Gym climbing is a safe way for one to learn how to climb and to get strong quickly. There is no need to wait for the weather to cooperate, you can climb day or night, and there is a climbing gym in nearly every large city in the United States. The gym offers protection from weather, bad landings, sunburns, bugs, and snakes. You can concentrate solely on climbing hard and working on your technique on forgiving climbing holds in air-conditioned comfort.

Paul Robinson competing at Send Fest, Salt Lake City, 2007.
STEVE WOODS

Similar to climbing outdoors, when climbing in a gym, be aware of those who are climbing with you and around you. Don't climb or walk under people climbing above. When you do climb, know where you may fall on the particular boulder problem that you are trying and warn others who may be in the landing zone. Don't hog the wall; there are others who want to climb too.

The gym's bouldering area will usually feature many color-coded routes. On some routes you are expected to use the same color-coded holds for both hands and feet (foot tracking). On others you are expected to use your hands on the color-coded holds, but are free to use your feet on any hold on the wall regardless of color-coding (open feet). The boulder problems will also have a specific grade attached to them. Familiarize yourself with the gym's ratings system before embarking up any walls.

There are many differences to note when you make the transition to climbing outside. Remember to always spot your climbing partner, and make sure the landings you are climbing over are safe and padded properly. Climbing outdoors requires a greater skill set, including the ability to evaluate rock quality and climb on or around loose holds. There are no holds marked with tape to show you where to climb, and the holds aren't predictable shapes. Climbing outside is all about climbing what the rock gives you. Don't tick holds with chalk unless it is impossible to find them otherwise. Always brush holds and tick marks when you are done. Never manufacture holds in any way. If you cannot make it to the top, leave the climb as you found it. Unlike gym problems, outdoor climbs will wait for you forever. Even if you never do it, someone else may find a new sequence and succeed on what you deemed impossible.

Don't damage the flora and fauna around you and always pick up after yourself—there's no vacuum to pick up your tape wads and trash at the end of the night. Leaving trash and manufacturing holds are a sure way to jeopardize access to the area. Set a good example for the people to come after you. Leave the area as pristine, if not more pristine (by cleaning up after others), than when you arrived.

Competition Climbing

Competition climbing is different from climbing with friends in the gym or outside on the rocks, mainly because of the pressure and rules involved. Climbing in a competition can be very intimidating for some because of the multitudes of people and the judgmental atmosphere. Some climbers excel under the pressure and climb flawlessly; others falter in the limelight. Think seriously about competing before you throw yourself into a contest, as you may not be fully prepared. For some a poor performance can lead to low self-esteem, while others can shrug it off or use it as motivation. Injuries also can occur from pushing your body too hard during training or competition. If you do not enjoy the atmosphere around competitions, don't compete.

Training for a competition should be very structured. If you know the format of the competition you are interested in doing, train in a similar fashion. If it is a redpoint competition, go around your gym trying as many climbs as you can as quickly as you can. Don't rest too much in training since a redpoint competition usually lasts only three hours. If it is an on-sight competition, set yourself some climbs of varying styles on varying wall terrain (maybe five or six) and try to do each one in five minutes; use a stopwatch. When you complete one, rest for five minutes, then try to do the next one in five minutes and so on. Most on-sight competitions will give you a bonus for flashing, so make sure your first effort is a 100 percent try. If it is an outdoor competition, climb outside a lot (if possible at the competition site) to become accustomed to climbing on rock.

On competition day, walk around the gym looking at the climbs within your ability. Find your warm-up climbs and pick out the climbs you think

Byron Voges on **The Shield** *(V11), Stone Fort, Tennessee, during the third and final leg of the 2010 Triple Crown competition.*
PAT GOODMAN

would make the best score for you. Warm up similar to your standard gym sessions; don't rush into hard climbs before you are ready. In a redpoint competition, watch others who are climbing around you and get beta. It is not cheating—it's called a redpoint competition for a reason. Watch others to figure out a sequence that will work for you. Make sure to try your best on every attempt—remember, every fall will be a deduction from your final score. If in your first few attempts you do not succeed, take a break and go find some other climbs that interest you. Watch others trying the climb you fell on to see if there are any alternative sequences that may be more suitable for you. Don't tire yourself out on one climb!

Do competitions with a friend. Not only will the two of you be able to figure out climbs to try, but you'll also be less nervous during the competition. For on-sight competitions with an isolation area, get to isolation early and warm up as you would at your local gym. Drink lots of water and take deep breaths to prepare yourself for the climbing ahead. Make sure you are fully warmed up and don't feel rushed at all; otherwise your climbing performance will not be at its best.

Cash prizes! Paul Robinson clutches his winner's check as he gets a ride over the crowd at the awards ceremony following the Horse Pens 40 leg of the 2006 Triple Crown.
PAUL ROBINSON COLLECTION

Success Story

During the winter of 2008, the only place you could find me was at the Colorado Athletic Training School (CATS) in Boulder, Colorado. There is a bouldering wall in the back of the gym where I spent a majority of my time training for the 2008 American Bouldering Series Nationals. The gym is small and not the prettiest climbing site in the world, but the plethora of small holds and steep angles on the particular wall made it the perfect place to train for a big competition. Nearly every day I was in the gym climbing on boulder problems my friends and I had set for ourselves to get ready for the competition in early February. I felt very strong that year but knew that it would take a lot to beat some of the best in the sport, including Chris Sharma.

When competition day came, I felt ready and made my way over to the Spot, another gym in Boulder where the competition was being held. The first day of the event, I finished in fourth place heading into the final round. I was a bit disappointed but knew I had another day to prove I could do better.

I had to get super psyched if I wanted to do well the following day. The next morning I woke up and made myself some cereal. I realized I was running a little late, so I ran out to the car, suddenly felt nauseous, threw up my cereal all over the road, got in the car, and drove to the competition. Maybe I was a little too psyched! Then again, sometimes a little extra psyche makes all the difference in the end.

When I arrived at the gym, I went into isolation and prepared myself. I was extremely nervous when they called my name and gave me the warning that it was five minutes until I was up to climb. With a packed house of over 700 people in the Spot, it was impossible to *not* feel a little nervous. I calmed myself the best I could with long, deep breaths and headed out to my first problem. I executed each move the best that I could and felt very strong on each of the four climbs.

By the time I finished, I felt like I had climbed very well. I sat down with some friends to watch the remaining climbers compete. It was hard to tell how I had done, but from what I could see and what my friends were telling me, it looked like I was in the running for first place. When the competition was over, I waited impatiently for the results to be announced.

I tried to stay cool as they began the ceremonies. The announcers ran through the list of top finishers from fifth to first. When they got to first, they announced my name! I was thrilled that all the training and hard work throughout my climbing career had paid off with a win at the 2008 American Boulder Series National Championship.

To celebrate the win I hung out with my friends who had also competed. It was great to feel like all the training was worth it in the end. It was now time to relax and celebrate a great day of climbing, then get out on the rocks again after being cooped up in a gym for months and months.

Highballs

What Is a Highball?

The term highball conjures up different meanings for different climbers. For some it means any problem high enough to scare them, regardless of risk. For some that could be 15 feet high, for others 30 feet or more. Other boulderers believe the term should only apply to problems where a fall would cause certain injury and put a boulderer out of the game for weeks if not the whole season. For our discussion we'll focus on serious problems with a high risk of injury. If you can safely jump or fall off a tall problem into a deep pit of foam, then the standard bouldering techniques discussed in this book will see you through. However, on a problem where you only have one go at the move and you'll get hurt if you blow it, you need to adopt a different approach. Don't get fooled into thinking you're highballing if the risk has been replaced by a heap of bouldering pads—this will just get you in trouble when you find yourself really highballing.

Why highball at all? Well, besides the awesome pics there is an adrenaline surge you don't get with less risky problems. The fight or flight (literally) response triggered by highballing can be very addictive. During a highball climb I don't feel the effects as much as I do shortly after topping; then my body starts shaking, my mind revs up like crazy, and if the downclimb is technical at all I'll have to wait out the shakes before I descend. It feels primal and powerful. Getting scared is part of the thrill too—like on a roller coaster. Learning to control your fear is a big part of it. So is the totally locked-in focus one gets while sending—I call it mind detergent—it washes out every thought in your mind except moving perfectly on stone. Highballing is the opportunity to put all your skills to the test in a genuine risk/reward situation.

Not everybody likes such tests. Some of us don't like getting scared. Others don't possess the focus. Highballing is definitely not for everybody. If you don't like it, don't do it.

Andy Salo on the first ascent of **Edge of Oblivion (V7)**, *Glacier Gorge, Colorado.*
ANDY MANN

New Zealand has some of the most spectacular limestone boulders in the world, and the locals aren't afraid to go high. Zac Orme on Koosti (V5), Spittle Hill, New Zealand.
DEREK THATCHER

Highballing for Kids

You must be kidding, Vern. No, I'm not, or should I say the French aren't. Hit the kids' circuit at The Elephant area of Fontainebleau and check out problem *16b*. It's over 20 feet tall with a potential hideous tumbling fall down a lumpy slab, and like any good highball the crux is right where it belongs, at the very top. Admittedly the holds are huge and one can climb next to a kid and probably stop a fall, but the point is the problem is there to build a head for heights from an early age. Either that or somebody seriously hates kids. I include this tidbit here to show that tall problems aren't just for experts. I got used to tall problems from day one of my career. With no pads back then, it was obvious you didn't want to fall once your feet were "above the basketball rim." This developed a cautious style that has helped immensely in other facets of my climbing, such as necky on-sight trad leads.

"Okay Junior, no allowance this week if you don't send 16b." Marcie Puskarik pressing out the summit mantel in a dish full of freezing water on a rainy November day.

My Approach

I'm from the old-school pre-pad highball camp that believes a fall from a highball must result in injury or it isn't a highball. I've put up hundreds of highball first ascents and have never suffered an injury highballing. Thirty-plus years of highballing—zero falls. To me, falling off a highball is the ultimate bouldering failure. In my mind, success lies not in bagging another summit but in demonstrating control over my mind and perfection of my technique.

I would rather back off a highball in control than climb it out of control. An out of control highball send is a failure.

I'm a lot choosier when picking highballs to try than I am with other boulder problems. If I'm going to risk a broken leg it had better be on the best of the best. Of course, this can lead to a dangerous obsession with a problem beyond one's limits. Highballing forces you to be honest with yourself as to your abilities. I prefer first ascents because of the extra mystery of grappling with holds never touched before—I don't have any preconceived notions as to how hard it will be, or thoughts as to whether the previous ascensionists were stronger or weaker than me. This helps remove the competitive aspect that can get one in trouble. However, if I'm with a bunch of buddies trying to bag the same tall first ascent, there's definitely competitive urges.

Putting those in perspective is important—I have fun with those urges on the ground but leave them there when I step on the rock. Once climbing, my focus is on the moves, not the first.

Once I pick a line I'll evaluate the descent (no Rule One Violations), the topout, possible bail-out points, rock quality, cleanliness of holds, landing, everything . . . I want to know exactly what I'm

"What the . . . hey, there's bolts up here." Paul Robinson boulders out a micro-sport pitch. Eldorado Canyon, Colorado.
ANDY MANN

This is absolutely not the time to think about a potential fall. A thin move leads up to the obvious chalked hold, then the real fun begins (read: you'd better have a lot of trust in your feet because you're edging on a pencil eraser and smearing a mosquito bite). Your mind better be thinking about executing the moves perfectly and nothing else. Pat Goodman bouldering at High Ridge, Northern Baja.

getting into and leave nothing to chance. If I can get a better view from a neighboring problem, I'll climb that.

On tougher highballs I will climb up and down a lot, getting a feel for the opening moves and examining the crux. Downclimbing skills are essential for the highballer—it's usually your only path out of trouble. Even on shorter problems I prefer

downclimbing to jumping to save wear and tear on the joints. I will often opt for a harder sequence that I know I can reverse over an easier move (say a lengthy dyno). If I am faced with a dyno, I will carefully evaluate where my feet should be planted and if they will or should come off. One-chance-only, irreversible moves are pretty freaky. To calm my mind I think of other problems I've done with

A climber preparing to rappel down and pre-inspect moves on Evilution (V11), Grandpa Peabody Boulder, Buttermilks, California.

similar moves. I tell myself if the move were right next to the ground it would be easy and I'd do it first try no problem—business as usual. And I will be sure in my mind that I can send all the moves above, because I'll no longer be able to back off.

The climbing up and down part of the process helps nip away at the fear. When I start on a new highball problem I'm plenty scared. However, when I actually climb it there is no fear. Instead there is the mind detergent focus mentioned before. One hundred percent of my thoughts are going into performing the moves—maintaining ideal posture to the rock, breathing properly, setting my feet well and weighting them, executing the sequence, switching to Plan B immediately if needed and Plan C if that doesn't work. If I start up intent on sending that try and find my mind isn't totally focused, I will back down and try to set my mind right. This might take a few more attempts. It might never happen—in that case I will leave the problem for another day and/or another climber. My list of highball sends is pretty long, but it's important to know that my list of uncompleted highballs is pretty long too. I'm cool with that. I place high value on the experience of trying a problem even if it doesn't culminate in an ascent. The adrenaline rush is still there, and I got my fix.

Other Approaches

In the twentieth century the vast majority of highball first ascents were done in ground-up style, the climber venturing into unknown territory with only one chance to get the move right. Comfort with the terrain and knowledge of the sequence were gained by climbing up and down until one could finally commit to send. Prior to the 1990s there were no pads, and stakes were very high indeed. Highballing was a practice of an elite few. With the advent of pads, many of the pre-1990s highballs were effectively neutered. Some climbers took advantage of the situation by bagging the former death routes with a cushy mountain of foam beneath them. Much chest beating ensued. However, pads did not kill highballing—there were still climbers out there willing to risk injury on the tall boulders; only now the boulders had to be much taller if there were to be a threat of injury from falling into a stack of pads. So whereas in the pad-free days, 20 feet was considered a tall problem and no-fall territory, since pads the bar has been raised to 30 feet and even higher. The combination of probable injury, a greater amount of air beneath one's feet, and the pump factor of more moves taxes the mind even more.

Nowadays some climbers espouse a top-down approach using toprope inspection and move rehearsal prior to a ropeless ascent of a tall problem. This allows lines to be tried with moves hard enough that the climber will take falls figuring them out. Basically one uses headpointing tactics to produce what used to be called a toprope-rehearsed solo, but calls the result highballing, just as if it had been done ground-up without employing ropes. Whether a twenty-first-century highball is established ground-up or top-down is rarely reported, the media and even some climbers being purposely vague with this detail. This creates a hazard to boulderers who might be lured into trying something ground-up that has only been done as a toprope-rehearsed solo before. Ask around if you have concerns as to what you're getting into, and regardless of the answer exercise good judgment while climbing.

CHAPTER ELEVEN

First Ascents

Boldly going where no man or woman has gone before can be a thrilling experience. There is an extra adrenaline rush when you commit to a move with no idea of whether it will go or not. There's a sense of accomplishment, and quite often social perks that go along with that. There can be the reward of pitting yourself against a challenge set before you by nature, not by other climbers. Or, if competitive fires drive you, there can be the kick of picking a plum before your rival or buddy does. Whatever the reason one chooses to do a first ascent, one should put some thought into the project first.

How Much, If Any, to Clean

Much of the responsibility involved in first ascents centers around the initial cleaning of the problem. There are ethical and environmental considerations. Usually the ethical considerations are tied closely to environmental factors. For instance, in some of the densely forested country of the southeast it might not raise any eyebrows if someone ripped fifty pounds of kudzu off a boulder to access a problem. On the other hand, I know of some Hueco locals who would gladly pummel anyone who removed a single leaf from one of the rare ferns in the park. In the southeast that kudzu might all grow back in

a few months. In West Texas that fern might never recover. Before going at a boulder with your wire brushes, consider the effects it will have on the ecosystem.

Look at a problem objectively (this is hard with first ascent stars twinkling in front of one's eyes). Will it be a classic that others will want to repeat? Or an embarrassment that will dishonor you and your entire clan? Doing a first ascent for the sake of doing a first ascent is the lamest reason I can think of. If the problem is not going to see much future traffic, perhaps it's best to clean it minimally or not at all. Maybe you'd be better off ignoring the problem altogether. Or you can climb it as nature presented it. Climbing on dirty holds is not impossible and is actually good practice should you ever get hooked on mountaineering. (I reckon one reason top boulderer Mark Wilford is also such a great alpine climber is because he is not afraid to tackle a boulder problem without cleaning it. To him part of the challenge lies in effectively dealing with dirty holds while he climbs. After all, nobody was going to brush clean the North Face of the Eiger before he soloed it.)

Okay, you're convinced that people will wait in line and buy tickets to get on your proposed first. How to approach it then. Do you rip off every loose flake in sight, rent a grader to smooth out

Kevin Jorgenson on the first ascent of Sticks or Stones (V8), Hueco Tanks, Texas.
ANDY MANN

Oh yeah, this one's gonna be classic. Chris Hill scopes an obvious line on a virgin boulder in High Valley, northern Mexico. He didn't succeed on this trip, but came back later and made the first ascent.

An Alternative to First Ascent Mania:
Another Ego-Bloating First-Person Account

I have spent much of my bouldering career in the southwestern United States. Time and again I would find an incredible virgin line to scale. Often I would succeed and come down grinning with the satisfaction of putting another feather in the cap of the Great White Boulderer, explorer and developer of the finest problems in the land. More times than I care to remember, I would later discover that Bob Murray had been up the problem before me. Well, pluck my cap like a Christmas goose. Usually this discovery would come months or years after my ascent. By that time I was hot on some other first I had just done, so the disappointment was softened. Still, it became a recurring theme in my career. Strangely, it had a very positive effect. I grew to admire Murray's taste in problems immensely—after all, we were drawn to the same walls. More importantly, I realized that being first didn't mean that much—it was the sense of adventure that counted. When I was up on those problems, I was jacked up on so much adrenaline that I'd shake uncontrollably as soon as I pulled over the top. It's great when several climbers can get a first ascent buzz from the same problem. For all we know, Bob may not have been the first up either.

In recent years I've done a number of fine probable firsts. In the spirit of multiple first ascents, I haven't shown others these routes. At one point, however, I suffered a lapse. Far out in a little-visited desert, I climbed a huge boulder with no easy route to the top. Confident that I was first to stand on top, I cockily stacked some tiny flakes into a 2-inch-tall cairn on the summit. I strongly doubt any other boulderer will ever find or climb that rock in the future, but if he or she does, I hope I will have returned first and swept that cairn off.

the landing, then call in the Air Force for an Agent Orange strike to devegetate it? This would be overkill. Once again, I suggest thinking objectively. How would the problem look if nobody cleaned it but a hundred people climbed it? All those ascents would rub the dirt and lichen off the hand- and footholds, snap off the loose flakes that people might actually pull on, leave the loose flakes that nobody would pull on, and so on. To avoid overcleaning, imagine what the climb would look like after that many ascents, then clean it to that point, but no further. You'll save yourself time (which you can spend on more problems) and you'll avoid excessive environmental damage (and maybe future access hassles).

Tools of the Trade

Some boulderers make a career out of doing first ascents; others make a career without ever doing one. Sometimes one may be fortunate enough to meet a virgin boulder problem that requires no hold cleaning. Usually, however, holds collect dirt, leaves, cactus spines, pine needles, and broken glass or are covered with varying amounts of moss, lichen, poison ivy, etc. Often it can take longer to clean a problem than to actually climb it.

Wire brushes are the primary tool of the first ascensionist. A standard steel-bristled paint scrubbing brush (12-inch handle, 5 inches of bristles) found at any hardware store works well. In areas of

The author on the first ascent of Instagator in the central Sierras, California. There was no easy way to the top of this boulder, so I had to clean on the go, carrying my brushes on a Gammon Reel. From this point to the top was pretty mossy, and it took a lot of energy to hang on with one hand and scrub with the other. I had to be careful to save enough energy to safely downclimb between goes. It was worth it though, because this is one of the sweeter FAs I've been privileged to do in the last few years.

Cleaning Tips

- Clean from the top down for the same reason you sweep stairs from the top down.

- On sloped holds and rounded bulges, clean not just the fingertip edge but also the spots where your palm and/or forearm will rest against the rock. The extra friction on your palm or arm can be crucial to success.

- On holds that stick out like sore thumbs after they're cleaned, feather the edges of your cleaning job to blend in with the surrounding rock.

- Don't overclean. This is a waste of time that could be better spent climbing. If you find that a problem needs more cleaning, you can always go back and clean it further.

soft rock, such as sandstone or limestone, steel bristles can damage the rock, actually carving grooves if too vigorously applied. In these cases a brass-bristle brush, such as for scouring pots, is a better choice.

To clean thin cracks, tight corners, and pockets that the larger brush can't fit into, I use round plumber's brushes. These come in varying diameters and reside in the plumbing department at most hardware stores. Get the smallest (1/2-inch diameter) and a 1-inch too.

To clean holds you can't reach, make an extendobrush. Mine has the longest wooden mop handle I could find at the hardware store. A standard brush is hose-clamped to one end, a plumbing brush to the other end. I also have a skyhook bolted to the plumbing brush end, which I use to test loose flakes. The wire handle of the plumbing brush can be bent to angle in to hard-to-reach holds. If bent too frequently, however, the wire handle will fatigue and break.

On tall problems you may have to clean holds on the go. I once had a small wire brush on a string around my neck. This was uncomfortable and the bristles threatened to scrape off the manly chest hair I had worked so long to grow, so I was psyched

when I learned of the Gammon Reel. This is a surveyor's gadget that has a retractable string threaded into a plastic case the size of a dental floss box. It's like those retractable key chains janitors wear, but very light. I wear the Gammon Reel on my chalk bag belt, and have a nylon brush and a wire brush on the string. I can reel out the brushes, clean a hold with the appropriate brush, then just drop the brushes and they snap back to my hip.

Safety glasses or goggles are helpful for keeping grit out of your eyes.

Evaluating Loose Holds on Virgin Lines

You can save yourself injury if you test loose holds before you pull on them. When I can reach a hold from the ground, I test it with my fingers. Sometimes I will get a lot of flex and sense imminent breakage, yet the hold does not come off in my fingers, or I give up before I snap it into my face. Through much trial and error I came up with the following additional test: I stick the plastic handle of my toothbrush behind the suspect hold and twist. If the hold snaps, it most likely would have snapped

The Big Decision: Yet Another Blood-and-Guts Tale of Bouldering Action

Many years ago I had the privilege to be turned on to an incredible boulder garden in the mountains. Very few people had been there, fewer still seem inclined to boulder there, yet there were literally dozens of killer boulders to develop. I was in boulderer's heaven. Here I could climb by my rules and develop an area as I saw fit. I got in a pattern of climbing one day, then cleaning problems the next day. As most of the boulders had never been climbed, there were a fair number of loose flakes adorning them. Some of these fell off with a brush of the hand, others with a gentle tug, and some withstood testing and remained to be used as holds. To test layaways out of my reach, I would take a shovel, put the corner of the blade behind the suspect flake, then, holding on to the end of the handle, I'd give a twist. (This may sound like overkill, but the actual torque you can exert this way is fairly low, probably not much more than with the toothbrush test.) I had climbed partway up one exquisitely beautiful problem, but was spooked by the flexing layaway I would have to pull on—the only hold in an 8-foot span of rock. I gave it the shovel test: Sure enough, it snapped off, but in such a way as to form a hold twice as big. The problem seemed substantially altered and I felt bad, like I'd doctored a hold instead of breaking a loose flake. I gave the resulting hold the same test, but it held fast. I told myself I wasn't a bad person and worked on the problem. It turned out to be so hard that I would never have stood a chance had the flake withstood its initial test.

A few days later in the same area, I was testing a hold on another classic line. This hold also failed and dropped in the dirt at my feet. Like on the first problem, it was the only hold adorning a long blank stretch. Unlike the first problem, there was nothing left when it snapped off. The problem was gorgeous, a three-star candidate in any area. Now it wouldn't go for anyone less than 8 feet tall. I knew that with a little glue I could have that problem back. Carefully done and nobody but myself would know. Furthermore, there was a fair chance that I'd be the only person to ever try that problem; my choice would be entirely personal. Still, something didn't feel right about that tactic. At the base of the problem was a thick flake, half the size of a garage door. It leaned a few inches out from the wall. I placed the broken hold atop it and left to sleep on my decision.

A few days later I made up my mind. If I were to glue that hold back on, then by the same token I should glue back all the holds I'd knocked off testing. To do otherwise would be to take nature's hand out of the decision. By removing the luck of the draw, I'd also remove much of the adventure of bouldering. I didn't want to be in the business of creating problems instead of cleaning them, so I walked over to the problem, picked up the broken hold, and dropped it down the narrow gap behind the starter flake. I would never be able to retrieve that hold, and I would never have doubt again about where I draw the line between cleaning and creation.

if I pulled on it climbing. If the brush just flexes or snaps itself, the hold will probably support weight if treated correctly (see the section on Dealing with Loose Rock in Chapter 2). Rarely would a hold fail that passed the toothbrush test. Testing with a stouter tool, say a screwdriver or cleaning pin, can be overkill and might potentially bust off a usable hold. After all, given a big enough crowbar, you could pry North America off the planet. To test holds out of reach, a skyhook attached to the end of a stick can be used. Pull on the holds in the directions you will pull on them while climbing. There's no sense in pulling off a hold by yanking on it at some oddball angle you wouldn't use while climbing.

Whatever method you use to test loose holds, remember that you usually won't have your entire weight on that hold. The hold might only need to support 30 pounds for you to do the move. If this is the case, don't test it to 180 pounds. If you do, your problem might end up shy one hold.

Rappel Cleaning

Some climbers will clean lines on rappel; others feel bouldering should be a rope-free pursuit at all times—including when cleaning. Others fall somewhere in between and will get a friend to clean something on rappel but not divulge any information about the moves or holds.

Glue

Glue is too often used as a substitute for technique. In the past I have felt that gluing a hold back on was sometimes justified when a hold snapped off a classic problem. I felt others deserved to try that problem in the same state as the first ascensionist. Now I'm not so sure. Broken holds can be viewed as part of the evolution of a problem. Gill's famous *Right Eliminator* and *Standard Mental Block* problems (at Horsetooth Reservoir in Colorado) are examples of problems that have evolved substantially,

hold-wise, through the years, but are still regarded as classics.

If you resort to the glue pot to realize your ambitions, do the climbing community a favor: Don't just drip glue around the edges of a hold to reinforce it. This causes a visual mess and is a weak fix. Instead, pull the hold off (you might find out you can't and therefore don't have to monkey with it), then clean off the back of the hold and the rock where it pulled off. Apply your glue to these surfaces and press the hold back on. You will have a much greater surface area to glue, hence a stronger bond. Also, the glue will be hidden behind the hold—all that will be visible is a hairline crack where the hold snapped off. Go easy on the glue, as most glues used by climbers are space-filling epoxies. If you use too much, the hold will stick farther out, look stupid, and change the problem to boot.

There's a special place in Hell for people who turn the boulders into gluey messes: All the holds suck. Your chalk bag is empty. And your partner always botches the spot.

Doctoring versus Cleaning

Where does one draw the line between what constitutes cleaning a problem and what constitutes doctoring it? I believe the crucial factor is intent. If the preparation of the problem is done with an eye toward creating a problem of a certain difficulty—say four holds broke off when tested and two were glued back on—then you most certainly are doctoring the route, and you've brought shame upon yourself, your friends, your family, and your country. If you have chiseled in a new hold or filed down one that was too sharp for your piggies, then you too are a world-class loser. Using glue or a chisel to bring a problem down to your level permanently alters the problem, and everyone, not just you, has to live with your bungling. If nature doesn't provide the challenge you're looking for (or too much of a challenge), then go to the climbing gym to create your own routes.

Putting It All Together

As I write this I'm still buzzing from a first ascent I did yesterday. I spotted the line a week before and just couldn't get it out of my head—a dead horizontal 15-foot roof 13 feet above a flat rock shelf. Nice landing until the lip moves, then it was a full-bore wheelchair zone as the shelf dropped away another, hell, I don't know how many feet. I didn't check because a fall from the lip moves was out of the question. There were a couple V-double-digit sit-downs on the wall, but the proudest line was just waiting there, and I couldn't get it out of my head how the V14 climbers could have left this plum unclimbed.

It looked to be big moves through intriguing features—make a big layaway to a double-hand cow tongue match, bust out to an obvious slot of indeterminate depth, cut the feet and spin 180 degrees to stuff in double heel-toes in a porthole that went all the way through the roof, cut loose on the heel-toes, do a bat hang rest, go for the abdominizer crunch up to twist and grab the groove in the lip, match there, cut the feet loose, heel hook above my hands on the lip, and power through to a juicy orange-size knob. Stand up, wave to the throng of adoring fans, and be carried back on their shoulders to the car and libations. At least that's how I previsualized the sequence. Now let's walk through the process of how the FA really went down. Not only was it a super-kickass climb, but it involved a slew of different techniques and strategies to pull it off.

First, I'll say I was very intimidated by this line, which was a huge part of the attraction. The thought of climbing it seemed audacious, like being a geeky freshman and asking the head cheerleader to take you to the senior prom. I wasn't sure I'd be ready to try it this trip—I'd shown up in Rocklands very weak after double knee surgery and being hospitalized with pneumonia. I wasn't expecting much, but one day a switch seemed to flip on and things started really clicking with my bouldering the week prior to the send. I was feeling stronger and more comfortable contorting my body. I was climbing like I knew how to climb. This may seem peripheral to the first ascent process, but in reality being in the right frame of mind is very important. You'll be climbing into the unknown—no beta from prior ascensionists, no assigned rating, no knowledge that the moves will actually go—your head had better be screwed on straight.

Yves, a strong Swiss boulderer, wants to check out the latest V14 on this newly developed wall, so along with his girlfriend, Sandra, and *Boston Legal*'s AJ we hike out to the wall. Yves is quite strong and reasonably tall, hence a good choice to spot. And should he blow the spot, well, AJ is a lawyer. It had rained the day before and I was worried about the lip being slippery. So first thing I scramble around to the top of the wall to check things out. It's dry up there so I can safely downclimb to the edge.

The lip is only a few feet thick and there are a couple hairline fracture lines. I had carefully examined these hairline fractures from above and below on a previous recon and am certain they don't intersect or continue through the whole thickness of the lip. Still, I want to be sure the whole lip won't break away when I crank on it. Hanging on positive holds on the wall above, I stand on the lip and gradually put more and more weight on it. If it breaks, I should be able to catch myself on my handholds and scramble to safety. I'm wearing my helmet just in case. Now I've got full weight on the lip. I jump up and down a bit to test it to double or more of my body weight. Still good. I step over to the more suspect part of the lip by the hairline fracture, gradually weight it, then give it a hop as well. All good so far. I've already considered what might happen should the hairline fracture crack under my weight while climbing and create a loose block—the angles of the potential block and the way the block rests against the other side of the lip are in my favor—even if the fracture busted all the way through, the shape of the block would wedge it in the lip groove like a chockstone. Hmmm, that geology degree is paying off.

I brush off some dirt, loose twigs, and a smatter of lichen. Okay, good to go there. A bigger concern is the solidity of the knobs over the lip—should one snap it would be *hasta la vista* career. I grab a couple positive handholds and kick the knobs hard. Good thing I checked because one busts off. I clean the dirt along the fracture line where the knob came off. The other knobs pass the kick test. I downclimb a bit farther to where I can drop my leg through the crazy heel-toe porthole and sit securely on the lip. Now I can let go with my

hands, and I check every hold I might use for soundness with a rap of the knuckles. They all sound and feel solid. Oh crap, no excuses left to bail on this project. Time to go to the base.

At the base Yves, AJ, and I have a discussion about how to spot this problem and how to set the pads. It's agreed that once I start pulling the lip they can no longer safely spot me without risking a plunge over the edge themselves—I'll be on my own at that point. We talk over potential fall angles. I'm worried about a partial crack in the first big layback hold—I tell them which direction I'll fall if it snaps so they'll be ready. (I've already climbed up to this hold and fully weighted it with one hand, with my other hand on a good hold well to the left—if it failed this test my left handhold would swing me out of the way of the cantaloupe-size chunk. Helmet on again just in case. Even though the hold passed this test, I realized I'd be pulling outwards on it

I'm reaching out and giving the cow tongue a good rap with my knuckles. Sounds good, so it's time to commit my weight to it.

to do the problem, not just downward, and perhaps this different pull could snap it.) Next we discuss the cow tongue. The crazy-ass hold looks a lot like a cow tongue, but as I'll be grabbing the tip of the tongue then matching behind that, I'll be putting a lot of torque on the attachment point. Rocklands quartzitic sandstone is real stout stuff, but I'm checking in myself at 175 pounds. If the tongue snaps I'll be going headfirst straight down. My spotters are ready for that. After that my worries about hold snapping diminish—the slot looks sound and I've checked the porthole and lip holds from above. Next, the spotting discussion surrounds what to do should my feet get stuck in the heel-toe jams—I'll be in a bat hang and my spotters will have to push me straight upward so I can release my feet; when I do they'll need to grab me by the armpits and flip me upright so I land on my feet—a tricky move, so I'm glad we've talked over how to do it. As previously discussed, once I leave the security of the hole and grab the lip I'm on my own. Spotting prep done, I spit shine the soles and heels of my climbing shoes. Time to climb.

I cut loose for the 180-degree swing to the porthole. In the background you can see AJ moving the pad as planned before the attempt.

With my new sequence in hand, I manage to get my right leg into the porthole. With it crammed to the hilt, I'll be solid and Yves will move the pad to the right for the lip moves.

Up to the cantaloupe layback and reach out to the cow tongue. The layback feels solid with no flex, the end of the tongue is beautifully shaped to wrap my hand on, but first I give it a good rap to listen for hollowness. It sounds good so I take a deep breath, weight it, and bring my right hand over to match. I've near full weight on it and it's holding fast—this rock is crazy good.

I reach to the slot and it's not as deep as I'd hoped, but good enough. I cut my feet off the wall, swing 180 degrees, paste a toe on the ceiling, and stretch my left foot out to the porthole. Up to this point everything has gone just as planned, but now I realize the angle my foot naturally jams in is not in my favor—I've just got a heel hook, not the heel-toe cam I'd hoped for. Releasing the tongue seems dicey, so I pull my foot instead, hang straight down, and drop off. My heart is pounding and my whole body is abuzz with adrenaline. Holy crap that was scary, but now I know the holds are sound. While I take a break to de-pump and calm down, Yves makes short work of the V14. I ponder different foot sequences for the tunnel.

I give it another couple goes. My new foot cam sequences don't work as I'd hoped, but I find a way to release the cow tongue and grasp a hard-to-see fin near the slot. Armed with this new knowledge I de-pump and de-adrenalize, then give it another go. My new sequence works and I manage to pull my left heel out of the porthole and stuff my right foot in it. That feels better. I grab a handhold on the side of the porthole, pull up, and stuff my leg in as deep as I can until my knee is poking above the lip and my entire calf is wrapped around the lip groove. Damn, I could hang off this leg bar long enough to eat lunch.

What next? I'm hanging upside down looking at 3 feet of the weirdest climb I'd ever seen. Grabbing the base of the lip groove was no biggie, but getting out of the leg lock was going to be problematic. I'd have to make up some serious new techniques on the go. I'm not all that clear on what happened next—all I remember was that I was doing some wicked moves with my legs that would have an MMA champ tapping out in seconds. The good knobs always seemed just inches beyond my reach during this wrestling match. Eventually I ended up hanging off two slopers, throwing my right leg over the lip and laying it in the groove, then eventually working my foot back down the tunnel from above for another solid leg bar. By all rights I should have been scared out of my gourd, but I was very calm. Work it out. Climb the moves. Climb like you know how to climb. Falling never entered my mind until after the ascent, when I realized how risky hanging the slopers at the lip was. At the time though, the clock was ticking, so I opted for the easiest moves instead of hanging out longer to find a more secure sequence.

Grabbing the knobs was triumphant, gratifying, relieving, and just plain a happy moment. Walking down from the summit I felt one hundred pounds lighter—flying high on adrenaline and accomplishment.

One of the fun parts of first ascents is naming the problems. Somehow my best problems usually end up with my lamest names. This was no different. As this problem was on the same wall as *Vlad The Impaler,* and as I had drunk my fill on this one, I dubbed it *Verm The Imbiber.*

Going MMA on the lip moves. Left: Yves and AJ spot me as long as they can without risking being carried into the void with me. Right: Yves and AJ have stood down; now my only spotters are the pack of rabid baboons lurking in the dark pit below.

A Woman's Perspective

By Angie Payne

When I wrote the first edition of *Better Bouldering*, women at the boulders were a rare sight. Now women are well represented in the sport and nobody represents as strongly as Angie Payne, the three-time American Bouldering Series National Champion. For more on her story let's go straight to the source.

—JS

Hungry for More

I still remember the first 5.10a I climbed in the gym. It was the route that I had to complete before I could learn to lead climb. And if I could lead climb, then I could climb out the big roof, and then maybe I could climb a 5.11, and then and then and then . . . My eleven-year-old brain was overwhelmed by all of the possibilities. I tried the route over and over again, and the last move kept booting me off. When I finally succeeded, I wasn't thinking about the fact that I was a beginner or the fact that I was a girl in a male-dominated sport, and I most certainly wasn't thinking about contributing to the progression of climbing. At that moment I was just a psyched young girl who had sent her project, and I was hungry for more.

I started climbing just a few years after becoming the first girl to play in the local peewee football league. That career was short-lived, and when the team weight limit reached 120 pounds, I removed my 60-pound self from the league to avoid certain death. So when I discovered climbing, I was thrilled to find a sport where my light weight and small fingers were an advantage. Because I was small and lacking in strength, some moves were too long or powerful for me. Fortunately I was scrappy and stubborn, and I learned to work around such moves, building my ability to read the rock and decipher new sequences. Women are generally more flexible than men, possessing greater hip turnout and high-step ability. I used these assets to my advantage, finding and utilizing alternative body positions that my male peers could not match. With every climb I tried, I added a unique new move to my so-called "vocabulary of movement." Although I have gained muscle in the passing years, I still find this "vocabulary" to be the most valuable physical asset to my climbing. While women should by no means be afraid to be muscular and powerful, it is important to remember that the ability to employ creative

*Angie Payne on **North Face of Firepit Rock (V9)**, East Cochise Stronghold, Arizona.*
JOHN DICKEY

Angie Payne
JOHN DICKEY

body positions and some good old-fashioned technique can go a long way.

It is easy to focus on the physical aspect of climbing, especially as a beginner, when physical improvement is typically fast and obvious. It is harder to remember the less tangible mental component of the sport, which is arguably more important. I have found that refining my mental game allows me to better apply what physical strengths I have. There are countless women who are much stronger than I am, but I can still compete with them by using my mind to make up for what I lack physically. I have achieved my hardest goals by

choosing climbs that play to my strengths, keeping a positive attitude, eating well, and finding the proper balance between training and resting. So whether you have big shoulders, small fingers, superior flexibility, tall stature, small stature, strong-willed personality, calm demeanor, etc., etc., etc., engage your mind and use your body to your advantage.

Being a female in a male-dominated sport never intimidated me. After my football experience I never thought much about being the minority gender, and if anything it worked to my advantage during my early years in climbing. I climbed mostly with males in my youth, and I quickly learned

Lisa Rands was one of Angie Payne's inspirations. Lisa brings both power and technique to the table. Here she applies her jamming skills at Stanage Edge, United Kingdom.
WILLS YOUNG

Angie Payne on The Automator *(V13), Chaos Canyon, Rocky Mountain National Park, Colorado.*
JOHN DICKEY

that strength is contagious. The more time I spent climbing with people stronger than me, the faster I progressed. I was constantly pushed to try things that I otherwise wouldn't have, and I often surprised myself with my own strength or ability. At the same time, if a situation arose where I couldn't keep up with the guys, I would get frustrated and attribute my failure to the gender difference. This temptation to play the "gender card" is one of the ways that women hinder our progress in the sport. The best way that I have found to eliminate this temptation is to climb with other women. After all, if you can't keep up with the women around you, it's certainly not because of your gender. Being openly competitive with the same sex can be incredibly beneficial. Although society seems to discourage this behavior in women, I feel it's important to do everything you can to engage in healthy competition with the same sex. This can have a huge impact on your climbing—it has on mine.

Recently I found myself sitting at the base of *The Automator* (V13). It seemed that a lifetime had passed since I redpointed that pink 10a in the gym, but there I was again, falling at the end of my project. Fifteen years of climbing had brought me to this point, and I was fighting to bring back that beginner's mindset. I had let myself forget that I will always have something to learn, no matter how experienced I think I am. I forced myself to remember that I was pushing my limit, just like I did on the pink route, and that doing so required a willingness to learn and possibly fail. I prepared myself and pulled on. It took everything I had, but I struggled through the last few moves to the end. As I stood atop that boulder, I wasn't thinking about the fact that I was still part of the minority gender in climbing or about the small step I had made in the progression of women's bouldering. At that moment I was just a psyched woman who had sent her project.

And I'm still hungry for more.

More Bouldering Games

If you're not bouldering or training for bouldering, you're resting. If you didn't plan a rest day, then find a way to get out bouldering. Below are some suggestions when your project is out of condition or you're just looking for a change of pace.

Circuit Bouldering

France's Fontainebleau is the spiritual home of circuit bouldering, where circuits of twenty to over seventy problems of roughly the same grade were created, originally to mimic the demands of long alpine routes, but later simply to test boulderers. Circuit bouldering tests your skills unlike any other form of bouldering as each circuit contains a wide variety of problems—slabs, mantels, dynos, arêtes, roofs, etc. You move through each color-coded circuit in a mapped order, and you can't skip problems and still claim the circuit. It forces you to get on problems you would otherwise avoid. Say you consider yourself a V8 boulderer, but you suck at V5 mantels—welcome to the V3–V4 circuit. When you complete that you can move on. Few other areas have set up circuits like Fontainebleau, but it's easy to set up your own. Go to a bouldering area that has a guidebook and force yourself to do all the problems of a certain grade in the order they appear in the guide. Don't skip any. In the gym, knock off all the similar-graded problems across the wall from left to right, then go back right to left knocking off the next grade up. It will help you identify and work on your weaknesses, and give you a great workout to boot.

Bouldering in the Dark

Night sessions usually turn into some of the most fun. The sun goes down, conditions cool off, and the atmosphere often seems more relaxed. Just don't trip over the whiskey bottle.

This problem on the Roche aux Sabot, Fontainebleau, blue circuit was so fun it convinced me to go back and climb the entire forty-six-problem circuit.

Marsha Tucker on Heavenly Path (V1), Happy Boulders, Bishop, California, just one of fifty-eight problems she did to celebrate her fifty-eighth birthday.

Dave Yarwood tried Witness The Sickness *(V11) multiple times on his Rocklands road trip, but to no avail. The season was winding down and the days were getting warmer. He decided to give it one last go on his last evening there to get the cool nighttime temps. Voila!*

Bouldering in the Rain or Snow

One of my most memorable bouldering sessions was at the Sugarloaf Boulder in Banff, Alberta, Canada. Snow covered the boulder, and we needed multiple attempts just to scale the third-class walk-off. By the end of the session, we were climbing problems we couldn't step off the ground on an hour before. We learned how to freeze our gloves to slopers, create holds with packed snow, brush snow off without smearing it, and so forth. For all I know, the hardest problem we did might have been 5.2, but it sure as hell didn't matter. We were having a blast, and the glove-freezing trick came in handy for me years later on the Eiger. Bad conditions don't equate to bad bouldering. Use the opportunity to learn something new. Raining? Try bouldering with

A memorable day sending the kids' circuit at The Elephant sector of Fontainebleau in the rain. Hillary Haakenson celebrates upon topping out the thirty-second and final problem.

your socks on the outside of your shoes—this trick goes back to the days before rock shoes. Practice having fun.

Locals enjoying brisk sending conditions at Flock Hill in New Zealand. James Morris on Acapulca (V11).
DEREK THATCHER

Ice Bouldering

All the fun of rock bouldering with ten times the risk. Bouldering in crampons and dry-tooling with axes is great practice for mixed climbing. But just as it is foolhardy and dangerous to fall ice climbing, so it is equally foolhardy to fall bouldering with all those knives strapped to you. Toproping is probably a better choice. Nevertheless, some climbers do boulder on rock with their ice tools. If you do this, it is best to stay off established boulder problems and practice somewhere obscure. Crampons leave permanent scrape marks and dry-tooling puts incredibly concentrated stress on holds with high potential for breaking them. Bouldering on ice is good practice too, and doesn't suffer from these drawbacks. Beware of tools popping off holds or out of the ice—they have a habit of heading straight for your face. Pad or remove your adzes when not in use, and wear a helmet and eye protection.

Aid Bouldering

No, I'm not talking about power spots. Many a climber learned direct aid techniques on the boulders before heading for the big walls. As a result, ugly old pin scars festoon many boulders. This is the twenty-first century, however, and clean aid techniques have proved to be faster and less destructive than pitoning. Boulders can be a good place to learn hooking and nut craft. As with dry-tool bouldering, it is best to practice on an obscure boulder—stay off established free climbing problems. Hooks place tremendous strain on the holds that support them. A hold that supports a 200-pound boulderer by the fingertips of one hand may snap when hooked by a 110-pound climber. Like ice tools, when hooks or nuts pop they seem to ignore the laws of physics and head straight for your face. Wear a helmet and eye protection. Aid falls are sudden and often unexpected, making for rougher landings. Again, toproping is a good answer if you want to push your limits safely.

Temps top 100 on summer days in Moab, Utah—perfect conditions for "bivering" above the Colorado River, as Lisa Hathaway proves here.
LISA HATHAWAY COLLECTION

Buildering

Buildering is bouldering on buildings. Buildings often have far fewer surface flaws than boulders. This stark geometry forces precise technique. Buildering can be great practice and great fun. For some, it is an end unto itself. The liability is that it is sometimes illegal and in most U.S. locales viewed as suspicious in the post–9-11 days.

Bouldering by Instinct

Leave the guidebook at home one day. Go out to an area with no knowledge of grades and lines and see what you climb and how you climb it. Do you shy away from problems requiring you to face your weaknesses? Do you get on stuff you find attractive and send it because you try harder than on other problems you merely tick for the grades?

Canadian Sonny Trotter experiencing the incredible syenite bouldering on See Spot Run (V6), Hueco Tanks, Texas.
ERIC ODENTHAL

Road Trips

When I wrote the first edition of this book, road trips solely for bouldering were viewed with suspicion—now they're all the rage. Travel is a great way to expose yourself to different rock types, different techniques and approaches, different standards, and of course different cultures. If you haven't hit all the areas featured in this book, get cracking. Befriend the locals to get full value from your trip. Come back with an expanded skill set.

Some U.S. airlines charge $200 one-way baggage fees for bouldering pads. I have found, however, that if you fold a standard 3 x 4 foot pad over (no easy trick with stiffer pads) and crank them down with compression straps they configure to within most airlines maximum HxWxL stats. Check your airline's baggage regulations before you get to the airport and an expensive surprise. Some of the more popular destinations offer pad rentals.

When arriving at a new area, take some time to learn the rock characteristics—this could take a session or two. For instance, just because you've logged a lot of time on Colorado sandstone doesn't mean you understand southern Illinois sandstone. When looking back on my record of bouldering injuries, I realize half of them occurred on the first or second day at a new area—including both my bouldering concussions. Cockily misjudging rock friction is a shortcut to the emergency room.

Welcome My European Friend!

We're glad you've come to visit the United States. We have a lot of great bouldering for you to experience, and we're very proud of our bouldering areas. Right away you might notice that American areas are missing something found in Europe's boulder gardens. That's right, our boulders aren't surrounded by a galaxy of feces and used toilet paper. We'd like to keep it that way. So if you didn't plan ahead and last night's burrito supreme comes knocking, do everyone a favor and walk (or run) at least 100 meters from the boulders and dig a hole at least 25 cm deep to poop in. Don't throw your toilet paper in the hole—put it in a ziplock bag and pack it out. Bury that poop deep, and if possible roll a big rock over the grave. There are lots of dogs roaming our boulders and it seems some love to dig up and eat feces. These "chocodile hunters" also really love licking people in the face, especially those who don't speak English. We train them that way.

Notice something else missing? Yep, you can't find the popular problems by counting the cigarette butts at the base. "Pack it in, pack it out" is the motto over here. If you toss your butts or candy wrappers, don't be surprised to find them back in your pack later—with maybe a few other surprises.

And one last thing—no pof, no rosin, no pof, no rosin, no pof, *no pof!*

Thanks for helping keep our boulders clean, and have fun in America.

Physical Training

By Dave MacLeod

I spend so much time bouldering that I don't have time to train. Lucky me. However, I realize not everybody chooses to lead a nomadic lifestyle moving with the seasons to boulder full-time in prime conditions. Chances are if you're stuck with a mortgage, family, or God forbid, a full-time job, you don't get out to the boulders as frequently as you'd like and would benefit from some off-the-rock training. That's why I've brought in Dave MacLeod to write this training chapter. Dave's got degrees in exercise physiology and sports medicine, not to mention he sends 5.14 X trad climbs. How does he physically prepare for these climbs? He trains on V13s.

—JS

To be a good boulderer, you need good technique, tactics, and strength. In practice these three ingredients work together to make your total ability to throw at a boulder problem. In training, however, your efforts improving one ingredient can work directly against the others if you get things wrong. In this chapter, I'm going to take you through the fundamentals of training for bouldering.

If you observe a cohort of boulderers who've been at it for a decade or more, you'll see three common categories. First, there are those who have mastered the development of all three performance ingredients, without their training of one aspect sabotaging the other. These are the ones you tend to have heard of already because they have become the elite. Second, there are those who are super strong but somehow fail to translate it to V-double-digit climbing. The reason is usually that their strength training activities have eroded their technique, although it's not always obvious to the untrained eye. Third, there's the analog of the second category except that all the focus on pure strength training got them injured. They ended up with both poor technique and strength because they lost so much time to layoff. My goal in this chapter is to equip you with the basic training information to get and stay in the first category.

Dave MacLeod keeping fit on his V13 testpiece **Sanction,**
Dumbarton, Scotland.
CLAIRE MACLEOD

Harry Crews
flexing in Rocklands,
South Africa.

Outdoor Bouldering as Training

The first major constraint that will affect your approach to your training plan is whether you actually train at all! Some readers will be lucky enough to have access to essentially unlimited outdoor "real" bouldering year-round. Lucky you. It's a big advantage, so milk it well. The big advantage of climbing on the same terrain, even the same problems as your ultimate bouldering goals, is that it's much more efficient to train technique while simultaneously training strength. You are pulling hard on the holds because you really want to do the problem, so you are creating a good stimulus to get strong. Yet at the same time, you are constantly trying to find the easiest way to climb the moves, so you are learning new technical tricks. This is

why you sacrifice gains in technical climbing skill whenever the training is "synthetic," i.e., based on a climbing wall or basic strength exercise. The goal in strength training is to make an exercise as hard as possible and use as much force as possible so as to stimulate strength gains. In "real" climbing the goal is to get the strength stimulus by trying harder problems that force you to give 100 percent, but the basic idea of finding the easiest way to do the moves is never altered.

So what kind of extra training should the permanent outdoor climber do? Well, you might have guessed I'd say there is little need to add any extra training, even at a high level. The only problems you might face with always climbing outdoors is when the rock type is sharp or conditions are

Lisa Rands on **Crimp Ladder,** *Way Lake, Sierra East Side, California.*
WILLS YOUNG

poor—then skin damage limits the total volume of climbing and thus stunts gains in technique and strength. In this case some additional basic strength or climbing wall sessions will help to achieve enough volume. But there are other, more important, concerns too.

First, an important skill for any athlete is to be able to separate "training" and "performing" mode. The loosely defined nature of climbing without the formal competition of other sports compounds this problem for us. Permanent outdoor climbers have a tendency to always be in "performance" mode, i.e., arranging everything so you climb your best today, or tomorrow. Long-term thinking tends to go out of the window. What happens is that you get hung up on saving skin—saving energy and focusing only on particular problems you're desperate to send—at the expense of getting the volume and variety you need to progress. You might even sacrifice training intensity if you get too focused on staying fresh for attempts on a technical problem at your limit. Freshness is important when you really are close to an important send, but the rest of the time you need to work yourself hard to make incremental progress.

The answer to this problem is to find a good routine of switching between training and performing mode. Say you have a two-week trip to a bouldering area. The first week you could spend in training mode, doing lots of attempts on small

This crew punched a trail out here a couple days before and shoveled away the snow over the top moves of the Checkerboard to let the rock dry out. Now they've returned with perfect crisp sending conditions.

sections of projects, dialing the moves while physically working hard. Mix in enough other easier problems to keep the volume high. The second week, you take some good rest, lower the volume, and focus on better quality attempts and sending projects. Your goal is to finish your climbing sessions strong, but not exhausted, to save energy for the next day.

This switching between performance mode (where the "here and now" takes priority) and training mode (where your focus is on building for future performance) is basic periodization. The underlying principle is that of saving and spending; the currency here is training time. You save up by investing training time working hard on your weaknesses. During this time you sacrifice performance because you aren't always fully rested and you are spending time doing the elements of climbing you are worst at. All of this means your grade takes a hit! Then you "cash in" on that effort by resting more and "performing" on problems that play more to your strengths. How you balance your time throughout the year between training and performing mode is totally up to you. Olympic athletes are at one extreme of the balance, barely seen for four long years until they reappear and (hopefully) have their moment of glory. Climbers are so often at the other extreme, getting frustrated when they can't climb their best grade every session of the year.

Bizarrely, climbers often experience the benefits of training mode at the very time they are trying to perform—on trips to special climbing areas. If you don't get the chance to go on trips all that often, you might have noticed that you are at your fittest just after you come home from a trip. Climbers are so keen on the trip that they agonize over taking a rest day and instead climb far more than they would at home. Skin and muscles are trashed, and it's usually pure motivation that keeps them going. There's nothing wrong with this obviously! But what's going on is that on the trip some real training is happening, hence the progress you notice afterward.

The moral of the story is to train harder before the trip, then take lots of rest days during it, if you really want to squeeze an extra grade out.

The next concern for those permanently outdoors is to avoid entrenching your weaknesses. At one extreme, the disadvantages of basic strength work, such as campusing, is that the movements are not varied enough. However, if basic laddering strength really is your weakness, campusing forces you to attack it; there is no other way to campus other than to pull hard. But if you only climb outdoors, you are free to climb a given problem according to your existing strengths, i.e., in your personal movement style. For outdoor climbers, something to force you to attack your weaknesses head on is exactly what you need. You might not even notice your weaknesses unless you are sharing the attempts with friends of a similar strength level. Noticing what moves your friends can do that you can't will help you identify those weaknesses and plan your training accordingly. Maybe your body tension is poor. Then you should deliberately seek out problems that depend on it, or isolate this weakness by climbing indoors with tiny dinks for footholds.

Achieving a Good Training Effect from Outdoor Bouldering

- Only go into performing mode when you are going for a flash or a redpoint you know you are close to. At other times, boulder in training mode, keeping your work rate high during sessions. It may help some to view training as a performance itself—one to be done completely and with good form. Pay attention to the technique you use and compare it to friends'. Try to find the easiest way at all times, but isolate your weaknesses by targeting problems with specific types of moves you are rubbish at.
- Look out for sacrificed volume due to sore skin on sharp rock, or getting hung up on always being fresh.

- Vary the rock/problem type. Spend more time on the types you can't climb your normal grade on.
- Climbing in bad (warm) conditions is good training, but sometimes risky for injury. Be careful but milk this as training, then come back and send when a crisp day comes around.

Indoor Basic Strength Training for Bouldering

What about the rest of us, those who don't live next to Hueco Tanks or Fontainebleau and who make up the bulk of our yearly training on walls, boards, and other contraptions for hurting our fingers? Before discussing what to do on bouldering walls, etc., it's a good idea to understand some basic muscle and training physiology.

Dave MacLeod training on his home board.
CLAIRE MACLEOD

Muscles and Muscle Adaptation

The strength of muscles is dependent primarily on their cross-sectional area, but some other factors are important too: the makeup of different fiber types (slow and fast twitch), the recruitment of fibers during contraction, and the firing frequency and synchronicity. When you start to train a muscle, the earliest adaptation is in the neuromuscular coordination of muscle fiber firing (recruitment, firing frequency, and synchronicity). If you have a session on the fingerboard for the first time in ages, you can see this in action clearly. You get stronger hanging on even *during* the first session and make a significant jump in strength by the second session. Afterward, the progression slows markedly. Muscles have adapted to inhibit their full potential for firing as a protective measure. Maximum force is very dangerous for injury. So full muscle firing is usually only possible in emergency "fight or flight" situations under the influence of strong waves of adrenaline. However, repeatedly producing maximum voluntary force in training helps reduce this reflex inhibition. The muscle learns over time that it's okay to lower its guard a little and allow higher recruitment and firing rates. The long-term adaptation of muscle is the growth of new fibers (hypertrophy), and this is where the really substantial gains lie. Whereas recruitment improves in days and weeks, hypertrophy progresses over years, unless you are in your late teens with plenty of growth hormone floating about.

Because muscle growth, especially in our rather weedy upper body muscles, happens so slowly, it's important to keep reminding the body constantly, day in, day out for years. That's why it's impossible to shortcut strength gains (without cheating with steroids). If you try to build muscle by bouldering or campusing nonstop, the body simply cannot adapt fast enough and you get injured. So the first principle of strength training is to *take it slow and steady*—keep showing up, keep doing your moves month after month—and eventually you'll get strong. You can't speed it up by downing protein shakes (it's the ephedrine/caffeine in them that makes you feel great, not the protein), or anything else really. Aside from regularity of strength training stimuli, steadily over years, the only other thing you can do to increase the rate of strength gains is tweak your training to maximize the volume you can do without getting injured.

One big problem for boulderers in strength training is that strength to weight ratio is important for climbing. Low body fat percentage is seriously important for climbing well (in the presence of good technique). Low lean (muscle) mass is important too. Ideally we want to have not too much muscle, as it's really the forearm muscles that are the limiters for force production in climbing. Sure, you need to be able to deliver power from the whole body to make steep bouldery moves between spaced holds. But use of momentum in your technique plays an important part in development of this power during moves (power equals force times velocity). Too much muscle becomes counterproductive. There are some famous exceptions to this general rule who manage to climb well on big muscly bodies. They manage it by having genes that distributed a lot of their muscle bulk in their upper body. On the whole, more male climbers could do with being a little lighter than those who need bulking up. It's a different situation for female climbers, who quite often lack the upper body musculature to move between the holds. Where their male friends cannot hang the small holds because of heavy bodies, females can often hang on easily but struggle to make the reaches between holds. They need to target the juggy, powerful problems as much as possible. This is one of the rare cases when a little weight training might not be a bad idea as a supplement for a few months, just to get started. All that said, the common situation is for climbers to blame lack of strength when struggling on powerful moves, when it's lack of momentum use that's the real problem.

All this presents some knock-on nutritional considerations. It's not possible to put on muscle on a calorie deficient diet. So indefinitely sustaining an extreme weight loss program while trying to gain strength has very limited potential. Climbers for whom weight is a concern will probably do best by keeping a "training weight" that is manageable for most of the year and trimming down a couple of pounds while tapering down their training shortly before it's the sending time of year.

Bouldering Strength Principles

Progressive Overload

The fundamental principle underlying strength gains is that of "progressive overload." To make progress, the body must be served up a stimulus it's not constantly used to. The way to ask the muscles to get stronger is to make them pull as hard as you can. Sounds simple, but believe it or not a lot of climbers don't manage it. We are social beings, and all sorts of quirks of our psychology get in the way of delivering maximum activation of the muscles. In gyms, showing off is a major concern for a large proportion of climbers, even if they don't realize it themselves. And if not showing off, you might just be making sure you don't look bad. This happens in a few different ways. First, if you spend your climbing time thinking about how you look or compare to others, you cannot give your full focus to the climbing. In other words, you're simply distracted from the task at hand. Second, how you want to perceive yourself also influences the content of your training. Let's say you can't compete with the "beasts" on the steep board, but techy, balancy problems are your thing (girls, I'm talking to you!). Feeling good about how you climb is addictive, so you get drawn, subconsciously or otherwise, to spending more time on your favorite angle and less on the angle you really need for improvement. You're mistaking competing for training again. Competing (at what you know you're best at) is fun, but if you do it all the time there is no time left over for training, and hence progression.

Accommodation

Once you climb on any one board, angle, type of move, etc. for too long, your body gets used to it and stops improving. In sports science it's called the principle of "accommodation." Lots of climbers go to the gym and ask themselves, "which board should I train on?" The answer is: If you've been training on this board for a few weeks or months, it's now the wrong board. Pick the one you're least familiar with or worst at. That will be the right choice.

Specificity

"What you do in training, you become" is the simplest way of explaining the principle of specificity in training. If you always crimp, you'll always be weak on pockets. If you always avoid big powerful moves, you'll always struggle with them. If you always do lots of campusing, you'll climb everything like it's a campus board. Remember, your goal is to get really good at finding easy ways up hard bits of rock first, and to get strong fingers second. A great many boulderers assume they should concentrate on the secondary goal and the first will happen by itself. It won't. Here's how to make sure things work out well.

Training Strength on the Bouldering Wall

More than any other training tool, the bouldering wall is by far the most effective for achieving the goals of learning to climb well and getting strong in the process. The reason is that you are doing real moves, learning real technique. And although you should be on the hardest problems possible to maximize the stimulus for your body, the basic game of bouldering—finding the easiest way to do a move—is never altered.

Climbers tend to get hung up on whether they should be doing short sessions on superhard problems they can't yet complete, lots of mileage on easier problems they can flash or complete in a few

tries, or a mix of both. In my experience a mix of both works best for strength and technique gains. But the exact makeup of your session is almost always better guided by simply what motivates you on the day. If you're fired up to try one particular project all session—great. If you end up doing mileage on lots of problems, that's fine too. The only way you'll sacrifice gains is when you stick to one extreme for too long. Spending weeks of sessions always on problems where you can't string more than one move together sacrifices volume too much. But never trying moves that are right at or above your limit means you miss out on that explosive recruitment stimulus, not to mention the technical aspect that forces one to look in greater detail at every subtle movement within a climbing move. Just climbing what looks good at the gym or what you feel psyched for keeps motivation high, and that's always good for training gains.

When climbers worry excessively about the exact intensity of the problems they try, they are distracted from a much more important factor determining the gains they will get—the character and setting of the problems. The character of the problems at your local gym comes down to three crucial factors: the shape of the boards, the variety of holds used by the gym, and the setters who make the problems.

At first you might think, "There's nothing I can do to influence those factors." But you must! If the shape of the boards is limited, mix it up by climbing in different gyms, or alternatively, build a board yourself. To influence the holds used and the setting of the problems, you have a couple of options. First, you should get to know the person who sets and encourage them to use the types of holds they have been neglecting. Even if you like problems with wild athletic moves on big blobs, ask them to set at least a handful of problems in the opposite style, for the training benefit. You might also be able to persuade the gym manager to call in some well-known route setters on a regular or seasonal basis.

Got an extra ten grand burning a hole in your wallet? Then you too could build a sweet home wall like this one. Marco burns a hole in Kevin's head with the laser pointer during a game of add-on.

Lastly, you could become the setter yourself and get free reign on what types of problems get set. It's a real skill and not everyone is good at it. But it's actually quite a good exercise in technique learning because it forces you to visualize how moves fit together. Even if you don't get paid for the work, at the least you could earn yourself free gym membership and total control over the types of moves you'll be climbing on. The hardest part is actually setting problems you know you'll be terrible at, rather than playing to your strengths. If your gym has a board with no set problems and just holds everywhere, make sure you climb with enough different people so you aren't limited to your own style of setting or that of one or two friends.

Supplementary Strength Training

For climbers this means hangboarding, campus boarding, weight training, and various other basic strength exercises. Generally speaking, there are only two situations when it's necessary to use any of these and hence miss out on the vital technique training that real bouldering provides: First, if you are at a high level of climbing with many years of experience behind you and need a stronger stimulus to keep making strength gains. Obviously this applies to very few indeed. Second, when your available resources for training are limited enough that you're left with a particular strength weakness. In my opinion such basic, generic strength training tends to be overused in general by climbers. Sure, those that do it right do get a little stronger, but it's all too often at the expense of technique, and so their ultimate climbing ability stays the same or gets slightly worse.

How does this happen? Well, think about an elite level climber who is training for the World Cup. A full session including a long warm-up, hard problems, mileage problems, and some endurance work at the end might add up to 1,000 moves climbed. In a gym session he or she might do twenty sets of ladders on the campus board, or 100 moves. That's a 1:10 ratio. A much less experienced climber needs the technique training far more than a hardened competitor, and yet so many choose to spend their time and energy campusing. That climber is more likely to do only around 300 moves of real bouldering per session, but will still do the same amount of campusing, a 1:3 ratio. That's a huge difference in the makeup of the training. It's this overuse of basic strength training relative to the volume of real climbing done that results in poor technique, stagnation, and probably injury too.

The lesson here is to introduce or increase basic strength training in your schedule only in parallel to increased real climbing, never instead of it. Are you ready to do this? Probably not. But the majority of climbers would make better progress by getting on with real climbing and addressing the points in the previous section about the quality and variety of the diet of climbing moves.

It's different if you don't have a good gym or crag to go to, week in, week out. If you are starved of climbing due to where you live or work, then basic strength training is your only option. My advice is that when you do get the chance to climb, focus on volume—make sure you rack up as many moves as you can. But when you can't, just pulling hard on your fingers several times a week on whatever contraption you have access to is way better than nothing.

Hangboards

If used as a true supplement to real climbing, hangboards are great tools for improving raw finger strength, or specific grip types you are weak on. A general pattern for many climbers is to start off crimping a lot because it allows you to pull harder on holds as a beginner with weak fingers. But, unfortunately, the habit sticks until the reliance on it results almost inevitably in finger pulley injuries down the line. Even with injury it's really hard to break the habit of crimping everything once it's ingrained. You are just so weak on open-handed holds by comparison that it feels "wrong" to open-hand. The hangboard lets you escape this problem and attack head on the grip types you are weakest at. Take your newfound strength and work these grip types into your habitual climbing.

To gain strength you need to produce a near maximal force. The problem with hangboards is that most people can easily hang onto finger edges with two hands but find one hand is impossible. So it's hard to get the intensity correct. The aim generally is to achieve a hang of five to eight seconds that feels as hard as you can manage, i.e., you simply cannot hang on longer than this. To find the correct loading on the fingers, your two main choices are to use one hand and take body weight off with some sort of support, or to use two hands and add extra weight. Be inventive, and use what you can to tweak the difficulty so you really have to try hard to hang on for several seconds.

Design your sessions by doing several sets (three to five is good) per grip type, and work through each grip in turn. You should work through open-handed grips with three and four fingers, as well as crimped and two-finger pocket grips if you are at a high enough level to manage them. For a lot of climbers, using a full crimp grip with the thumb over the top is quite aggravating for the fingers and elbow joints. This depends to some degree on individual finger lengths. Maybe you'll have no problem with it, but often using a "half-crimp" with the

Jason Chinchen working the hangboard at Tai and Mary's home wall in Bishop, California. The hold on his head? Jason asked me to Photoshop in something to cover a thin spot.

middle knuckle (PIP joint) flexed but without using the thumb feels a lot more comfortable and safe.

Less is more when it comes to hangboarding. A session consisting of a ten-minute warm-up of progressively harder hangs and pull-ups, followed by sets of six-second hangs with one-minute rests in between can be completed in thirty to forty minutes. If you're doing it on the same day as bouldering, do the hangs first, while you are fresh. You'll get less training benefit from hangboarding in a fatigued state, not to mention the increased risk

of injury. If you have ample resources for regular climbing, then two to three sessions of hangboarding per week will be a good supplement for an intermediate level climber. If you can only climb once a week or less, you could build up to using your hangboard every day. But be careful. If you feel sluggish and full of aches and pains, don't be afraid to back off for a few weeks. Your body is trying to tell you that you're doing more hangboarding than it can handle.

Campus Boards

WARNING: **Campus boarding is the most injury-causing activity a climber can do. This is true both from sudden-onset injuries to fingers, elbows, or shoulders and from insidious injuries that build up over time. Sometimes, accumulated damage caused by using the campus board excessively will show up only after several months, and the symptoms of injury may show themselves only in your real climbing at first, causing you to miss the true cause of the injury.**

Campus boards? Dangerous, yes, but young males can't get enough of them. Logan Jauernigg won't let recent thumb surgery get in the way of some quick burns.

Taking the above into account, the same rules for hangboarding apply to campus boards—less is more. Trouble is, they are addictive. They are so simple and easy to measure. Yet overusing them is totally counterproductive. All the gains you make in strength you lose in climbing by forgetting how to use your feet. Unless, that is, you stick to the very high ratio of real climbing moves vs. campus moves I described above. This problem of campusing negatively affecting your technique is even more accentuated in relatively novice climbers. In the first several years of climbing, a novice climber's technical repertoire is still being formed. Campusing subconsciously teaches you to relax and forget about the lower body, while pulling as hard as you can with the fingers.

Campus boards are of use as an extra stimulus if you are already doing a stack of climbing *and* have expert level technique. Basic laddering should be more than sufficient. Start hanging on the bottom rung with both hands, snatch to a higher rung with one hand, and pull straight through to a higher finishing rung. Match hands and you're done—the basic campusing set. A good workout (following a thorough warm-up) is to do five to ten sets of a ladder you can't do every time (e.g., 1-4-7) followed by five to ten slightly easier mileage sets (e.g., 1-4-6 or the slightly harder 1-3-6). It's a good idea to use an open-handed four-finger grip on the campus board. Crimping while laddering on a campus board is the single quickest way to destroy your finger pulleys. Anyone considering the most dangerous exercise—plyometric double dynos—will only get enough benefit from it to justify the risk if they have a long history of hard training to build up the necessary injury resistance.

If you decide to add campusing as a training supplement, a few sessions (a few weeks at most) a few times a year is a good amount of work to do. Campusing week in, week out, year-round is a dead cert for injury.

Body Tension Exercises

Body tension is the ability to maintain force production through all your points of contact, especially your feet, in steep powerful climbing. Climbers often speak about it as a purely strength component, but it's not. It has both a technique and strength component. The technique part is interesting. We are hardwired to feel more in balance when we make ourselves more upright. Yet in overhanging climbing, we can maintain pressure on the footholds by pushing our hips inward and making ourselves more horizontal. When you're not used to it, it feels weird. It's a learned technique and one of the few technical skills in climbing that is rather counterintuitive. It's also very natural when grabbing a distant handhold "in extremis" to concentrate all of our mental energy on delivery of force to that hold. In the process we subconsciously

forget about the lower body and allow it to relax, just at the moment when the feet are most likely to cut loose. The ability to focus on both ends of your body at the same time as you hit the hold is another learned skill that takes tons of practice. That's why the best body tension training is just to do steep boulder problems with small, awkwardly placed footholds and quite big moves (but not dynos).

Climbers often supplement this with basic strength exercises like front levers. A much easier version is to allow your trunk to remain vertical and only pull up your legs. These are good fun if you like brutal exercises and great for impressing others at the gym. But a more effective exercise is to hang on two good holds on a steep wall and simply attempt to move your feet around on distant and sloping footholds. Working hard moves on a tensiony problem with poor footholds but

*The handholds aren't jugs and the footholds aren't winners either, so Paul Robinson utilizes substantial body tension to keep his feet from cutting loose on **Never Ending Story** (8b+), **Magic Wood**, Switzerland.*

Bouldering legend Jim Holloway busting a textbook front lever in the mid-1970s. In the Olympics you don't get credit for a front lever unless you can hold it perfectly for three seconds. Despite primitive training methods and a 6-foot 4-inch frame, Holloway could hold a front lever for half a minute while holding a relaxed conversation at the same time. Few, if any, boulderers possess such incredible lever strength today.

JIM HOLLOWAY COLLECTION

reasonable handholds will also do the same job. When it comes down to it, the climbers who have the most impressive body tension on the rock aren't the ones doing front levers all day, they're the ones doing steep, technical cave problems nonstop.

Antagonist Training and Other Injury Avoidance Techniques

Sustained training for powerful steep climbing appears to cause characteristic postural faults in climbers that may contribute to or cause upper body injuries. The classic climber's posture is an overdeveloped back, shoulders projecting forward, and upper arm bone turned inward (inwardly rotated). Repeated pulling down and in and inward rotation of the arm causes overdevelopment of the internal rotator muscles such as the latissimus dorsi and teres major. A corresponding weakness of the external rotators results in the scapula and upper arm bone (the humerus) being held in an unnatural position, which eventually causes a plethora of possible tendon, nerve, and muscle injuries in the arms and shoulders.

Stretching the muscles that tend to shorten

and training the "antagonist," or opposing muscles, offsets this problem. It's a tricky business though, because the list of potential muscular or postural imbalances is huge and varies massively depending on the individual and the training he or she does. If you pick the wrong exercises, at best you'll waste your time and at worst you'll contribute to injury development.

A varied diet of climbing is your first line of defense. Climbing on every angle and type of move or hold helps to work and stretch more of the muscles on both sides of the upper body joints. The next thing you can do is to look out for the classic signs of climber's posture. A "slouched" shoulder posture and hollow chest is common, with the pectoralis minor muscle becoming too short. The upper arm bone often becomes internally rotated. The olecranon bursa (the large bony lump on the point of your elbow) should point straight backward with your arms at rest. If it points a little out to the side, and the crease of your elbow points toward your body instead of straight ahead, your arm bone has become inwardly rotated. This is reported to contribute to development of the elbow tendonosis problems referred to as "golfer's" and "tennis" elbow. There are countless other signs and symptoms that are far too complicated for a nonexpert to either spot or design an appropriate response.

All this leaves you with two options: Ignore it and then wish you hadn't in x number of years, or go to the best physiotherapist you can find and have a full assessment of your upper body posture. If there are faults in your posture, and there probably will be, do the exercises the physio gives you religiously and keep going back to reassess until you've realigned your bent-over shoulders. If you truly cannot afford to sacrifice a few beers to save up for your appointment, then a few sets of press-ups, external rotator exercises, and stretches of the internal rotators and pectoralis minor done as part of your warm-up routine are a good basic preventative measure.

Endurance

Most of the time bouldering is an explosive discipline that is not heavily dependent on anaerobic or especially aerobic endurance. However, a significant proportion of boulder problems can take more than thirty seconds of sustained effort, and a few are more like routes, taking several minutes to climb. Any boulderer who neglects to train endurance on this type of problem will see a critical performance limitation on any sustained sequence of around twelve moves, maybe less. Problems of ten to twelve moves or less primarily utilize the body's short-term energy replenishment source, phosphocreatine. When you finish a problem of this length, you are likely to be breathing hard but not really pumped in the forearms, and you can produce a similar effort just a few minutes later. Problems of fifteen to thirty sustained moves are getting into the anaerobic endurance–dependent zone, where glucose is broken down in the muscle to provide energy at a very high rate, without using oxygen.

Things get even more complicated when we look at longer duration climbing of a couple of minutes or more, either sustained or involving shakeouts en route. Cave problems, highballs, and traverses can easily be this long and depend on both anaerobic and aerobic endurance capacity to succeed. When most people think of aerobic endurance, they consider the adaptations of the cardiovascular system (e.g., heart ventricle expansion). But endurance adaptation has both central cardiovascular and peripheral components. "Peripheral" in this sense basically means "within the muscle being trained." It is these peripheral components that are of interest to climbers. The puny muscles of our forearms cannot use enough oxygen in climbing to make the heart work hard enough to really stretch it, as happens in running or cycling. Instead, the limiting factors in peripheral aerobic capacity are the density of the capillary network inside the muscle that supplies the blood to sustain aerobic work and the levels of microscopic proteins that drive metabolism inside muscle cells.

*The author on the FA of **Hot Buttered Pump** (5.12-), Rocklands, South Africa. This boulder traverse starts out of sight at the left end of the wall, and at 60 meters long is twice the length of most sport pitches. Despite overhanging 10 to 15 degrees its entire length, there is no single move over 5.9, but few under 5.7; hence it's a race to the finish against the peripheral aerobic clock.*

The point of the physiological explanation is to say that climbers shouldn't worry about general cardiovascular training like running to help their climbing endurance. What we are after is forearms packed with glucose-burning enzymes that can run metabolism as fast as possible in the muscles, and a dense network of forearm capillaries to supply oxygen and remove metabolic waste.

Sport climbers must do large volumes of easier routes to gain the necessary endurance adaptations. For boulderers, aerobic adaptations are lowest on their training priority list, Some regular long routes or circuits of large numbers of relatively easy problems done back to back without rest is sufficient to maintain it.

Anaerobic training for boulderers is definitely important, and the method of choice for this is interval training. Interval training is basically doing a series of bouts of high-intensity climbing, with shorter rests than you would normally take if you were redpointing. The length of the intervals depends on what you want to train for, but thirty- to sixty-move intervals work well, with two- to four-minute rests in between. The critical thing to get right in interval training is the intensity. If the interval is near your limit, you simply won't be able to complete it enough times with short rests to get the gains. Let's say you are training to manage a thirty-move V6 and that will be a limit performance for you. A V4 or maybe even V3 of similar length and character would be ideal to train for it. You could train on the project itself by repeated links of long sections of it with much shorter rests than if you were having a serious attempt at it. But it's more likely you'll have to replicate it by climbing a sustained gym route or boulder circuit you've set yourself.

Anaerobic intervals are an extremely time efficient form of training. They are easy to fit into the rest of your training regimen, so there's really no excuse for boulderers to lack this aspect of fitness. Completing seven circuits of thirty moves with four-minute rests between circuits takes less than forty-five minutes. It's ideal to do this after your strength training, so you can easily fit it into the end of your gym session.

There are a few key aspects of anaerobic circuits to make sure you get right. First, don't be afraid to work yourself hard. You want to finish the session feeling like your arms are about to explode. Second, volume is important; to see decent gains you'll want to do at least three sessions of circuits a week. Elite level sport climbers will do more than five per week to make gains. Third, gains in anaerobic endurance develop fast. By the third week of circuits, you'll be able to do far more than in the first week. But this type of training cannot be sustained through the whole year. Boulderers shouldn't need to anyway. (More on scheduling this in your training year below.)

The most important aspect of anaerobic training routes/circuits to get right is the character of the climbing. Ideally the circuit should have no real crux, just a totally sustained sequence of moves with no places to stop and rest. If there is a hard crux, you'll end up falling there before you've had a chance to really push your anaerobic system. Being a good problem setter is really useful, so you can make up a circuit and change and evolve it as your fitness changes or if you realize it's not perfect. There is a great psychological benefit of anaerobic circuits too. You are getting yourself used to feeling

100 percent "maxed out" and battling through the next move. If you've trained at this effort level day in, day out in your circuits, you'll be battle hardened and able to keep a cool head and good focus in the most heated of "send" moments, when you really don't want to blow it.

Making a Schedule

"How much training should I do? How much rest? What's the best routine?" There are no definitive answers to any of these questions. Moreover, what is right for you depends completely on your individual background, level, and goals and countless other things. Below are some crucial points to help you make a schedule that keeps you improving.

Listen to your body. The patterns of its responses to the training you subject it to are the single best clue you'll ever get to make the right choices. Do what seems to work. If it stops working, something needs to change. If you tried everything and you're still on a plateau, the change wasn't drastic enough. This isn't easy, but everyone is in the same boat, constantly experimenting with new tweaks in their routine to stay on the ladder of improvement. If your body is in pain, it's telling you to back off. But if the pain is centered on one particular joint or muscle, it's more likely that a technique or training error is overstressing it and needs correcting.

The training stimulus can be improved by changing many different variables. Too often people go for increased intensity, but a change in volume, type of training, and variety could yield better results.

Three climbing sessions per week of training is a good rule of thumb for seeing improvement up to a reasonably advanced level. Strength gains are possible from very little stimulus so long as it's regular. But it's nearly impossible to gain technique without putting some decent hours in.

Strength gains require high forces to stimulate the muscle strongly, and you can't produce high

Alex Puccio on **Dead Serious** *(V10), Hueco Tanks, Texas.*
ANDY MANN

forces when you're wasted. If you've been bouldering for hours and your strength level is going
through the floor, you're no longer training, you're
just extending your recovery time. Go home, rest,
and come back tomorrow. Shorter, more frequent
sessions are nearly always better.

Strength gains after the initial rush happen really
slowly. So it's important to pull hard on holds year-
round to keep improving. If you have a break from
training, don't try to shortcut your catch-up with
more intense training than normal, such as campusing—you'll only get injured.

It takes a fraction of the volume of training to
maintain a given level than it does to increase it.
Use this to your advantage. It's impossible to keep
training full bore year-round. Take time out during
the year and do other important things in life like
work, holidays, study, partying, etc. Maintain your
level with just a little training. This will refresh your
body and then you can pick up where you left off.

Long-term plateau or burnout is often a complicated problem with more than one cause that's
extremely difficult to tease out. Big changes in most
or all aspects of your game are the answer. Usually they are the changes you hadn't thought of
or wouldn't consider because you are too close to
the canvas to see them or don't have the necessary
expertise. That's a good time to have a chat with a
really experienced coach.

*Hip turnout like a run-over frog: Cody Roth
warming up at the Planfontein sector, Rocklands, South Africa.*

Flexibility

Climbing isn't so much dependent on overall flexibility as it is merely dependent on a minimum
level of flexibility in a few key joints. The most
important of these is the ability to high step and
turn your hips out. Wide bridging is also important
from time to time. But the issue of flexibility in
climbing is not as simple as doing a few stretches
to improve the range of motion (ROM) in these
joints. Stretching for performance and stretching for
injury avoidance are two different things.

Stretching for Performance

Active flexibility is what is important, rather than
passive flexibility, especially for high steps. Passive
flexibility is the range of motion of a joint when it
is assisted by an external force, such as using your
own body mass in the splits, leaning against a wall,
or pulling your limb using your arms. In climbing we need active flexibility, which is the range of
motion of the joint when it is moved under its own
steam using the antagonist muscles of that limb. Try
high stepping at the climbing wall as high as you

Jesse Althaus using superior hip flexibility on **Ketron Classic, Happy Boulders, Bishop, California.**

can. Now use one hand to help pull your leg higher still. If it will go higher, then your active flexibility could be improved.

Some female climbers can put their male friends to shame when it comes to passive hip flexibility.

However, female climbers often lack the muscular strength to realize their full range of passive flexibility. Male climbers more often have the strength to move closer to the end range of the joint and hence don't seem to be limited as much as you might expect by poor passive range of motion. The solution? Stretch tight limbs to improve passive range of motion, but don't neglect to build the strength at those extreme joint angles (able to pull your leg into a high step without your bum sagging).

Don't mistake poor technique for lack of flexibility. Getting those crucial extra inches out of your high step comes down as much to technique as it does to flexibility. High steps require careful positioning of the lower foot to allow a twist of the trunk and arch of the back to turn the pelvis as much as possible. If you do this correctly, you can get lots more out of your current active range of motion. On overhanging terrain often the problem is that you don't maintain enough body tension to allow you to lift one leg in control without feeling like you're going to cut loose. Inhale, tension up, and focus on delivering lots of force through the stationary foot so you're stable and ready for the high step.

It's crucial to practice high step, wide bridging, and frogging moves regularly on the boulders or gym wall so you develop strength at the limit of your hip range of motion, and learn the technique to get the most out of that range. Time spent stretching to improve passive ROM without doing this as well is time wasted—you'll never realize any gains. Getting this practice can be a real problem if you set your own training problems. You'll subconsciously choose foothold arrangements that work within your current hip ROM and never actually train its limits.

It takes a lot of sustained stretching to make real progress, so be focused in your stretching routine. If your stretching program includes many muscles, it will take a lot of time. This is fine if you have time and enjoy stretching. Many people do. But if it's a chore for you, choose your tightest muscles and work on them. Most male climbers could prioritize a simple "sit and reach" hamstring stretch, an appropriate version of the splits, and frog stretches for hip turnout—and you're done.

Stretching for Injury Avoidance

Stretching during warm-up and for injury avoidance is a totally separate issue. Current consensus is that stretching is not actually necessary in warm-up. But in real life most climbers will want to stretch muscles that are stiff from previous training or recovering from tendon injury. The current evidence (which is far from thorough, just an indication) is that a warm-up stretching routine doesn't protect you from injury during the session. Body temperature, pace of the increase in activity, and types of moves being done count much more.

Stretching for injury avoidance might not be critical during warm-up, but it certainly is a huge issue in maintaining good posture. A large proportion of climbers develop significant postural faults around the shoulder that predispose them to shoulder, back, and elbow tendon pain after several years of climbing. There are many muscles that control the shoulder, and muscle length and strength imbalances have countless variations and intricacies. After experiencing elbow problems related to poor shoulder posture myself and studying the field for many years, I have settled on one simple recommendation for all climbers: Every year have a session with an expert physiotherapist to assess your shoulder posture, strength balance, and movement. Have the physiotherapist recommend appropriate stretches and exercises to keep everything well aligned. It is almost guaranteed to lengthen your career as a climber. Because the range of postural problems caused by climbing are so complex, there is no substitute for expert assessment and advice.

If your physiotherapist identifies a postural fault in your upper body (if he or she doesn't, lucky you!), you'll have to stick to your stretching regime with monastic zeal to correct it, or face the painful consequences in years to come. Sorry to sound gloomy, but every over thirty-year-old climber who has spent years battling shoulder impingement or elbow tendonosis will share my plea to the younger generation.

two concussions, stitches

permanent tinnitus in both ears from anti-inflammatory use

bad '80s haircut

tendon & ligament damage in four fingers, dislocated index finger

rotator cuff tears (both shoulders)

biceps tendon tear

tendinitis in both elbows

partial paralysis of left arm from botched elbow surgery

degenerative back pain, scarification

torn tendon

broken wrist

bilateral hip replacement

tendon & ligament damage in four more fingers

torn meniscus in both knees bilateral knee surgery, tendinitis behind both knees

bone-deep shin lacerations

avulsion fractures and ruptured ligaments, fractured heel

bunion city

broken seismoid

Injuries and Injury Prevention

By Nico Brown, PT

The Injured Reserve List and How to Stay Off It

No athletic activity is without risk, and everyone's risk is different. Boulderers have different tolerances for taking risks depending on climbing style and experience. But they also have different risks for injury because of variations in body type, age, connective tissue characteristics, and past medical history. Two basic characteristics of bouldering inherently increase the chances of injury. First, most boulderers do many more hard moves in a day than they would if they were roped climbing. Second, every bouldering fall is a ground fall.

The purpose of this chapter is to keep you having fun on the boulders and also provide some simple guidance when things go south—when you get hurt or overdo it and have to rehabilitate and heal. If you prefer to blow off this chapter or if you already have an injury, the bottom line is simple: *Consult a properly licensed health-care professional before beginning any rehabilitative or exercise routine.* Believe me. I boulder and I've hurt myself *and* I am a licensed sports physical therapist, but I consult my colleagues and get their advice when I'm injured. Most importantly, I do what I can to prevent injuries and I always give myself time to properly heal. That's the beta.

Be aware: Good boulderers have excellent body awareness, so be aware of your body and listen! Just

Check out this photo of me circa 1991. If you need advice on how to get injured, I'm your man. But as injuries have never served to advance my bouldering, I feel you'd be better served getting advice on how to avoid them. That's why Nico Brown is writing this chapter. He has a master's degree in physical therapy and heads the Edwards branch of Howard Head Sports Medicine, part of the Vail Valley Medical Clinic in Colorado, meaning he works on loads of patients from the prestigious Steadman-Hawkins Clinic, meaning he is the physical therapist to the stars. He's worked on my knees, other famous boulderers' ankles (patient privacy doesn't allow us to name these Big Names, but you've heard of them), and countless athletes from the NFL, MLB, NBA, and NHL. When he's not doing that, he's out cranking 5.13s at Rifle or hitting the local boulderfields.

because "Plastic Joe" can pull every day without rest doesn't mean you can. Everyone has different soft-tissue strengths/characteristics; therefore everyone has a different breaking point. Your awareness of your personal threshold for injury is what will keep you in the game progressing toward your individual bouldering goals.

This chapter gives pointers for taking care of common bouldering injuries. But remember—being proactive is always better than reactive! The boulderers who become the strongest are the ones who spend their time training and bouldering, not rehabbing injuries.

The key to bouldering at your limit without injury is a mixture of proper risk assessment and biomechanical efficiency. Biomechanical efficiency varies for each individual and depends on finding the correct length–tension ratio for your muscles, which means finding the balance between muscles that are long, weak, and floppy versus muscles that are short, tight, and overdeveloped.

The following will improve your biomechanical efficiency and help keep you off the injured reserve list:

- Developing and using good posture.
- Improving flexibility.
- Stretching and strengthening the stabilizing muscles of the core and shoulder.

Sounds great on paper, but how do we accomplish this in real life? Simple, work on your weaknesses. For instance, if your shoulders have given you issues in the past or you have trouble with shouldery moves, work on your shoulder stabilizer muscles. Same thing goes for posture. I would also recommend for any climber a consistent routine of basic stretches for the hip muscles and shoulder stabilizer exercises.

How Injuries Occur and Heal

Injuries occur when your tissues are stressed beyond a certain threshold. Remember Silly Putty? If you pull it fast, it breaks quickly—like screwing up on a highball problem and breaking your ankle. If it is stressed a little over time, it gets floppy and weak with micro-tears at the ends—this would be a bit like some elbow issues like tendonitis/tendonosis. When you're injured, your body reacts in a systematic fashion involving three stages. The time required for healing depends upon severity of injury, location of injury, associated signs like decreased range of motion (ROM) or strength, and associated complications due to the injury.

The first stage of healing is the acute or inflammatory phase, which can last forty-eight hours to seven days or more. Proper use of the PRICE method will help you limit this phase and get to the good stuff. The second phase of healing is the subacute or proliferation phase, where your body is sending cells to the site of injury to help begin the actual healing. This phase lasts ten days to six weeks. The final healing stage is the chronic or remodeling stage, which can last from six weeks to twelve months or more depending on the injury.

Injury Types

There are two main types of injuries: acute and chronic. An acute injury is one of rapid onset from a specific cause. For example, Verm snaps a topout hold, falls, and twists his ankle—ouch. A chronic injury is one of longer duration, typically involving repetitive motions or movements. For instance, Verm gets tendonosis of the vocal cords from repeatedly telling us how it was "back in the day when we didn't have those sissy pads." Both types of injuries are common due to the nature of bouldering.

Acute Injuries

Acute injuries are not so cute—a basic understanding of first aid and a healthy dose of common sense go a long way in serious situations at the boulderfield. It is highly recommended that you and your climbing partners take a basic first-aid class, or better yet, a Wilderness First Responder course.

Basic First-Aid Tips

- Use the PRICE method to decrease pain and inflammation during the first forty-eight to seventy-two hours after an injury. PRICE stands for protection (splinting/buddy taping, etc.), rest, ice (twenty minutes on, then no icing for at least thirty minutes to prevent frostbite; ice no more than two hours total per day), compression (Ace bandage), and elevation (above the level of the heart, the higher the better).
- Know who to call and where the nearest phone coverage might be for major emergencies.
- Carry a basic first-aid kit, and make sure the

Can you say "Adios, finger tendons"? Moves like this feet-free dyno off a shallow two-finger pocket put the boulderer at risk for a tendon pull. To minimize overloading the fingers, John Stackfleth uses the momentum from his foot push to accomplish the move, not a pull on his fingers. Further protecting his fingers is his use of an open-hand grip. Nevertheless, after snagging the target hold, the fingers in the pocket could get overloaded trying to control the lower body swing—a better option would be to find at least one higher foothold to dyno from so the foot would remain on the wall to prevent a body swing.

contents are up-to-date and you know how to use them.

- Bring a spotter, or at least let someone know where you are going bouldering.
- Stay calm.

Chronic Injuries

Chronic injuries are the most annoying. The best treatment is prevention, but you just had to try that problem a few more times . . . Now you're in pain and can't even climb your warm-ups. Sucks, but it is what it is—time to fix it.

Tips for Chronic Injuries

- Give it a rest—don't return to climbing until resting and moving pain has ceased.
- Brace/tape to support healing tissues—for some wrist issues, night bracing has really worked to help those tissues catch some zzz's.
- Be patient and give the tissues adequate time to heal—the longer you have had an injury, the longer it will take to heal.
- Ice only when inflammation is present—no more than twenty minutes at a time to avoid skin irritation. Take off twenty to thirty minutes between sessions and don't exceed two hours total ice time per day.
- Keep yourself sane—for shoulder issues try one-handed problems, for ankle issues try one-footed problems, for head issues . . . talk to one of the other kinds of therapists.
- Be deliberate about your return to bouldering. Get a calendar, set a schedule, and stick to it! Being psyched is one thing, but being foolish is another—stick to your schedule.
- Strengthen closer to the core—many chronic wrist and elbow issues could be much improved with a regime of rotator cuff and abdominal stabilization exercises while resting the injured area. A strong foundation makes for a strong building.
- Get professional help. Find someone who understands climbing and with whom you can

PRICE

- **P**rotection
- **R**est
- **I**ce
- **C**ompression
- **E**levation

Why You Want to Avoid the Knife

The following list contains typical rehabilitation times for common surgeries before a full return to climbing:

- Shoulder—six to eighteen months
- Knee—one to twelve months
- Ankle—four to twelve months
- Finger—two to eight months
- Wrist—two to twelve months
- Spine—six to eighteen months
- Elbow—four to twelve months

Time frames will vary based on the individual and the specific surgery received.

connect. Consider surgery only after a course of conservative treatment has failed or would be ridiculous to even consider (e.g., a severely broken bone).

Ankles

Since all falls in bouldering are ground falls, the ankles take a beating. Crash pad technology has improved, but certainly not perfected, our drop zones. Good spotting practices also increase safety.

The dreaded "edge hit" is a boulderer's nightmare. Here, Yves Hangi has come up just short on a monstrous huck. Now he's landing with his foot on the seam between pads. Yves escaped an ankle sprain only because his momentum carried him straight backward onto his ass. Had there been a sideways component to his fall, the result would likely have been a sprained ankle. With a stack of pads like this, the top pad should be the softest (less ankle-rolling edge-strike action) and positioned to cover the seam between the lower pads.

Nevertheless, bad falls happen, and when they do the ankle is a common victim.

If you can't walk it off and the ankle swells, it is highly recommended to get an X-ray to rule out a fracture. Ankle sprains, especially lateral ankle sprains, are the most common type of ankle injury to plague the boulderer. Chronic ankle sprains can lead to ankle ligamentous instability; therefore it is better to take proper care of the issue the first time.

For acute or recent ankle sprains, always begin with the PRICE method. Crutches or a cane may be needed during the protection phase. As soon as possible, begin to work on regaining ROM by writing ABCs with your foot. These should be pain-free, as pushing into pain will only increase swelling and decrease ROM. When pain, swelling, ROM, and walking have returned to normal, it is time to begin strength and balance work. A full return to bouldering (and falling) might not be wise, as the ligaments are still healing and a big fall may lead to a longer recovery. A gradual return to bouldering over the next six weeks is a smart approach—you could even venture over to the roped world while your ankle is mending.

Chronic ankle instability is common if you have sprained your ankle many times, because the ligaments have been stretched beyond their functional range. We cannot tighten the ligaments without surgery, so you have to work on strength and balance if you are to avoid the operating room.

Exercises to Improve Strength and Balance in Ankles

Writing the ABCs with each foot is a good way to build ankle strength. Better yet, do this standing on one foot. If you don't dig the alphabet, floss your teeth while standing on one foot, then brush them while standing on the other. Too easy? Then try it with your eyes closed. Also good is playing catch with a soccer ball or basketball while standing on one foot until your leg muscles burn.

Fingers

Strong fingers are key for hard bouldering. Finger injuries are the most common of rock climbing injuries, and the most common injury to fingers are pulley injuries—specifically the A2 and sometimes the A4 pulleys.

The pulley is a nice little piece of gristle that keeps the tendon close to the bone. It is so important because it acts as a fulcrum for your tendon, allowing your fingers to hold that nasty little crimper. Sometimes those nasty little crimpers bite back with a loud pop—if you hear the "pop," end your session and start icing.

Acute pulley injuries vary in severity but often involve the dreaded pop, followed by a feeling of instability in the finger, pain that increases with bending, and swelling. Basic treatment consists of two phases:

Ice, rest, and protect the finger until full, pain-free ROM is achieved. During this time it is highly recommended that you work on shoulder and core stabilizer muscles. This phase can last anywhere from one to eight weeks, depending on severity of injury.

Once full, pain-free ROM is achieved, begin work with a very light hand strengthener—such as a squeeze ring, putty, or ball—for both flexors and extensors, then begin a *gentle* return to climbing using a pulley ring or pulley taping techniques so that your climbing progression is pain-free. A slow, progressive increase in climbing difficulty coupled with a slow, progressive decrease in the support level from the ring and taping is recommended until you

The A2 and A4 pulleys marked. The A2 ring finger pulley is the most commonly injured. Note how the fingers are curling into a protective open-hand grip on the brew.

Extreme crimping is a recipe to pop pulleys. Here Chad Foti uses a toe cam to move his hips close to the overhanging wall and reduce the weight borne on the crimper. **Pen Dragon (V11), Rocklands, South Africa.**

A pulley ring is a little plastic splint used to support and protect an injured finger pulley.

are able to fully climb without tape. Also, do not crimp in the beginning! Start with the open-hand position and gently work into crimping, as crimping adds much more force and you risk reinjuring your finger. This phase can last from two to twelve weeks.

Healing takes time. If you rush phase two, you will cause further damage and have to return to phase one. You might even need surgery for your chronically injured finger. When in doubt, see a specialist that understands climbing.

"Can't I just tape the pulley back on?" Well . . . no. However, I do think that taping can help support a strained pulley and give a friendly reminder during your return to full climbing rehabilitation. Alternatively, a pulley ring can be used to help support the pulley as you return to functional activity.

I do not recommend taping a healthy finger to prevent injury. Your body adapts to the stress put upon it; therefore, decreasing the stress on the pulley with taping will cause that pulley to have less overall structural support than if no tape was used in the first place. Chronic finger injuries, however, may require consistent taping. Listen to your body and do what feels best for you and your digits.

Wrists

Wrist sprains after bouldering falls happen—use the PRICE method initially. An X-ray is recommended to rule out fractures because certain bones in the wrist get very poor blood flow and will not heal properly if ignored. In the absence of a fracture,

Tom Helvie on a low V9 traverse problem at The Buttermilks, California. You can see this move is putting a lot of torque on his right wrist, putting it at risk for a TFCC injury.

gently increase ROM. Once ROM is full, you can resume climbing.

Boulder problems with lots of underclings and slopers rule! They can also rule your wrist—especially a little disc on the pinky side of your wrist called the TFCC (triangular fibrocartilage complex). If it clinks, pops, and is painful on the pinky side of your wrist, then this is likely your issue.

Using a splint at night to allow the tissues to get some much needed rest can really help symptoms. Don't wait until symptoms are severe, as chronic TFCC issues are difficult to treat without surgery. When ROM is pain-free and full, resume climbing, easing into the types of movements that pissed it off in the first place.

Elbows

Oh the dreaded 'bows . . . an ounce of prevention is worth . . . well, it's worth your season—I will let you put a price on that! Epicondylitis, tendonitis, tenosynovitis, angiofibroblastic tendonosis, etc.—it all means the same thing—pain, swelling, tissue damage, and not climbing. The term "tendonitis" is really a bit of a misnomer—tendonosis is a more correct term given the micro-trauma at the origin of the forearm muscles.

Nevertheless, this is an overuse injury—which means your workload was too much for your body to handle. There are varying degrees of severity. Elbow overuse injuries strike in two places—medial and lateral. Medial refers to the inner part of your elbow and lateral refers to the outer part of your elbow. Medial is most common because those muscles pull your fingers and wrist toward your palm. Lateral can happen with loads of crack climbing and also crimping with the wrist in an extended position combined with poor proximal strength of shoulder and core stabilizers.

Symptoms of tightness and mild pain after climbing are common warning signs of bad things to come and should be heeded. If you do not alter your training/climbing, these symptoms will get worse. Recurrent micro-trauma at the origin of the forearm muscles causes inflammation. Inflamed tissue becomes even more inflamed if the stress, in this case climbing, continues.

Signs that things are getting worse are increased pain, pain that resolves with warm-up but returns later in the session, and pain with activities of daily living or nonclimbing-related activity.

Prevention is the key to long-term success and happiness. Remember that everyone has different soft-tissue strengths/characteristics and therefore everyone has a different threshold for injury or breaking point.

Okay, you got cocky and now your elbow hurts . . . don't be dumb! Follow these guidelines:

- Take some time off climbing—your body needs time to heal. Give it that time (or do one-hand slab problems with the good arm and work on your footwork).

Cross-friction massage of elbow.

- Cross-friction the tissue 0.5 to 2 inches from the elbow in the direction of the wrist five to ten minutes twice daily to decrease scar/fibrotic tissue and promote blood flow for healing. This should not be excruciating! Begin with gentle resistance and increase gradually.
- Easy, pain-free stretching—try to warm muscles prior to stretching using a heat pad or gentle massage. Hold stretches for thirty seconds each, completing multiple reps throughout the day.
- Gentle, progressive strengthening. Begin with shoulder and core stabilization exercises until resting pain is minimal. Then begin pain-tolerable forearm exercises—start with eccentric

A Note on Vitamin I

Ibuprofen is a nonsteroidal anti-inflammatory drug, or NSAID, that many boulderers pop like candy. The over-the-counter variety is indicated for arthritis and as a painkiller when inflammation is present. The maximum daily dosage is 1,200 mg. I advise caution with prolonged use due to various adverse effects including gastrointestinal and liver issues. Moreover, taking ibuprofen, which is a painkiller, can mask or dull injury symptoms and therefore lure you into a false sense of security that could increase risk of further injury.

Kinesiotape job for elbow tendonosis on Robyn Erbesfield-Raboutou's four-time World Cup champion forearm.

(lowering) exercises to minimize load on tendons and muscle shortening.

- Ice for ten minutes after exercise or feeling any sort of tweak. Do this a minimum of twice daily, but no more than two hours total per day maximum.
- Symptoms should be minimal during warm-up and resolved after warm-up, prior to a gradual return to full crushing.

I am not a big fan of the large compressive elbow braces for climbing . . . but some people love them—go with what works for you. I have found kinesiotape to be useful for supporting muscles during the return to the climbing phase. It is fairly easy to use and apply—follow the directions and don't

put it on too tight. Use bracing and taping to return to climbing, then slowly decrease usage.

A note on fractures and prolonged immobilization: After the doctor removes the cast, remember to focus on range of motion prior to strength. An elbow that cannot fully extend will make every reach a lot farther and may cause long-term problems.

Elbow Exercises

The best way to prevent elbow problems is to do stabilization exercises for the shoulder (see below) and normal and reverse eccentric wrist curls. With eccentric curls you use your free hand to help raise the weight, then slowly lower the weight with your exercising arm.

Shoulders

Strong shoulders are good bouldering shoulders. Strong shoulders have balance between the large mover muscles (lats, biceps, deltoids) and the smaller stabilizer muscles of your rotator cuff. The rotator cuff consists of four separate muscles that act together to maintain the dynamic stability of the ball of the arm bone in the shoulder blade socket during movement.

Another very important factor when considering the shoulder is the role of the shoulder blade (scapula). The scapula is considered the foundation of the shoulder. Bouldering without a good foundation will put a lot more stress on the shoulder and significantly increase the risk of shoulder injury.

A simple way to tell if you might have a "foundation" issue with your shoulder is to have someone watch the way it moves when you raise your arm as if to grab a hold. If healthy, your shoulder blade should move as well, but not shoot out to the side. If the scapula "wings" or shoots outward away from the midline, then this indicates a possible crack in your foundation—better add some scapular stabilization exercises to your daily routine.

The Hulk *is one of the most coveted V6 ticks in the Bishop area, but you'd better have some strong-ass shoulders if you want to hang the dynamic cross-through to "the boss" without endangering the front of your shoulder capsule. Ben Connor demonstrates.*

A big, poorly controlled cross-through or fall on the outstretched hand can cause excessive stress to the front of the shoulder capsule. If this stress is too great your shoulder will dislocate. It's cool if the shoulder relocates (pops back in) on its own, but *do not force it.* I know you saw *Lethal Weapon* and all, but don't do it! You can fracture the front of the socket, which will make your injury much, much worse and seriously postpone your return to the boulderfield.

If you have ongoing pain and weakness in the shoulder that is worse with overhead motion, and you cannot sleep on that shoulder, then you might have a rotator cuff injury. These injuries vary in severity, and you would be well served to seek professional advice for your particular injury. Rotator cuff tendonitis and partial tears do quite well with good conservative treatment. Full-thickness tears will require surgical intervention and significant physical therapy to return to climbing.

This is definitely a time when prevention and maintenance pays off big time! Improving your shoulder stabilizers will also decrease the level of stress upon the rest of the arm. Therefore, with any chronic elbow, wrist, or hand injury it would be smart to spend some time on the shoulder.

Shoulder Exercises

The following shoulder exercises are recommended: external rotation for the rotator cuff and prone horizontal abduction progression and prone horizontal extension progression for the scapular stabilizers.

External Rotation

Dave Bainbridge doing an external rotation exercise for the rotator cuff. It's important to position the elbow slightly behind the rib cage (slip a pillow or rolled-up sweater between your ribs and arm for proper alignment). Keep the elbow in that position throughout the movement—imagine a spit running through your elbow to your shoulder and your upper arm rotating back and forth around the spit. Now do enough reps until you feel the burn; it only takes a weight of about three to five pounds (a rock works fine) to really work the shoulder. Raise and lower the rock about a foot—a greater range of motion will not increase results. This exercise can also be done with a sport cord (aka Theraband) while standing—just don't forget the towel for shoulder positioning. Dave's got Shiva inked on his delt, so that's four extra shoulders to work out—better bust out an extra set.

Prone Horizontal Abduction Progression

For the prone horizontal abduction progression, lie prone on a picnic table, Swiss ball, or other support that allows your straightened arm to hang all the way down. With the arm hanging down, raise the elbow up to the side with the forearm dangling until the elbow is even with the shoulder. Next, extend the forearm out to the side to shoulder height with the palm facing down. Finish it off by rotating the hand and giving the thumbs-up. Each day, knock out two to three sets of ten to fifteen reps. You can add weight slowly to increase the burn.

Prone Horizontal Extension Progression

For the prone horizontal extension, use the same prone position. Letting the forearm dangle limp, raise the elbow backward along your side until at hip height. Next, extend the forearm to hip height with the thumb pointing to the ground. Finish by rotating the thumb out to the side. Again, do two to three sets of ten to fifteen reps each day; add weight as desired to feel the burn.

Hips and Knees

Hip and knee issues are less common but do happen. Hip instability and pain can occur with multiple falls. Knee strain from deep drop knees and high hand-foot matches can also happen. Maintaining strength, balance, and flexibility in your legs is the best medicine, as well as avoiding situations that "just feel wrong."

John Stackfleth working an extreme drop knee on Gleaner (V6), Happy Boulders, Bishop, California. Deep drop knees like this can cause meniscus tears.

Core Stabilizers and Spine

Are you hard-core? Well, even though an awesome six-pack might get you a date, it won't get you more core stability. What? Blasphemy! No, it's true: The six-pack abs (rectus abdominus for the anatomy dorks out there) are not actual core stabilizers! The transverse abdominus and the multifidus muscles are the true core stabilizers, whereas your six-pack muscles are primarily mover muscles that allow your trunk to flex. Maintaining muscular balance between the movers of the body (e.g., the rotator cuff versus deltoids and biceps) and the stabilizers will help improve your climbing. Ignore them and risk having a pity-party at the doctor's office.

Eric Daniels has the typical climber's posture. Note the shoulders are slumped and rolling forward. This indicates the presence of muscle imbalance: Specifically the pecs and internal rotators of the shoulder are too tight or overdeveloped. This situation significantly increases risk of injury. Postural stretching for the pecs and thoracic spine coupled with shoulder stabilization exercises are the cure for climber's posture.

Bouldering has its share of back and neck injuries. These injuries can range from a minor back strain, to a pinched nerve, all the way to paralysis. It is important to get any spinal injury with nerve symptoms checked out by an expert. Symptoms of a possible nerve injury are abnormal sensations like numbness and tingling in your arms or legs.

Since we are talking about the spine, it seems wise to mention the head. Head injuries (and not just ego injuries) can happen while bouldering. Like all injuries the severity of head injuries varies, but the latest research indicates even mild injuries have the possibility to cause significant disability. Use good spotting techniques, common sense, and a helmet to help protect your melon.

Your posture, or lack thereof, is an indicator of possible muscle imbalance and core stability deficits. Don't be a knuckle-dragging fool! Stand up straight—it will help your reach too.

Here are some postural stretches for you:

This roller stretch helps loosen the thoracic spine. Align the roller perpendicular to your spine, then reverse crunch to wrap your back around the roller. Concentrate on pushing your shoulders down toward the ground to create the desired stretch (use your hands interlaced behind your neck to keep your head up and chin tucked—don't bend your neck backward). Do five reverse curls in one position, then roll the foam roller down your back a couple inches and repeat. Work from the base of the shoulder blades down to the small of your back.

Stretching the pectorals is as simple as putting your hand against a boulder or wall and rotating your torso until you feel the stretch in your chest. Hold the stretch for thirty seconds. Stretch each shoulder several times a day. The cigarette? Not recommended, even if you're a Euro Stud. If you're a smoker you need to be doubly careful about maintaining shoulder strength and stability because many orthopedic surgeons refuse to do shoulder reconstruction surgery on smokers. Nicotine-ravaged tissue frequently fails to heal.

Rehab doesn't get any easier than this, as climbing coach Robyn Erbesfield-Raboutou shows. Acquire a 6-inch-diameter, 3-foot-long foam roller from your PT or medical supply outlet. Align the roller parallel to your spine and simply lie down on it for five minutes, letting your shoulders relax and droop down toward the ground. You can add to this stretch by doing "snow angels" in this position or bringing the arms parallel with the spine and/or doing karate chop arm swings.

Conclusion

Bouldering is about having fun, and it's not fun to be hurt. Get a tune-up when your body's check engine light comes on and stick to the maintenance plan.

Remember that muscular power alone is not enough to maximize your climbing performance and ability. Every muscle has its role. When your muscles become unbalanced, your performance will suffer and your likelihood for injury increases dramatically. Your stabilizer muscles are crucial for maintaining efficiency and preventing injury—so use a combination of the exercises in this chapter that fits your needs best. If you only have ten minutes a day to devote to improving your bouldering through preventative measures, I recommend doing the foam roller stretches, as well as the rotator cuff external rotation exercises and the scapular stabilizer exercises. Doing these exercises regularly will help prevent you from developing climber's posture, thereby keeping your joints and muscles aligned for maximum biomechanical efficiency.

When in doubt about a bouldering injury, get professional treatment. I use a variety of techniques to help people, including deep tissue, joint mobilization, trigger point dry-needling, ultrasound, taping techniques, neuromuscular reeducation, stretching, strengthening, etc. Most health-care providers think rock climbing and bouldering are the same as hiking . . . so it's worthwhile to find a health-care provider who understands climbing.

Sources

Dutton 2004; "Current concepts of Orthopaedic Physical Therapy," 2006; "Hand Injuries in Rock Climbers," Kubiak et al., 2006; Climbinginjuries. com, Aimee and Kyle Roseborrough, 2009; "A2 and A4 Flexor Pulley Biomechanical Analysis," Mallo et al., 2007; Brown AW, Elovic EP, Kothari S, Flanagan SR, Kwasnica C (March 2008). "Congenital and acquired brain injury. 1. Epidemiology, pathophysiology, prognostication, innovative treatments, and prevention." *Archives of Physical Medicine and Rehabilitation* 89 (3 Supplement 1): S3 8. doi:10.1016/j.apmr.2007.12.001. PMID 18295647.

Jason Kehl on first ascent of To Die For (V5), Hueco Tanks, TX.
ANDY MANN

Taking It to the Next Level

Bouldering careers are filled with peaks and dips and seemingly endless plateaus. How best to keep improving? By attacking your weaknesses, not training your strengths. First, realize that time spent training your strengths will pay only small dividends—you're already far enough along the effort/reward curve that more effort only results in tiny rewards. Instead, spend that time addressing and working on your weaknesses. Does your footwork suck? Are you paralyzed at the thought of falling? Are you toting an extra twenty pounds? Can you only do half a pull-up? The tricky part is coming up with an honest assessment of your weaknesses. Few of us can be totally objective about our climbing—time to lean on a blunt experienced friend or professional coach to tell you where you're lacking or slacking.

Charlie Barrett on **Spectre** *(V13), Lydia Boulders, Bishop, California.*
WILLS YOUNG

Expanding Your Comfort Zone

Time to revisit the comfort zone paradigm. It's scary to try new types of problems that expose your weaknesses. Way more comfy to just poke about on the stuff you excel at. You might feel that jumping on slabby boulders will cost you your hard-won strength on thuggy problems. In reality it takes only minor effort to maintain strength, much more to increase it. Toss in a few thuggy problems if you're worried about strength loss, then spend the bulk of your time attacking a weakness.

Seek out variety. Try a new area with a different rock type. Differing rock types are climbed with drastically different styles, even on problems that may appear of similar angle and hold size. If you're stuck in the city, try a different gym with different route setters and hold sets. Better yet, call in sick with boulder fever and get outdoors—Mother Nature is the ultimate route setter—she has an endless hold set, and unlike gym route setters she doesn't design her walls to be climbed. Indoor routes are molded to fit the climber. Outdoors the climber must mold his or her body and technique

Adge Last palming a gritstone arête at Robin Hood's Stride, United Kingdom. As a rock type, gritstone appears fairly simple. Most grit is not overly steep and the friction can be top-notch, but grit still demands loads of body tension and precision. Grit imparts a new level of body awareness—a shift of the hips an inch one way or the other can be the difference between sending or peeling off.

In winter, boulderers from around the world congregate at this abandoned gravel pit. The Pit is probably the least scenic campground on the Sierra East Side (no really, that's how awesome the East Side is)—you should log some time there.

to fit the route—your technique will feel like you just punched in the turboboost.

Climb outdoors early in your career. Gym climbing is a great way to get strong fast. Climbers who start out physically strong delight in muscling their way up problems. Physically weaker climbers can't do this; hence to get up the same problems they develop good footwork and technique. Gyms are lousy places to learn footwork—the footholds are relatively large, they nearly all protrude, and they're marked out for you to boot. If you stay too long in a gym before bouldering outdoors, you will receive a rude welcome. Throughout your career, the difference between success and failure on

your projects nearly always comes down to nailing every move just right. You can't do that with lazy footwork.

Climb with new partners. Bouldering is a great opportunity to climb with those better than you or with radically different styles and/or strengths—learn from them. Often problems of varying difficulty will be in close proximity, allowing climbers of all abilities to boulder together. Unlike roped climbing, where a more experienced climber must hold back to drag an inexperienced climber up a route, in bouldering everyone can give their all and not interfere with each other's progress. Watch how the better climbers work a problem and how they analyze their performances between burns. Notice that they fall a lot, learning a bit more each time. Notice that just like you they have their weaknesses. Maybe they take falls personally and lose their cool. Perhaps they have crappy flexibility. Perchance they can't jam their way out of a wet paper bag. Emulate what they do well, and avoid what they do poorly.

Road trip to the hotbeds of bouldering activity. Get used to the standards being set. The only reasons a physically able person can't rise to the highest standards of the day is lack of desire and lack of commitment. Sure it takes sacrifices, but that's part of desire. It also takes an assload of hard work, but that's part of commitment. Bouldering isn't brain surgery—you can learn the bulk of the techniques in the first week (this book ain't that thick and I tried not to use too many five dollar words). The rest is just getting comfortable with the techniques and that takes repetition, which means bouldering tons (yeehaw!).

Perceptions of Difficulty

Difficulty is what you perceive it to be—if you think V13 is impossible, you will never climb that grade. If you think because others are climbing V15 there's no reason you can't, then barring injury, you too will climb V15. As stated above, the techniques of bouldering can be acquired quickly. Furthermore, good strategy is a skill that builds quickly with concentrated practice. Then if you're reasonably fit or better yet, young and athletic, it should only take four years or so of dedicated (read full-time) training and bouldering to get strong enough to crank near the top of the scale. Free your mind of the thought that V15 is hard (after all, ten years from now somebody will be climbing V19, why wait until then?) and you'll be able to blow the sport apart.

The reason John Gill and Jim Holloway were so ahead of their contemporaries is they didn't listen to "conventional wisdom" with regard to what

Jim Holloway at Morrison, Colorado, 1970s.
JIM HOLLOWAY COLLECTION

was possible. This was easier in the 1960s and '70s, as the climbing magazines rarely mentioned bouldering back then and open-ended ratings systems hadn't hit the country yet. Today's climber gets brainwashed by websites and magazines and videos to think we're reaching the limits of the humanly possible. This is bull. The "best" climbers these days are mostly privileged layabouts. Some are born with the gift of small fingers and low body mass, but not enough to say the sport has reached a mature

Fall trying. Neil Crancer whipping off The Entrée. Neal took a purported 2,000 such falls before finally feasting on success.

Cutting the end of his own index finger off with a power saw has not deterred Tommy Caldwell from taking it to the next level on **Shark Arête (V10), Rocklands, South Africa.**

ANDY MANN

stage where all the successful participants are built the same a la Tour de France riders. Imagine what today's best could do if they weren't constantly rewarded for just pecking away at the envelope. Strip the media adulation and most would quit or fade away, but a few would persist for deeper, more personal rewards. One of the lot would put down the bong and start training like a real athlete. When that person rethinks the concept of difficulty, then we'll see the next Gill.

I asked master boulderer Fred Nicole, "If you had one tip to give a boulderer wishing to improve, what would that be?" His reply: "As long as you like it, invest as much energy into it as you can. Don't take scales and grades too seriously; you might miss the real point!"

Refine Your Approach

Work on climbing faster without sacrificing good execution. Most of us pause excessively during problems, gathering ourselves to try a daunting move while our strength ebbs, instead of just getting on with it. On the ground is the place to think these things out. Then get on the rock and execute. Get a stopwatch and time your ascent. Now go back and see if you can do it a bit quicker, but just as smoothly. Most hard boulder problems don't allow rests. If you're not resting you should be climbing.

Use momentum. Dyno to save energy on moves to good holds even if you can do those moves static. You'll save strength for later moves and move faster to boot.

Climb the same problems both crimping and open-handed to develop both kinds of strength equally. Jim Holloway climbed all of his problems with an open-hand grip. His testpieces went unrepeated for twenty to thirty years and still challenge the best climbers today.

Use fear of embarrassment to your advantage. Tell your friends and partners your goals and your time frame. If you keep that stuff to yourself, it's too

Many climbers use the "I'm thirty (or forty or fifty)" line as an excuse not to shred anymore. Jo Montchaussé, sixty-five, has made the decision not to tolerate a decline in performance. Here he is busting out another classic at his cherished Roche aux Sabot.

easy to weasel out of the hard work and just make-believe the goal never existed. Your friends can help you stay on track by offering to drink your beer so you can maintain fitness, etc.

Rest as hard as you climb. By that I mean eat well and lay off the beer bongs. The difference between real professional athletes (Olympians and the like) and fauxfessionals ("pro" climbers) is that the real pros are paid to rest, not pose for videos. When they aren't training or competing, they sit instead of stand and lie down instead of sit. Their bodies need this to achieve maximum recovery in time for the next brutal training session. Someone with a job might be sitting at a computer instead of lying down—the desk jockey is not getting as good a recovery.

Fall trying. If you bail off a move because you don't think you can do it, you've just taken the same fall you would have had you tried the move and pitched. Unless it is a hazardous, hard-to-spot fall, fall trying.

Setbacks

You will have setbacks—injuries, illness, a job transfer, whatever. The better boulderer realizes every session isn't going to be a victory and keeps sight

"Can you do the iron maiden fist jam section again?" Professional climber Pat Goodman is glad it's 38 degrees so he can't feel the pain through the numbness on this photo shoot.

of his or her goals. Victory or not, every session is a learning experience. Coaches and books can teach, but *you* have to do the learning.

The best boulderers get injured the least. They listen to their bodies more attentively and sometimes simply have genetically stronger connective tissue. While others are clawing their way back to a former level after injury, they are pushing themselves to new levels. Learn to listen to your body. Don't let the prospect of short-term success lure you into an injury that could set you back months. I've lost count of how many times I thought, "gee, that move kinda felt funny in my finger; well I'll just try it one more time, and if it hurts again I'll shelve this problem for awhile." Sure enough, next try, *pop* goes the tendon pulley. In thirty-five years of bouldering I have never once regretted backing off a problem. I have, however, regretted *not* backing off far too many times.

Barring injuries, illness, or old age, a decline in performance is there only because you let it happen. Hey, if your mom gets sick and needs your help and you choose to blow off training to help, that's a noble thing. It is, however, a choice you consciously made, so be aware of your priorities in life and make decisions accordingly. Is the weather looking ideal to send your multiyear project on November 1? Maybe you should skip that Halloween party. Your decision.

Turning Pro and Taming Lions

The goal of many a young boulderer is to turn pro, go bouldering the rest of his or her life (which seems to end at thirty), and get paid for being so cool. Most "professional boulderers" have three things in common—free shoes, a trust fund, and a business card declaring they are a "professional climber." The truth is there is a pathetically small amount of money in this sport, and this won't change until people start paying to watch boulderers in action and Vegas puts a betting line on bouldering comps.

The other embarrassing truth is that while the majority of "pro climbers" are excellent climbers, some are just excellent self-promoters. There are loads of climbers with the talent and résumé to go pro, but they don't want to be sucked into that scene, preferring instead to work a real job and climb on their own terms. These are the climbers that become mysterious cult heroes.

Climbing salaries are a jealously and poorly kept secret. If rumor is correct, the "greatest climber of our day" pulls down no more per year than a minimum wage utility infielder riding the pine in the MLB. The second best makes way less than that, and the average pro climber makes less than a junior manager at Burger King. Combined with extreme frugality this can fund some cool road trips where you'll have to climb on demand for a bunch of photographers (can you say sunrise photo shoot?) and blog about your greatness every few days. Don't forget to get any significant send on unedited videotape or it doesn't count. Sounds great, huh?

Okay, I did what a good friend is supposed to do and tried to talk you out of it. Now for the true story of Dave Hoover. Dave's parents asked the boy what he wanted to be when he grew up. "I want to be a lion tamer." His parents told him he couldn't do that, that he needed to pick something else. Dave refused. His parents' friends tried to convince the boy that he couldn't be a lion tamer, but Dave just dug his heels in harder. Exasperated, his parents took him to a priest to talk some sense into the kid. The priest sat Dave down and explained to him why he couldn't be a lion tamer, but Dave was so adamant that a lion tamer was what he'd become that the priest finally came around and told him, "The world needs lion tamers too." Hoover became a famous lion tamer. Now go hone that footwork and hit the fingerboard.

Paths to Success

There is no single sure-fire path to bouldering success. The right path for you is the one that gives you the greatest satisfaction. The right path will depend on your temperament as much as your physique and ability. Following are quick sketches of the paths taken by some notable boulderers.

John Gill—The Genius

The originator of modern bouldering strayed far from the path other climbers took during the 50s and 60s. He eschewed "three-points-on-at-all-times" technique and started dynoing for holds on purpose. Unheard of. Furthermore, he directed his immense climbing talent toward bouldering as an end—not just as training for roped climbing. Hence many of his fellow climbers regarded him as a kook. Now he is seen as a genius and somewhat as a Zen master of bouldering.

Gill applied not just gymnastic technique and strength to the boulders but also a gymnastic mindset. To Gill, form was just as important as difficulty—a good gymnastic routine depended on both. Gill would repeat his problems over and over until he flowed across the rock, gaining maximum kinesthetic awareness. He didn't climb for the limelight or to compete with others. He climbed for the love of movement. Had he focused more on difficulty, his problems would have been that much harder. Anyone who has attempted to repeat his training tricks, like the one-armed front lever, can attest to that.

Gill put up hundreds of problems throughout the country. By virtue of their difficulty and history, Gill problems have become the most sought-after testpieces in American bouldering.

Bob Williams—The Competitor

Bob Williams loves to compete with others. It's where he gets his drive. As long as he is winning, he is psyched. This made him one of the great boulderers of the late 1960s and early 1970s. He cranked second ascents of more famous Gill problems than anyone else, including *The Scab* in the Black Hill's Needles and the *Pinch Route* on the Mental Block at Colorado's Horsetooth Reservoir. On the latter he one-upped Gill by starting with both feet on the rock instead of with a swing start.

Williams also hates losing. When he felt others would eclipse his track record, he bowed out of bouldering, only to come back fifteen years later to feel the joy of burning off kids half his age.

John Gill on **Fenton's Corner***, Estes Park, Colorado, 1963.*
JOHN GILL COLLECTION

Jim Holloway—
Pure Strength, Pure Motive

It's one thing to put up problems your peers can't repeat; quite another to put up problems that have stumped boulderers for twenty years and continue to baffle them. Jim Holloway took bouldering standards in the 1970s and pushed them further than anyone has before, since, or likely forever. He did this by competing against himself, not others. He trained hard, but in a primitive fashion, and despite a congenital skeletal defect in his lower spine, reached levels of strength most of today's climbers only dream of.

Holloway was a purist. He didn't care for ratings, sit-down starts, cheater stones, or even having a spot. Mention power spotting today and his face registers disgust. He started on the ground after every attempt. He felt that the honorable way to establish a new problem was to climb an entirely new stretch of rock, not just add hard moves to an existing route. He was known as an exceedingly smooth climber, and when told that he was so good only because he was 6 feet, 4 inches tall, he would crunch himself up and send problems using short persons' sequences. His most stylish trick, though, was the way he would pause in the midst of a crux move, reach back, and adjust his trademark painter's cap.

Bob Murray—
The First Ascent Machine

Bob Murray is quiet, shy, and a bit of a loner. He preferred to boulder by himself. He also didn't care to repeat problems. He is therefore one of the most prolific boulderers in American history, having put up hundreds of first ascents in the 70s and 80s. Compared to Holloway, style didn't carry much weight with Murray. If a landing looked bad, he was happy to self-belay on a toprope, and even to hangdog moves while doing so. He couldn't have cared less what others thought; he just wanted to

Bob Murray sinking bare toes in pockets at Box Canyon, Socorro, New Mexico.

climb new problems and do ever thinner and harder moves, preferably dynamics.

Murray looked undernourished until pulling up on a problem; then muscles seemed to come out of nowhere and power him up. His fanatical training begot a remarkable strength-to-weight ratio. Rather than relying entirely on his arms, however, he did many of his desperates barefoot, so he could use his toes like fingers.

In the American Southwest, the term "Murray Problem" is said with reverence. Nonetheless, because Murray never sought publicity and rarely received any, many of his problems may never be found again.

Jim Karn—Move Master

Jim Karn is best known for his success as a sport climbing competitor, but he also compiled one of the best bouldering records of any American in the late 1980s and '90s. Karn successfully used an "I'm going to do lame so I've got nothing to lose" attitude to free his mind before sport comps. Winning these competitions was a necessary evil that granted him the financial freedom to pursue other ends, such as bouldering with his friends. Out at the boulders, he ditched the negative energy approach in favor of friendly competition with his bros. They would rip on each other mercilessly but in good humor, prodding each other to try harder.

Karn rarely used his strength and expertise to put up new problems. To him it didn't matter who did a move first, only that he himself could do it. He used boulders as training apparatus, doing multiple laps on hard problems and making those problems even harder by cranking them static or powering past intermediate holds. When he was younger, he sought out ever harder and harder moves to do. Later he looked to master moves and climb as smoothly as possible. To him the best way to do a problem was not the most efficient way, but rather the most aesthetic.

Fred Nicole—Swiss Powerhouse

I remember the first time I heard about Swiss boulderer Fred Nicole. A couple friends came up to me in Hueco one evening and declared, "We've just seen the world's strongest boulderer. You won't believe it, the dude's forearms are so huge they swing about like an old lady's triceps." Sure enough,

*Fred Nicole at his home turf on **Auffahrt, Ticino, Switzerland.***
FRED NICOLE COLLECTION

Nicole's forearms were otherworldly, so much so that his precision footwork was often overlooked.

Nicole's quest is to push himself to the maximum in terms of physical difficulty on the rocks. He's set new standards not just in his native Switzerland but also at Hueco Tanks, Rocklands, and other areas. The first boulder problems rated 8b,

8b+, and 8c are all attributed to Nicole. "I was always afraid of height," Nicole admitted in an interview, "so bouldering became the way of expressing myself in climbing." To keep the focus on pure physical difficulty, he picks projects with minimum risk in terms of height and bad landings, frequently employing sit-down starts. He describes his movement style as "a very slow climber compared to the modern dynamic style. I like to be precise on my movements."

When asked if he ever gets burnt out trying a project, Nicole has this to say: "The idea itself of a project is what fascinates me most. How to figure out a line out of a rock. How to adapt myself to the given line of holds. It's a micro-cosmos that needs my total commitment. To solve a project, time does not really fit in it. It's becoming accessory to me on my quest. And yes, sometimes I can get burnt out and very seldom I can even abandon a project. But I prefer the idea of putting it on the side for later. Even if I might never go back . . ."

Nicole's motivation comes not just from the quest for pure difficulty but also the desire to keep progressing even several decades into his career. As well, he enjoys discovering new spaces for his activity, whether it be a new area, a new line, or the discovery of a new variation to an existing line. "I love the dimension of bouldering, the simplicity of a single rock where the climber needs to find a way to solve the problem," says Nicole. "My fascination for this interaction between human and rock has not disappeared with the years. I'm still astonished by the climbing. It's a process that I still don't completely understand."

Lisa Rands— Muscle Power, Mind Power

In the early 2000s, Lisa Rands dominated the competition circuit. Rands earned a reputation for just flat out trying harder than her peers, and the results prove it. Rands was the first American woman to

Lisa Rands at the Happy Boulders, Bishop, California.
WILLS YOUNG

win on the international bouldering circuit, attaining the world number one ranking in 2002 after taking a World Cup win and the prestigious Open des Ecrins at L'Argentiere title.

Outside the competition circuit she crushed it as well. "I remember when I began to climb harder than my male friends, and this was awkward. For a long while I was held back, thinking that if my male climbing partners couldn't do something, then I surely wouldn't be able to do it. At the time, there weren't other women out there proving this wrong, so it was up to me to try to get over that hurdle and push on!" Push on she did, becoming the first American female to climb at the V11 standard. She is also the first woman to climb Yosemite's iconic *Midnight Lightning* without toprope prerehearsal and the first woman to climb Buttermilks's classic *Mandala* (V12). If that isn't enough, she also sports an impressive resume of highball sends.

"In the past I used to have more power and pure arm strength," Rands admits, "and would use this to compensate for lack of body tension or skill. These days, since I am no longer bouldering exclusively but doing more of other styles of climbing, I move more statically and have better all-around body strength and technique. This makes up for the loss of sheer power in most situations."

Paul Robinson—From Gym to Rock

Paul Robinson could be the poster child for the new generation of boulderers. Bred in a gym starting at age eleven, he excelled in the competition circuit, then was released outdoors to tear a swath

Paul Robinson on **Esperanza** *(V14),*
Hueco Tanks.
PAUL ROBINSON COLLECTION

through the bouldering hotspots of the world. At age twenty-three now, Paul checks in at 5 feet 10 inches and a scant 125 pounds. He has a minimal attention span for anything that doesn't have to do with big-number sends. This immersion leads to his mission to repeat and establish the hardest problems in the world. Unlike some of his peers, he doesn't play the "modesty card" by refusing to rate problems. Instead he'll slap a provocative grade on a first ascent, then let the challenge to repeat it just hang out there. His Buttermilks first ascent of *Lucid Dreaming* checks in at V16 and at the time of this writing has yet to see a repeat.

Angie Payne—V13 and Beyond

Angie Payne started as a gym climber at age eleven, focusing on roped climbing until getting her driver's license at age sixteen and going bouldering to exercise her new-found independence. Payne excelled at bouldering, three times becoming the American Bouldering Series National Champion. A self-confessed "gym rat," she enrolled at the University of Colorado, moving to Boulder as much for the gyms as the outdoor climbing and the school. Rocky Mountain National Park and Mount Evans became two of her favorite bouldering areas.

Payne acknowledges that her bouldering style is like her personality, fluid and controlled, not explosive or dynamic. She enjoys the problem solving involved in finding alternative sequences and body positions to avoid thuggy moves. This ability allowed her to bag the first female ascents of problems like *No More Greener Grasses* (V12), Mt Evans, Colorado, and *European Human Being* (V12), RMNP, Colorado.

During a gym training session in 2008, Payne took a routine fall but missed the pad and badly injured her ankle. At the time she was evaluating the role of bouldering in her life versus her focus on school and an eventual veterinary career. A very competitive person, Payne was unsure about returning to the sport unable to compete at the standard she expected of herself. During her time off for surgery and rehab, however, she realized how much she missed other aspects of bouldering—the social scene, travel to new areas, and "escaping the craziness of this world."

Payne returned to bouldering and training with unsure expectations but fresh motivation. Her self-admitted desire "to rise to the top of whatever I am doing" became reality in 2010 when she left her mark as the first woman to climb a consensus V13, *The Automator* in Rocky Mountain National Park.

John Sherman—The Author

Two things I share in common with all of the above climbers: I love bouldering and I have a strong desire to succeed. My style is composed of bits and pieces taken from some of those above. Like Murray I seldom repeat problems, instead preferring to constantly experience new terrain. Like Holloway I value purity of ascent style. I have driven many of my spotters nuts: If I bump into them, or even if my shoelace brushes against them, I feel I haven't truly climbed the problem and must try it again "cleanly." One great advantage to such a pure style is that no matter how much flak I caught for my vocal opinions or my brash and unrefined character, I never caught any flak for how I did an ascent.

Unlike most of the above boulderers, I hate to train. At times I have been competitive like Bob Williams (especially when I'm smoking the old geezer off a problem). Then there were all the months spent bouldering alone in the desert during the "Dark Ages" of the mid-1980s, when partners were hard to come by. In those days it was the beauty of the sport alone that drove me on.

Different approaches have worked for me at different times. When the accumulation of injuries eroded my physical potential, I switched my focus to the mental challenges of highballing. I'm still addicted to that passion, but now also enjoy discovering and developing new areas in the United States and making pilgrimages to classic bouldering venues outside the US. So far in my career I have visited over 600 bouldering areas and climbed over 20,000 problems, thousands of them firsts. Fake hips, bum arm, multiple concussions—I wouldn't trade my career for anyone's.

The Best Advice in the Book

If you learn only one thing from this book, let it be this: There are many paths to a happy and successful bouldering career—don't try to copy another boulderer's style and technique verbatim. Find what works for you and stick with that. Don't try to become the next Bob Murray or Fred Nicole. Forcing yourself to climb like someone you aren't will minimize results. Be yourself instead. Pick the parts of others' styles that work for you; discard those that don't. If your reasons for bouldering change throughout your career, there is nothing wrong with that.

A Last Reminder

Bouldering is what you make it each time you go out. Though much of this book is devoted to helping you improve, you needn't be obsessed with always cranking harder and harder problems. There's nothing wrong with spending a session goofing around with your friends, seeing who can run farthest up a slab, or who can climb a problem with a hand in a pocket, and so forth.

Stay thirsty mis amigos.

L to R, Dave Yarwood, Cody Roth, and Chris Kelk chill out between burns during a night bouldering session at Rocklands.

Appendix A

Bouldering Ratings

There are two main ratings systems used internationally—V grades and French grades. V grades tend to dominate in the Americas, New Zealand, and Australia. French grades are commonly used throughout Europe, Africa, and Asia. Some areas, like Rocklands in South Africa, have a mix of both depending on which sector of boulders was developed by which nationality of climbers. The Brits? They can't seem to decide if they hate American grades or French grades more, so they seem to use both.

"V" Grades

The V system originated at Hueco Tanks in the late 1980s. It is open ended: the bigger the number, the harder the problem. It starts at V0 and as of this writing extends to V16, though someone is sure to claim a bigger number any day. Whether a problem is intimidating, scary, loose, or has a bad landing has no effect on its V rating—only the physical difficulty counts, that is, the technicality of the moves combined with the demands on one's power and endurance. The rating would remain the same whether the route was toproped or bouldered. Hence a scary V2 may be more difficult for some to boulder than a safe V5.

Relative Bouldering Scales

(US) Vermin	(Fr) Fontainebleau
VB	3
V0-	4
V0	4+
V0+	5
V1	5+
V2	6a
	6a+
V3	6b
V4	6b+
V5	6c
	6c+
V6	7a
V7	7a+
V8	7b
	7b+
V9	7c
V10	7c+
V11	8a
V12	8a+
V13	8b
V14	8b+
V15	8c
V16	8c+

French Grades

The French system hails from Fontainebleau. Like the V system it is open ended: the bigger the number, the harder the problem. Ratings currently go from 3 to 8c+. The numbers and sub-letters look the same as those used to rate roped climbs, but they're not equivalent. For example, the moves on a 7a boulder problem would be much harder than the crux of a 7a roped pitch. The French system also has a "traverse grade," which uses the same numbering but is reserved for long boulder problems that require more endurance than power. The moves on a 7a traverse problem would lie somewhere between the difficulty of a 7a boulder problem and the crux moves of a 7a roped pitch.

"B" Grades

B grades are rarely used today, but if you are savvy enough to delve into the career of John Gill, you will be exposed to them. Gill's B system was the first ratings system used exclusively on boulder problems in America. It had three grades: B1, B2, and B3. B1 had moves as hard as the hardest roped climbs of the time. Gill says, "B2 is quite a bit harder. And B3 . . . should be a completely objective climbing rating. B3 is something that is done once, is tried frequently, but is not repeated. If it is repeated, then it drops automatically either to B2 or even B1." (Though Gill's definition of B grades evolved throughout his career, this definition, which appeared in *Master of Rock* [1977], is the most commonly used.) B grades were intended to slide as standards increased. In 1969 Gill defined B1 as 5.10, in 1977 as 5.11, in 1987 around 5.12. This system allows people to judge themselves against the standards of their own generation. It also points out the fact that a climber doing B2 today is pushing no harder than a climber doing B2 thirty years ago, even if today's route is more difficult. The disadvantage with the B system is that it requires constant regrading of problems. This goes against human nature, as few climbers are happy to demote their B2 ascent to B1 to keep the system valid.

WARNING: Boulder problems are hard to rate because dozens of variables can greatly affect how hard an individual finds each single move. As most problems are only a few moves long, a difference in a single move makes a lot more difference than on a full rope-length pitch, where such differences tend to even out after many moves. Furthermore, ratings rarely correspond between different areas. Take all ratings with a grain of salt. If you are unsure about a problem's difficulty and your ability to attempt it safely, then pick a different problem you are more comfortable with. View ratings merely as a rough indication of but one component of a problem's overall makeup. Free yourself of preconceived notions of your ability; given time and honest effort, any problem is within reach. Learn to mistrust ratings and pity those who are slaves to them.

"If the routes stayed the same, but the gradings were suddenly all switched around, it would be interesting to see which routes people would be trying to do."
—JIM HOLLOWAY

Appendix B

Suggested Reading

Ament, Pat. *Master of Rock, A Lighthearted Walk Through the Life and Rock Climbing of John Gill.* Adventure's Meaning Press, 1992. The inspirational biography of the ultimate boulderer, John Gill. The extensive photo selection of Gill in action has served as a cult guidebook for boulderers since the original edition of this work appeared in 1977.

Ilgner, Arno. *The Rock Warrior's Way.* 2nd ed. Desiderata Institute, 2006. The original text on mental training for climbing, now in its second edition.

MacLeod, Dave. *9 out of 10 Climbers Make the Same Mistakes.* Rare Breed Productions, 2010. Heaps of in-depth coaching advice on mental, physical, and technical aspects of climbing.

Sherman, John. *Stone Crusade, A Historical Guide to Bouldering in America.* AAC Press, 1994. A history of American bouldering, complete with directions on how to get to over fifty of America's top bouldering areas. Lots of action photos.

Tilton, Buck. *Wilderness First Responder.* 3rd ed. FalconGuides, 2010. The third edition of the first teaching manual ever for the "Wilderness First Responder" course. This title represents the cutting edge in medical training for wilderness rescue and self-care.

Index

accidents. *See* emergencies; injuries and treatments

accommodation principle, 226

advice, best in book, 274

aid bouldering, 215

Althaus, Jesse, 37, 71, 84, 94, 238

ankle injury story, 48–49

ankles, treating and strengthening, 245

antagonist training, 232–33

anti-inflammatory drugs, 249

Arenz-Smith, Elaina, 31

arms. *See* handholds; hands and arms

Atkins, Ariel, 161

Autobahn story, 140–41

Ayala, Shadow, 46, 155

"B" grades, 277

bad landings, 22–24

Bainbridge, Dave, 252

barndooring, 98–101

basics of bouldering
common traps, 98–101
power, 98
resting, 98, 244, 265–66
See also footwork; handholds; hands and arms; legwork; overhangs; posture

beached whale maneuver, 87

Bénard, Stephanie, 95

beta
figuring out, not copying, 175
spotting, 36, 37
trying new, 175

bicycle move, 60, 63

Bleaussards, 69

blind boulderer (Dennis), 148

Blunk, Scott, 28, 29

body tension exercises, 231–32

Bogdan, Dylan, 77

Boland, Whitney, 97

book overview, xii–xiii, 274

books, suggested reading, 278

bouldering
about: overview of, xiii–xiv
author getting started, xi–xii
basics. *See* basics of bouldering; footwork; handholds; hands and arms; legwork; overhangs
best advice in book, 274
change-of-pace options, 211–17
defined, xiii
etiquette. *See* cleaning; etiquette
experiences possible, xiii–xiv
indoor vs. outdoor, xvii
range of difficulty, xiii
style vs. difficulty, xv–xvii
woman's perspective, 205–9

bouldering pads, 6–11, 38–43
best, 8
closure straps, 9
costs, 8
current trend, 8
density, 6–8
dog safety and, 44–45
fireman catch using, 41
minimal, with bad landings, 42–43
multiple pad use, 40–41
no-fall zones on, 38, 40
not having, 43, 44
positioning and butting, 8–9, 34, 38–41
single pad use, 38–40
sizes, 8, 39
slitting, 10–11
styles, 9
talus fields and, 41
tossing, 42
using, 38–43

waiters, 41, 42
when not to use, 43
See also falling and jumping

bouldering wall, strength, 226–27

Bradshaw, Steve, 93

bridging, 70

brush (tooth or bouldering), 5–6, 195–97

buckets (jugs), 77

buildering, 215

bump-and-catch technique, 32

burnout, 167

Caldwell, Tommy, 257

Camelio, AJ, 62

campus boards, 230

Carne, Alan, 20

carpet patch, 6, 8

catching boulderer. *See* spotting

cell phone, 17, 48

chalk, 3–5
cleaning off, 142–43, 148
courteous use of, 143, 147–49
forms of, 3–5
on holds, 149
liquid chalk, 5
tick marks, 147–48, 174, 180
two bags for, 5, 139
using, 138–41

chalk socks, 3–5

Charles, Olivier, 151, 176

Chastagnier, Quentin, 99

cheater stones, 150–52

chimneying, 133

Chinchen, Jason, 229

Chouvy, Pierre-Arnaud, 78

Chronic Excuse Syndrome, 163

circuit bouldering, 211

Clair, Fabrice, 19, 31

cleaning
brushes for, 5–6, 195–97

doctoring vs., 199
holds (chalk), 142–43, 148
natural matter off boulders, 193–97, 199
rappel, 199
shoes, 6, 144–47, 174
tick marks, 148
coefficient of friction (μ), 56–60
Collette, Simon, 104
Colorado Athletic Training School (CATS), 179, 183
comfort zone, 166, 260–62
commitment, 167
competition climbing, 180–83
compression and opposition, 53
Connor, Ben, 91, 251
Cooper, Carrie, 44, 65
core stabilizers, 255–56
corner torques, 64–65
Coulter, Poppy, 130
counterbalancing moves, 119
Crancer, Neil, 263
crash pads. See bouldering pads
Crews, Harry, 32, 220
crimping, 82
crux moves, 173

Daly, Mason, 175
Daniels, Eric, 255
dark, bouldering in, 211
Davis, Pete, 163
Decaria, Eric, 70, 145
Dempsey, Kayla, 51, 66, 87, 157
Dennis (blind boulderer), 148
difficulty, perceptions of, 262–65
dog safety, 44–45
double dynos, 103, 110
downclimbing, 45
drop-knee technique, 71
drying holds, 143
dynamics
    about: overview of, 103
    big mistake, 108
    committing to move, 108
    counterbalancing moves, 119

crouch and fire, 108
double dynos, 103, 110
excessive, avoiding, 108
extra pumps, 108–10
feet-off dynos (campus moves), 119
linked, 115–17
mid-path trajectory alterations, 119
other body part swings, 118
psyching up for, 108
sizing up moves, 137
standard, 103–10
swing starts, 111–13
using arms, 107–8
using legs, 103–7

edges, 76
edging, 52–54
Ego on the Rampage, 168–69
Ego-Swelling Combat Tales, 17, 29, 36, 140–41, 176–77, 195
elbow exercises, 250
elbow injuries and treatments, 248–50
embarrassment, fear of. See fear, failure, and falling
emergencies
    accidents, 48–49
    first-aid kit, 17, 243–44
    first-aid tips, 243–44
    See also injuries and treatments
emotional wiring, 157–58
Encinas, Tony, 164
endurance training, 233–35
Erbesfield-Raboutou, Robyn, 250, 256
etiquette
    America vs. Europe, 217
    asking permission to climb, 143
    "pack it in, pack it out," 217
    See also cleaning
evaluating performance, 174
excuses, 163, 177
exercises. See training

failure. See fear, failure, and falling
Fair, Kelsey, 45
falling and jumping, 19–28
    bad landings, 22–24, 42–43
    bouldering physics and, 56–60
    clearing bad landings, 23–24
    failure, fear, and falling, 155, 160–63, 173, 176–77, 265
    fall angles and, 25–28, 173
    good landings, 19–21
    pre-jumps and, 28
    risk management, 24
    running away, 22
    stone toss and, 28
    See also bouldering pads
false grips, 88–89
Farrell, Biff, 82
fear, failure, and falling, 155, 160–63, 173, 176–77, 265
feet. See footwork
feet-off dynos (campus moves), 119
Fehlman, Bryant, 150
finger injuries and treatments, 12–13, 246–47
finger jams, 124
fingerlocks, 121–23
fingerstacks, 124
fireman catch, 41
first ascents, 193–203
    cleaning guidelines and tools, 193–97, 199
    doctoring vs. cleaning, 199
    evaluating loose holds and virgin lines, 197–99
    glue and, 198, 199
    personal account, 200–203
    rappel cleaning, 199
first-aid kit, 17, 243–44
first-aid tips, 243–44
fist jams, 130–31
flagging, 72
flakes, 76
flexibility and stretching, 237–39, 242, 256

focus, 159
footwork, 51–69
    about: overview of, 51–52
    balance and, 66–67
    barndooring and, 98–101
    bicycle move, 60, 63
    Bleaussards and, 69
    bouldering physics and, 56–60
    coefficient of friction (μ) and, 56–60
    corner torques, 64–65
    dynamic movement and. See dynamics
    edging, 52–54
    hard-to-see holds and, 147–49
    heel hooks, 61
    heel-toe locks, 64
    keys, 66–68
    matching and, 89, 91
    overhangs and, 74–75, 231
    pockets and, 60
    power, strength and, 98
    precision and, 66
    rand smears, 62
    remembering footholds, 177
    smearing, 55. See also rand smears
    smedging, 65
    toe and foot jams, 65. See also jamming techniques
    toe hooks, 62–63
    trust and, 67–68
    See also legwork
Foti, Chad, 30, 91, 122, 246
Fox, Dale, 115
Fox, Erin, 172
frame of mind. See mental aspects
French grades, 277
friction, coefficient of (μ), 56–60
Full Service story, 176–77

gang spots, 32–33
gastons, 83
gear
    carpet patch, 6, 8

cell phone, 17, 48
essential, 1–11
first-aid kit, 17, 243–44
helmets, 13–15
knee pads, 12–13
skin kits, 12
toothbrush/bouldering brush, 5–6, 195–97
See also bouldering pads; shoes
Gill, John, xv, 87, 112, 114, 115, 165, 262, 269, 277
glue, 198, 199
goal setting, 164–65
Goebbel, Jessa, 86, 123
good landings, 19–21
Goodman, Pat, 31, 66, 83, 116–17, 189, 266
"grips," 75. See also handholds
Grossnick, Maki, 92, 104
gym, bouldering in, xvii, 68, 179–83

Haak, Fabian, 55
Haakenson, Hillary, 38, 174, 213
hand jams, 126–27
handholds
    barndooring and, 98–101
    beached whale maneuver, 87
    chalk and. See chalk
    crimping, 82
    drying holds, 143
    edges and, 76
    figure four, 89
    flakes and, 76
    gastons, 83
    "grips" and, 75
    hard-to-see holds and, 147–49
    huecos and, 80
    jamming and. See jamming techniques
    jugs (buckets) and, 77
    knobs and, 77
    laybacking, 83
    manteling, 84–87, 174
    matching and, 89, 91

open-hand technique, 82
overgripping and, 98
on overhanging faces. See overhangs
palming, 87
pinches and, 80–81
pockets and, 79–80
rosin and, 144
sidepulls and, 78
skyhook grip, 89
slopers and, 78, 98
tufas and, 81
underclings/underclinging and, 79, 84
wrist hooks and false grips, 88–89
hands and arms, 75–91
    about: overview of using, 75
    bouldering physics and, 56–60
    dynamic movement and. See dynamics
    legwork and, 51–52. See also legwork
    power, strength and, 98. See also training
hangboards, 228–29
Hangi, Yves, 137, 200–203, 245
hard-to-see holds, 147–49
Hathaway, Lisa, 215
head injuries, 16, 256
heel hooks, 61
heel-toe locks, 64
helmets, 13–15
Helvie, Tom, 248
Herbert, Tom, 78
high bouldering (highballing), 185–91
    about: overview of, xiv–xv, 185
    author's approach, 187–91
    for kids, 187
    other approaches, 191
    soloing vs., xv
Hill, Chris, 133, 194
hip injuries, 255
hip scums, 74

Hofer, Stefan, 41
holds
    cheater stones to reach, 150–52
    cleaning, 142–43
    hard-to-see, 147–49
    loose rock and, 45–47, 197–99
    tick marks and, 147–48
    See also handholds
Holloway, Jim, xv, 45, 232, 262, 265, 270, 277
honesty, with yourself, 164
Hsu, Audrey, 2, 79
huecos, 80

ibuprofen, 249
improving to next level, 259–67
    about: overview of, 259
    expanding comfort zone, 260–62
    perceptions of difficulty and, 262–65
    refining approach, 265–66
    setbacks and, 266–67
    turning pro, 267
indoor training. *See* training
indoor vs. outdoor bouldering, xvii
injuries and treatments
    about: overview of, 241–42, 257
    accidents and, 48–49
    acute, 242–44
    ankles, 48–49, 245
    anti-inflammatory drugs and, 249
    of author, xv–xvii, 160, 240, 241
    back and spine, 256
    causes of injuries, 242. *See also specific types of injuries*
    chronic, 242, 244
    elbows, 248–50
    fingers, 12–13, 246–47
    first-aid tips, 243–44
    head, 16, 256
    hips and knees, 255
    how they heal, 242

preventing injuries. *See* injury prevention
    PRICE method for, 243, 244
    shoulders, 250–54
    skin flappers, 12–13
    surgeries and recovery times, 244
    wrists, 247–48
injury prevention
    core stabilizers and spine, 255–56
    exercises for, 232–33, 245, 250, 252, 256
    general guidelines, 241–42
    skin flappers, 13
    stretching for, 239
instinct, bouldering by, 215

jamming techniques, 121–35
    basic, 121–34
    chimneying, 133
    drills for, 134
    finger jams, 124
    fingerlocks, 121–23
    fingerstacks, 124
    fist jams, 130–31
    hand jams, 126–27
    off-hands, 128–29
    off-widths, 132
    practice and drills, 134
    sizing up moves, 137
    thin hands, 124–25
    toe jams, 134
Jauernigg, Logan, 230
Johnson, Alex, 61
Johnson, Andy, 112
Johnson, Jeff, vi, 146
Jorgenson, Kevin, 171, 193
jugs (buckets), 77
jumping, boulder running and, 43

Karn, Jim, 271
Kearny, Walker, 33
Kehl, Jason, 81, 258
Kelk, Chris, 31, 275

knee injuries, 255
knee pads, 12–13
knees, techniques using. *See* legwork
knobs, 77

Lacasse, Melissa, 88
landings. *See* falling and jumping
Last, Adge, 260
laybacking, 83
Lee, Veronica, 113
legwork, 70–75
    barndooring and, 98–101
    drop-knee technique, 71
    dynamic movement and. *See* dynamics
    flagging, 72
    hands, arms and, 51–52. *See also* handholds; hands and arms
    hard-to-see holds and, 147–49
    hip scums, 74
    knee bars and knee scums, 70–71, 137
    on knees, 73
    matching and, 89, 91
    overhangs, feet and, 74–75, 231
    overhangs and feet, 74–75
    posting, 73
    power, strength and, 98
    stemming and bridging, 70
Leino, Julie, 80
liebacking (laybacking), 83
linked dynamics, 115–17
Long, McKenzie, 37
loose rock, 45–47, 197–99

MacLeod, Dave. *See* training
Mancuso, Brian, 90
manteling, 84–87, 174
Markert, Adam, 26, 35, 47, 106
Massey, Adam, 21
matching, 89, 91
mental aspects, 155–69
    being honest with yourself, 164
    burnout, 167

comfort zone, 166, 260–62
commitment, 167
emotional wiring and, 157–58
excuses, 163, 177
falling, failure, and fear, 155, 160–63, 173, 176–77, 265
focus, 159
frame of mind, 159
goal setting, 164–65
Midnight Lightning story demonstrating, 168–69
muscle memory and, 155–57, 173
next level and. *See* improving to next level
perceptions of difficulty, 262–65
positive thinking and trying hard, 159–60
previsualization, 158–59, 169, 171, 173–74
psyching up, 108, 159–60, 173
relaxation and, 159
results and, 167
role models and, 165
See also strategy
Midnight Lightning story, 168–69
mistakes, avoiding, 174–77
Montchaussé, Jo, 69, 265
Morris, James, 42, 53, 214
movement
    basic tenet of, 51
    bouldering physics and, 56–60
    coefficient of friction (μ) and, 56–60
    common traps, 98–101
    dynamic. *See* dynamics
    opposition, compression and, 53
    posture and, 92–94
    static vs. dynamic, 51
    See also footwork; handholds; hands and arms; legwork; overhangs
Moyles, Steve, 68
Murray, Bob, 195, 270–72

muscle memory, 155–57, 173
muscles and muscle adaptation, 224–25. *See also* training

next level. *See* improving to next level
Nicole, Fred, 40, 265, 271–72
night bouldering, 211

off-hands, 128–29
off-widths, 132
open-hand technique, 82
opposition and compression, 53
Orme, Zac, 186
other climbers
    less experienced, learning from, 175
    not relying on sequences of, 175–76
outdoor training, 221–24
outdoor vs. indoor bouldering, xvii
overgripping, 98
overhangs
    drop-knee technique for, 71
    dynamics for. *See* dynamics
    feet and, 74–75, 231
    physics of bouldering and, 57–59
    posture for, 94
    slopers on, 98
    straight arms for, 94–96
    torso twists for, 97
    upper body technique for, 94–97
    working slopers on, 98

pad waiters, 41, 42
pads
    bouldering. *See* bouldering pads
    knee, 12–13
palming, 87
Payne, Angie, xii, 205–9, 273–74
Payne, Lee, 61
permission, asking, 143
physics of bouldering, 56–60

pinches, 80–81
Pinter, Lev, 83
planning. *See* mental aspects; strategy
pockets, 60, 79–80
posting, 73
posture, 92–94
    bouldering physics and, 56–60
    core stabilizers for, 255–56
    "good" vs. climber's, 92
    muscle imbalance and, 255
    for overhanging faces, 94
    stretches for, 256
    for vertical / less than vertical faces, 92–93
power, 98
power spotting, 152–53
pre-jumps, 28
previsualization, 158–59, 169, 171, 173–74
professional boulderers, 266, 267
progressive overload, 225
psyching up, 108, 159–60, 173. *See also* previsualization
Puccio, Alex, 236
Puskarik, Marcie, 38, 164, 174, 187

rain, bouldering in, 213
rand smears, 62
Rands, Lisa, 25, 74, 176, 207, 221, 272–73
rappel cleaning, 199
ratings, 175, 276–77
reading rocks, 173–74
refining approach, 265–66
relaxation, 159
resting, 98, 244, 265–66
risks, xiv–xv
    focus and, 159
    highballing, 185
    ice bouldering, 215
    management skills, 24, 160
    muscle imbalance and, 255
    pads reducing. *See* bouldering pads

See also falling and jumping; injuries and treatments; injury prevention
road trips, 217
Robinson, Paul, xii, xiv, 23, 33, 47, 85, 118, 162, 179–83, 188, 231, 273
role models, 165
rosin, 144
Roth, Cody, 19, 73, 135, 237, 275
Rule One, xi
Rule One Violation, xi, 171

safety, 19–49
    accidents and, 48–49
    for dogs, 44–45
    downclimbing, 45
    loose-rock situations, 45–47, 197–99
    situational awareness and, 47
    See also falling and jumping; injuries and treatments; injury prevention; spotting
Salo, Andy, 185
Sather, Kelsey, 76
Schall, Phil, 80
setbacks, dealing with, 266–67
shoes, 1–3
    cleaning, 6, 144–47, 174
    current trend, 1
    edging and, 52–54
    fitting, 1–3
    industry, 4
    resoling, 3
    socks outside, 213
    styles and characteristics, 1–3, 4
    symmetric and asymmetric, 1–3
    trust and, 67–68
shortcuts, avoiding, 174
shoulders, injuries and exercises, 250–54
shoving boulderer, 32
sidepulls, 78
situational awareness, 47

skin
    flappers, fixing and preventing, 12–13
    kits for, 12
    moisturizing, 13
skyhook grip, 89
slopers, 78, 98
smearing, 55. *See also* rand smears
smedging, 65
snow and ice, bouldering in, 213–15
soloing, high bouldering vs., xv
spotting, 28–37
    beta, 36, 37
    bump-and-catch technique, 32
    calling off the spot, 36–37
    defined, 28
    Ego-Swelling Combat Tales, 29, 36
    fireman catch, 41
    focal-point lessons, 34–35
    gang, 32–33
    low problems, 36
    making catch, 31–32
    power, 152
    priorities, 28–29
    problems to avoid, 34–35
    qualifications for, 28
    recap, 37
    as sacred trust, 28
    shoving and, 32
    starting position, 29
    steering and, 28–29, 31, 32
    watching climber, 29–31
Stackfleth, John, 243, 255
stemming and bridging, 70
stone toss, 28
Strate, Rachel, 32
strategy, 171–77
    avoiding common mistakes, 174–77
    guidelines for developing, 171–74
strength. *See* training

stretching and flexibility, 237–39, 242, 256
Strong, Adam, 166
Stuckey, Sandra, 110, 137, 158, 162
Sturman, Shena, 39
Summit, Chris, 16
swing starts, 111–13. *See also* dynamics

talus fields, 41
thin hands, 124–25
tick marks, 147–48, 174, 180
toe and foot jams, 65. *See also* jamming techniques
toe hooks, 62–63
toe jams, 134
Tollefsrud, John, 160
toothbrush/bouldering brush, 5–6, 195–97
torso twists, 97
tossing pads, 42
towel-whacking, 142
training, 219–39
    about: overview of, 219
    accommodation principle, 226
    ankle exercises, 245
    antagonist, 232–33
    body tension exercises, 231–32
    bouldering wall, strength and, 226–27
    campus boards for, 230
    elbow exercises, 250
    endurance, 233–35
    flexibility and stretching, 237–39, 242, 256
    hangboards for, 228–29
    indoors, 224–35
    injury-avoidance techniques, 232–33
    muscle memory and, 155–57, 173
    muscles, muscle adaptation and, 224–25
    outdoors, 221–24
    progressive overload and, 225

schedule for, 235–37
shoulder exercises, 252–54
specificity in, 226
strength principles, 225–26
supplementary strength work, 227–35
traps, common, 98–101
tricks to avoid
    cheater stones, 150–52
    power spotting, 152
    tick marks, 147–48
Trotter, Sonny, 177, 216
trust, 67–68
Tucker, Marsha, 64, 212

tufas, 81

underclings/underclinging, 79, 84
upper body technique, for overhangs, 94–97

"V" grades, 276
Vale, Josh, 100–101
visualization. *See* previsualization
Voges, Byron, 181

Walsh, Jenn, 63
washing holds, 143
Wilford, Mark, 43, 166, 193

Williams, Bob, 176, 269
Wilson, Chaz, 70
Wilson, Russell, xi
Winthrop, David, 156, 167
woman's perspective, 205–9
Wood, Justin, 103
Woods, Daniel, 75, 96
wrist hooks and false grips, 88–89
wrist injuries and treatments, 247–48

Yarwood, Dave, 213, 275

About the Author

John "Verm" Sherman is arguably the most prolific and experienced American boulderer, in the last thirty-six years having visited over 600 areas and climbed over 20,000 problems, thousands being first ascents. During the mid-1980s to early 1990s, Sherman was the foremost developer of bouldering at Hueco Tanks, Texas. He established over 400 first ascents there, and while writing the first Hueco Tanks bouldering guide climbed all but one of the 900-plus problems in the book. In the process he introduced the V system of grading boulder problems. Sherman also designed the Kinnaloa Sketchpad, the first commercially available bouldering pad, upon which the majority of subsequent designs have been based. He is particularly fond of ground-up highball first ascents—high-risk propositions requiring outstanding skill and judgment—a passion that started in the pre-pad era and continues today.

FRANCOISE MONTCHAUSSÉ

PROTECTING CLIMBING ACCESS SINCE 1991

JOIN US
WWW.ACCESSFUND.ORG

Jonathan Siegrist, Third Millenium (14a), the Monastery, CO. Photo by: Keith Ladzinski